THE BATTLE OF BRANDY STATION

NORTH AMERICA'S LARGEST CAVALRY BATTLE

ERIC J. WITTENBERG

FOREWORD BY O. JAMES LIGHTHIZER

SERIES EDITOR
DOUGLAS W. BOSTICK

Charleston · London

THE
History
PRESS

OTHER WORKS BY ERIC J. WITTENBERG

Gettysburg's Forgotten Cavalry Actions (1998)

We Have it Damned Hard Out Here: The Civil War Letters of Sgt. Thomas W. Smith, Sixth Pennsylvania Cavalry (1999)

One of Custer's Wolverines: The Civil War Letters of Brevet Brigadier General James H. Kidd, 6ʰ Michigan Cavalry (2000)

Under Custer's Command: The Civil War Journal of James Henry Avery (2000)

At Custer's Side: The Civil War Writings of James Harvey Kidd (2001)

Plenty of Blame to Go Around: Sheridan's Second Raid and the Battle of Trevilian Station (2001)

With Sheridan in the Final Campaign Against Lee (2002)

Little Phil: A Reassessment of the Civil War Leadership of Gen. Philip H. Sheridan (2002)

Protecting the Flank: The Fights for Brinkerhoff's Ridge and East Cavalry Field, Battle of Gettysburg, July 2–3, 1863 (2002)

The Union Cavalry Comes of Age: Hartwood Church to Brandy Station, 1863 (2003)

The Battle of Monroe's Crossroads and the Civil War's Final Campaign (2006)

Plenty of Blame to Go Around: Jeb Stuart's Controversial Ride to Gettysburg (with J. David Petruzzi, 2006)

Rush's Lancers: The Sixth Pennsylvania Cavalry in the Civil War (2007)

One Continuous Fight: The Retreat from Gettysburg and the Pursuit of Lee's Army of Northern Virginia, July 4–14, 1863 (with J. David Petruzzi and Michael F. Nugent, 2008)

Like a Meteor Blazing Brightly: The Short but Controversial Life of Colonel Ulric Dahlgren (2009)

Published by The History Press
Charleston, SC 29403
www.historypress.net

Copyright © 2010 by Eric J. Wittenberg
All rights reserved

First published 2010
Second printing 2010
Third printing 2013

Manufactured in the United States

ISBN 978.1.59629.782.1

Library of Congress Cataloging-in-Publication Data

Wittenberg, Eric J., 1961-
The Battle of Brandy Station : North America's largest cavalry battle / Eric J. Wittenberg.
p. cm.
Includes bibliographical references.
ISBN 978-1-59629-782-1
1. Brandy Station, Battle of, Brandy Station, Va., 1863. 2. United States--History--Civil
War, 1861-1865--Cavalry operations. 3. Virginia--History--Civil War, 1861-1865--Cavalry
operations. I. Title.
E475.51.W57 2010
973.7'34--dc22
2009047450

This work is respectfully dedicated to the memory of the twenty-one thousand American cavalrymen who clashed at Brandy Station. It is also respectfully dedicated to the memory of Deborah Whittier Fitts, ardent preservationist, untiring advocate for the Brandy Station battlefield and friend.

Contents

CONTENTS

FOREWORD

In the late spring and early summer of 1863, Confederate forces seemingly achieved the impossible. Though outnumbered and outgunned, the Army of Northern Virginia, under the command of the audacious Robert E. Lee, crushed the Army of the Potomac at the Battle of Chancellorsville. A total Confederate victory finally seemed within reach, prompting Lee himself to pen a letter to a subordinate, explaining that he believed the army would be "invincible if it could be properly organized and officered." For the Army of the Potomac, the once bright hope for a successful campaign withered away following the defeat, as did morale within the ranks. In this hour of despair, one soldier wrote home, "We care not to ford rivers, sleep standing, and fight running when sure defeat always awaits such a *doomed army*."

In the following pages, my friend, historian Eric Wittenberg, takes us back to this critical moment in American military history, focusing on the momentous cavalry clash at Brandy Station. He follows the rapid course of events, as a confident Robert E. Lee persuaded President Davis and his cabinet to commit the Army of Northern Virginia to a second invasion of the North. As Confederate and Union troops begin to prepare for this next great chapter in military history, Eric presents an invaluable description of the opposing cavalry forces that would soon meet in combat.

As he brings us closer to the tumult of battle in Culpeper County, we learn of Confederate plans to utilize the Shenandoah Valley as the avenue of invasion and the role of Rebel cavalry in protecting Lee's main column of infantry. Similarly, the story of Federal troopers on their ride to intercept Lee is detailed and thrilling, highlighting the personal stories of these men who rode into battle in the summer of '63.

Up to this point in the war, much had been made of the superiority of Southern cavalry. Boasts were made about such supremacy, especially following J.E.B. Stuart's much vaunted "Ride Around McClellan" on the Peninsula in 1862. The Battle at Brandy Station would ultimately challenge that understanding. One of Stuart's own horsemen would write that Brandy Station "*made* the Federal cavalry…they gained on this day that confidence in themselves and in their commanders which enable them to contest so fiercely the subsequent battle-fields."

Though engaged in a bitter conflict, the Southern cavalry did not disappoint those who believed them to be the dashing cavaliers of their day. In the days preceding the clash at Brandy, several notorious reviews were held and are eloquently chronicled in the following pages. Such reviews did much to flaunt the pomp and circumstance of those who had "jined" the illustrious cavalry. The savagery of war as it presented itself at Brandy Station would, in part, dismantle this romantic view of soldiering and expose the brutal realities of combat in the nineteenth century.

This detailed narrative of the Battle at Brandy Station is a testament to Eric's fine historical research and attention to detail. The ebb and flow of battle across such infamous ground as Fleetwood Hill and Yew Ridge are presented with excellent clarity and will be a first-rate resource for new and seasoned battlefield visitors alike who wish to tour this hallowed ground. Adjoining the historical narrative is a driving and walking tour unparalleled in its accuracy, replete with exacting GPS coordinates that will allow visitors to apply the actions gleaned from the historical record to the actual ground. From the viewpoint of a lifelong student of the war, nothing could be more worthwhile.

Through the inclusion of his detailed and precise driving and walking tours, my friend has validated the argument that battlefield preservationists like myself have been making for years: that without the land, the original topography—the hallowed ground itself—it would be *impossible* to tell these stories.

As president of the Civil War Preservation Trust (CWPT), I cannot tell you how important it is to have a well-educated and interested public. As the famed historian David C. McCullough put it best: "History is who we are and why we are the way we are." The preservation of Civil War battlefields is essential to that understanding. These battlefields are educational resources that provide a tangible connection to our past and lessons for our future.

As Eric addresses the fight to preserve Brandy Station, I would be remiss if I did not mention that the fight continues. The struggle to preserve this blood-soaked ground has spanned several decades, but as I write this, the CWPT has assisted in preserving more than one thousand acres at Brandy Station. At such a crucial moment as that in which we now find ourselves, when our battlefields are constantly threatened, Eric's narrative could not be more important.

Ultimately, we will preserve only what we appreciate, understand and hopefully learn from. *The Battle of Brandy Station* illuminates and enlivens the past, which is our best hope for creating a new generation of stewards, preservationists, students and historians to care for these now deathless fields.

O. James Lighthizer
Washington, D.C.
June 30, 2009

PREFACE

For nearly fifteen years, I have studied the great clash of cavalry that occurred at Brandy Station, Virginia, on June 9, 1863. Along the way, I became involved with efforts to preserve the battlefield. When I first visited it in 1994, a developer was intent on building either an industrial park or a Formula One raceway at the heart of the battlefield. I was horrified by the prospect of such beautiful pristine ground—the subject of four different major mounted engagements during the Civil War—being destroyed so cavalierly and for such frivolous purposes. I became determined to do what I could to save that ground. Surely, the ground where the largest cavalry battle was ever fought on the North American continent was worthy of being saved.

Fortunately, through the stalwart efforts of a determined handful of local residents, led by battlefield historian Clark B. "Bud" Hall and assisted by the Civil War Preservation Trust (and its predecessor, the Association for the Preservation of Civil War Sites), as well as some very capable and generous lawyers from Washington, D.C., who worked for free, the overwhelming majority of the battlefield at Brandy Station has been forever preserved. Their long fight to save this ground is worthy of being chronicled independently, and I hope to do so someday. Long after my generation has passed from the scene, future generations will be able to visit the battlefield and see the same pristine fields that I came to love, and for that, I am grateful.

I decided to write this volume as a means of providing a good overview of the battle, with good maps, that not only focuses on the long preservation fight that led to the saving of most of the battlefield but also gives the reader a driving and walking tour (complete with GPS coordinates) of the publicly accessible portions of the battlefield. My whole concept was that this would be a book that could be taken out on the battlefield and used as a field reference.

One note of caution regarding this work is necessary here. This work is *not* intended to be the definitive work on the subject of the Battle of Brandy Station. That work, by Bud Hall, should be completed shortly, and I recommend it to you as the final word on Brandy Station. Mr. Hall has invested twenty years of research, writing and tramping the battlefield and is nearly finished with what will be the definitive work on the subject. This volume is not intended to be competition for that project. Indeed, Mr. Hall reviewed this work, made comments on it and was the impetus for the writing of this book. Anything that I know about Brandy Station is a direct result of my association with Mr. Hall, and in many ways, this book is intended as a tribute to him and his efforts.

As with any project of this nature, I owe major debts of gratitude to a lot of people. First and foremost, I am grateful to Bud Hall for his friendship and support and for his mentorship along the way. Likewise, I am grateful to Mike Block, a member of the board of trustees of the Brandy Station Foundation, for spending several days walking the field with me and helping me to better learn the terrain. Mike Noirot provided the modern-day photos that grace the driving tour at the back of this book.

Master cartographer Steven Stanley drew the superb maps for this book, based on the research of Clark B. Hall. Simply put, nobody does better maps than Steve, and I am indeed most fortunate to have his work included in these pages. Steve is the cartographer for the Civil War Preservation Trust and originally drew these maps for the CWPT. David Duncan and Jim Campi at the CWPT gave me permission to reproduce the maps here, and I am grateful to them for allowing me to do so. I am likewise grateful to CWPT president Jim Lighthizer for writing the excellent foreword. No battlefield better embodies the mission—and the success—of the CWPT than does Brandy Station, and it is my honor and pleasure to feature both here.

I am similarly honored to be part of The History Press's Sesquicentennial Series on the Civil War. I hope that this volume is a worthy contribution to that effort. I am grateful to series editor Doug Bostick for including me, and I am grateful to Laura All for her efforts to steer this manuscript through the publishing process.

Finally, I would be remiss if I did not acknowledge my long-suffering but much loved wife, Susan Skilken Wittenberg, for her endless patience with my compulsive need to tell the stories of Civil War soldiers. Without her love and seemingly limitless support, none of this would be possible, and I am forever in her debt.

Chapter 1

OPENING MOVES

Robert E. Lee and the Confederate Army of Northern Virginia thrashed Joseph Hooker's Union Army of the Potomac at the Battle of Chancellorsville, fought May 1–5, 1863. The spring campaign had begun inauspiciously. The Army of the Potomac broke its winter camps and began marching on April 27. Three Federal corps, the Fifth, Sixth and Twelfth, marched to Kelly's Ford, crossed the Rappahannock River and swung southeast toward Germanna Ford on the Rapidan River. The Federal Third Corps remained at Falmouth, while the First and Sixth Corps started moving toward the Rappahannock crossings at Fredericksburg. Thus, Hooker had more than 133,000 blue-clad infantrymen in motion by the afternoon of April 28.

By the night of April 29, Major General George G. Meade's Fifth Corps was poised to enter the Wilderness from Ely's Ford on the Rapidan, while Major General Darius N. Couch's Second Corps crossed the Rappahannock at U.S. Ford and moved toward Chancellorsville, a handsome tavern situated at a critical road intersection on Lee's left flank. By the night of April 30, four Union infantry corps were concentrated around Chancellorsville, ready to move against Lee's exposed flank. Lee did not know they were there and was unprepared to fend them off, as his attention was focused on the large force in front of Fredericksburg. However, instead of pressing his advantage, Hooker halted and ceded the initiative to the wily Lee, who shifted most of his army to meet the threat once he became aware of it.

Major General Joseph Hooker, commander of the Army of the Potomac. *Library of Congress.*

The battle around Chancellorsville began in earnest on May 1. Hooker's troops attacked the outnumbered Confederates of Lieutenant General Thomas J. "Stonewall" Jackson's Second Corps and shoved them back. Union infantry took possession of commanding high ground east of Chancellorsville. However, over the vehement objections of his subordinates, Hooker abandoned the strong position taken by his troops that day and instead pulled back to a defensive position at Chancellorsville, where he waited for Robert E. Lee to attack him.

That attack came on the afternoon of May 2. Lee gambled, dividing his outnumbered force and sending Jackson and the Second Corps on a seventeen-mile flank march, leaving fewer than twenty thousand men to contend with Hooker at Chancellorsville. In spite of warnings and evidence indicating that Jackson's corps was on the move, Hooker refused to act. The Confederate infantry crashed into the exposed and unprotected Eleventh Corps flank and broke it, sending its routed elements streaming back toward Chancellorsville late in the afternoon. That night, while out scouting, Jackson was shot by his own troops. He died a few days later. However, his flank attack shattered Hooker's confidence and cast the die for the Army of the Potomac's campaign in the Wilderness.

Hooker pulled back into a tight defensive position centered on Chancellorsville. On the morning of May 3, Jackson's weary infantrymen, now commanded by Major General J.E.B. Stuart, the Army of Northern

Virginia's cavalry chief, resumed the assault on Hooker's left. About nine o'clock that morning, a Southern artillery shell struck the porch where Hooker stood, stunning and probably concussing the army commander, leaving him incapacitated. Couch, the senior corps commander, found himself in de facto command of the Army of the Potomac, and he fought a superb defensive action against Jackson's determined veterans, who were joined by the rest of Lee's army. Couch was wounded twice in the action, and his horse was shot out from under him. The Army of the Potomac withstood the onslaught with heavy losses.

Meanwhile, the Union Sixth Corps crossed the Rappahannock River at Fredericksburg and drove the Confederate defenders from their strong position along a sunken road at Marye's Heights. They pressed westward, hoping to link up with Hooker from the east, but a stout stand by Major General Lafayette McLaws's Confederate infantry at Salem Church on May 4 repulsed this attack, preventing the Sixth Corps from reinforcing the Union position at Chancellorsville. Southern reinforcements then drove the Sixth Corps back toward Fredericksburg, ending any hope of linking up with the Army of the Potomac's main body.

General Robert E. Lee, commander of the Army of Northern Virginia. *Library of Congress.*

By now thoroughly beaten, Hooker pulled back into prepared defensive positions around the Chancellor House, with both of his flanks anchored on the banks of the Rappahannock River. The two battered armies spent May 5 glaring at each other, but there was not much fighting. On the morning of May 6, Hooker finally admitted defeat and began pulling the Army of the Potomac back across the Rappahannock at U.S. Ford. The Federals returned to their jumping-off point near Falmouth. Lee let them go, knowing that his outnumbered army had already accomplished as much as he might have hoped. Hooker's magnificent campaign, which had begun with so much hope, ended with a fizzle, a victim of the commander's hesitation at the critical moment on May 1.[1]

Having seized the initiative from Hooker, Lee wanted to gamble again. The Confederate high command convened a series of meetings in Richmond to discuss the next moves after the epic victory at Chancellorsville. After three days of intensive dialogue, Lee persuaded the Confederate leadership that the time had come for a second invasion of the North. Confederate secretary of war James A. Seddon later reported that Lee's opinion "naturally had great effect in the decisions of the Executive."[2] A northward thrust would serve a variety of purposes: first, it held the potential of relieving Federal pressure on the beleaguered Southern garrison at Vicksburg; second, it would provide the people of Virginia with an opportunity to recover from "the ravages of war and a chance to harvest their crops free from interruption by military operation"; third, it would draw Hooker's army away from its base at Falmouth, giving Lee an opportunity to defeat the Army of the Potomac in the open field; and finally, Lee wanted to spend the summer months in Pennsylvania in the hope of leveraging political gain from such an invasion.

With his bold plan approved, Lee returned to his army and began making preparations for the coming campaign. All seven brigades of cavalry assigned to the Army of Northern Virginia began concentrating in Culpeper County in anticipation of the campaign's opening. That concentration of cavalry proved to be an irresistible target for its Federal counterparts, who remained active and diligent, looking for opportunities to strike a blow.

On May 14, reports of Confederate raiders in Hooker's rear brought action. With a ten-year-old boy named Bertram E. Trenis as their guide, elements of seven Northern mounted units set out to pursue the marauders, rousting a group of Southern guerrillas in the process. Major J. Claude White of the Third Pennsylvania Cavalry led the pursuit, scouting the country to and around Brentsville. The Federals took a few prisoners, killing three horses and inflicting severe wounds on several enemy troopers with saber cuts.[3]

Brigadier General Alfred Pleasonton, commander of the Army of the Potomac's Cavalry Corps in June 1863. *Library of Congress.*

On May 17, Lieutenant Colonel David R. Clendennin's Eighth Illinois Cavalry received orders to go out on a lengthy reconnaissance into the so-called "Northern Neck" between the Rappahannock and Potomac Rivers in King George, Westmoreland, Richmond, Northumberland and Lancaster Counties.[4] Clendennin divided his command into three battalions, which traversed the entire length of the Neck, making their way to the confluence of the two rivers. They arrived at Leed's Ferry and determined that it was used for smuggling contraband across the Rappahannock. Clendennin decided to destroy the ferry. Six of the Illinois saddle soldiers dressed themselves in gray, took two prisoners with them and called out to the men on the opposite bank to bring the boat across. The deception worked famously, and when the ferrymen brought the boat across the river, they were promptly captured and the boat burned.[5]

Brigadier General Alfred Pleasonton, who assumed temporary command of the Army of the Potomac's Cavalry Corps when its regular commander, Major General George Stoneman, left the army to take medical leave on May 15, 1863, reported that the Illini horsemen

destroyed 50 boats, and broke up the underground trade pretty effectually, having destroyed some $30,000 worth of goods in transit. They bring back *with them 800 contrabands, innumerable mules, horses, &c., and have captured between 40 and 50 prisoners, including a captain and lieutenant.*

Pleasonton claimed that his horse soldiers caused more than $1 million in damage to the enemy war effort at the cost of one man severely wounded and two slightly injured. "Considering the force engaged and the results obtained, this is the greatest raid of the war," boasted Pleasonton.[6] The regimental historian of the Eighth Illinois noted:

It was found that some of the wealthiest citizens on "the neck" were engaged in the smuggling business, or contributing in some way to the support of the rebellion; and these gentlemen were made to pay dearly for their secession sympathies.[7]

Several infantry regiments also accompanied this expedition, raiding deep into the heart of Virginia. Captain George H. Thompson's squadron of the Third Indiana Cavalry joined them, making a lengthy march and successfully completing a dangerous crossing of the Rappahannock in leaky boats. The Northern saddle soldiers covered forty-five miles in just five hours that day. "We hid in the woods till next morning," reported Captain George A. Custer of the Fifth U.S. Cavalry, of Pleasonton's staff, who accompanied the expedition. "With 9 men and an officer in a small canoe I started in pursuit of a small sailing-vessel." They pursued for nearly ten miles until the Southerners ran their boat aground, jumped overboard and ran for the shore. "We captured boat and passengers," continued Custer. "They had left Richmond the previous morning and had in their possession a large sum of Confederate money."

Custer and a handful of men waded ashore and headed for the nearest house. Custer spotted a man in Confederate uniform lying on the piazza, reading a book. Although worried that he might be falling into a trap, Custer took the man prisoner.

Then, with twenty men, in three small boats, I rowed to Urbana on the opposite shore. Here we burned two schooners and a bridge over the bay, driving the rebel pickets out of town. We returned to the north bank where we captured 12 prisoners, thirty horses, two large boxes of Confederate boots and shoes, and two barrels of whiskey, which we destroyed.

Custer captured two horses himself.[8]

The Hoosiers successfully completed their march, capturing a handful of prisoners, a stash of Confederate money and fifteen horses, which they turned over to Pleasonton.[9] Custer, a scant two years out of West Point, was beginning to attract attention with his exploits. Hooker sent for him and complimented him highly on his conduct of the expedition, saying that it could not have been done better and that he would have more for Custer to do.[10]

Several days later, Michigan governor Austin Blair visited the camps of his state's troops. The colonelcy of the Fifth Michigan Cavalry was vacant, and Custer craved it. Custer asked Pleasonton to write a letter of recommendation for him, something that Pleasonton happily did. "Captain Custer," wrote Pleasonton,

will make an excellent commander of a cavalry regiment and is entitled to such promotion for his gallant and efficient services in the present war of rebellion. I do not know anyone I could recommend to you with more confidence than Captain Custer.

Hooker gladly endorsed the recommendation. "I cheerfully concur in the recommendation of Brig Genl Pleasonton. He is a young officer of great promise and uncommon merit."[11] Although the appointment instead went to Lieutenant Colonel Russell A. Alger of the Sixth Michigan Cavalry, Pleasonton nevertheless had great expectations and plans for Custer.

While the Southern high command debated its next move, the Army of the Potomac began itching for an opportunity to avenge the defeat at Chancellorsville. "The days rolled into June; and it seemed fully time to be doing something more about beating Lee, whose lieutenants were successfully screening their preparations for the coming northern invasion," observed an officer of a Massachusetts infantry regiment of the Twelfth Corps.[12]

Robert E. Lee recognized that the power and confidence of the Federal horsemen was growing with each passing day. "Every expedition will augment their boldness and increase their means of doing us harm," he wrote in a letter to Jefferson Davis, "as they will become better acquainted with the country and more familiar with its roads." The only solution, according to Lee, was for his cavalry command to receive reinforcements from the Deep South.[13] Lee's assessment was right on the money, as events in the upcoming Gettysburg Campaign proved again and again.

Once the Confederate leadership approved Lee's audacious plan to invade Pennsylvania, the Southern commander began shifting troops west for a strike up the Shenandoah Valley, set to commence on June 3. Jeb Stuart arrived in Culpeper County on May 20 and established his headquarters there to oversee the concentration of the Confederate horse in preparation for the coming invasion.[11] Within a few days, three brigades of Southern horse soldiers had arrived and established their camps in the lush fields of Culpeper County. On May 22, Stuart reviewed the brigades of Wade Hampton and the two Lees—about forty-five hundred of his command. "The grand Cavalry Review took place this morning and was one of the most imposing scenes I ever witnessed," recounted a Confederate staff officer.[15] "The most magnificent sight I ever witnessed," agreed Lieutenant Colonel William R. Carter of the Third Virginia Cavalry. "A Beautiful day & quite a large turnout of the ladies, considering the times."[16] The next night, Stuart threw a magnificent cotillion in Culpeper attended by his officers and the local ladies.

UNION INTELLIGENCE-GATHERING ACTIVITIES

Almost immediately, rumors of this activity trickled into Union headquarters. Within days of Lee ordering his cavalry to concentrate in Culpeper County, Colonel George H. Sharpe, of the provost marshal general's office and chief of intelligence for the Army of the Potomac, reported:

> *There are three brigades of cavalry 3 miles from Culpeper County Court House, toward Kelly's Ford…These are Fitz. Lee's, William H. Fitzhugh Lee's, and Wade Hampton's brigades…The Confederate army is under marching orders, and an order from General Lee was very lately read to the troops, announcing a campaign of long marches and hard fighting.*[17]

A few days later, a local citizen named G.S. Smith, who was known as a reliable source of intelligence, reported to Pleasonton:

> *This movement of General Lee's is not intended to menace Washington, but to try his hand again toward Maryland, or to call off your attention while General Stuart goes there. I have every reason for believing that Stuart is on his way toward Maryland. I do not positively know it, but have the very best of reasons for believing it.*

Pleasonton added his own incorrect analysis of the situation: "It is my impression the rebel army has been weakened by troops sent west and south, and that any performance of Stuart's will be aflutter to keep us from seeing their weakness."[18]

These reports provided the impetus for Hooker to "send all my cavalry against" the assembling mass of Confederate horse, in an attempt "to break... up [the offensive] in its incipiency."[19] Accordingly, Pleasonton ordered Brigadier General John Buford, commanding the First Cavalry Division, to join Brigadier General David M. Gregg's Second Cavalry Division at Bealeton and reconnoiter the area to try to determine the true object of the Confederate movement.

On May 28, Gregg reported that four brigades of Confederate cavalry were encamped in the vicinity of Culpeper Courthouse. Alarmed, Pleasonton asked Hooker for permission to send Buford's Reserve Brigade and a battery to reinforce Gregg at Bealeton.[20] Hooker wasted no time in approving the request and ordered Buford to assume command of all cavalry forces operating in the area. Reports also indicated that enemy patrols were operating on the north side of the Rappahannock near Warrenton, so Hooker gave Buford permission to engage the Rebels and push them back across the river.

The army commander concluded with the critical instruction that if Buford "should find himself with sufficient force, to drive the enemy out of his camp near Culpeper and across the Rapidan, destroying the bridge at that point." Hooker correctly guessed that the Rebel horsemen were gathering there to mask a Confederate advance down the Shenandoah Valley. Hooker specifically ordered Buford to spare no effort to find out the objective of the enemy movement, stating that "[a]t all events, they have no business on this side of the [Rappahannock]."[21]

Later that day, Pleasonton instructed Buford to drive the Confederates from Warrenton, stating, "The advance of the enemy's cavalry in the vicinity of Warrenton may have for its object to conceal a movement in force up the Valley. Spare no effort to ascertain the true object of the movement." On the twenty-ninth, Buford tersely announced, "The command is in motion for Bealeton."[22]

Buford's force arrived at Warrenton Junction after a grueling thirty-hour march. He immediately assumed command of the Union forces assembled there. After hearing that the Confederates had burned a nearby railroad bridge, Buford marched his troopers up the Orange & Alexandria Railroad. He discovered that no bridge had been destroyed but that Major John S. Mosby's Confederate guerrillas had torched a ten-car train of supplies, generating the smoke that had triggered the erroneous report. The independent cavalry

Brigadier General John Buford, commander of the First Cavalry Division, Cavalry Corps, Army of the Potomac. He commanded the right wing at Brandy Station. *Library of Congress.*

division of Major General Julius Stahel, which was not under the authority of the Army of the Potomac, pursued the guerrillas, inflicting a number of casualties. By interdicting the railroads and interfering with the flow of supplies and communication, the Rebels disrupted lines of supply and communication in both Stahel's area of authority and in Buford's.

Buford tackled the tasks of removing the wreckage of the train from the tracks and restoring telegraph communications. He reported that there was a good supply of water and grass for the horses near Warrenton and concluded, "I can hear of no rebel force. None has crossed the river below Waterloo Bridge. The horses and pack mules of the Second and Third Divisions are in wretched condition."[23] The next day, the railroad and the lines of communication were fully restored.

On June 2, Buford learned that three brigades of Stuart's cavalry had entered the Shenandoah Valley for unknown purposes. Pleasonton instructed the Kentuckian to

> *aid in fixing the locality and numbers of the enemy's cavalry especially, with a view to our future movements. Send us by telegraph all the news obtained,*

and have scouting parties active. The capture of prisoners, contrabands, etc., may give much information.[24]

Buford cabled Pleasonton that he intended to establish his troops along a new and shorter line anchored at Catlett's Station and that "no enemy save some of Mosby's are on this side of the Rappahannock. Orleans, Waterloo, Warrenton, and New Baltimore were visited yesterday." He concluded by stating that his entire command was "packed into an area 2 or 3 miles wide."[25]

Buford gathered his horsemen and set out to obey Pleasonton's instructions. On June 4, after a couple of futile days, army headquarters reported that a portion of the Confederate forces opposite the Union left had disappeared. Hooker ordered Buford to "keep a sharp lookout, country well scouted, and advise us as soon as possible of anything in your front or vicinity indicating a movement."[26] Uncertain of the enemy's whereabouts or plans, Hooker had every reason to be worried.

Buford's labors bore fruit the next day. "I have just received information, which I consider reliable, that all of the available cavalry of the Confederacy is in Culpeper County," announced the vigilant Kentuckian. "Stuart, the two Lees, Robertson, Jenkins, and Jones are all there. Robertson came from North Carolina, Jenkins from Kanawha, and Jones from the Valley. Jones arrived at Culpeper on the 3d, after the others."[27] Buford was incorrect in part of his report—the brigade of Brigadier General Albert G. Jenkins was not present. Buford correctly noted that the strength of the Rebel cavalry had increased but wrongfully suggested that, instead of bringing new units into service, Stuart had mounted infantrymen. "My informant—a refugee from Madison County—says Stuart has 20,000; can't tell his instructions, but thinks he is going to make a raid."[28] While the informant overestimated the number of Confederate cavalry by double, Buford provided army headquarters with insightful intelligence of the enemy's whereabouts and dispositions, and Hooker made good use of the information.

A correspondent of one of the New York newspapers correctly observed, "This force is the largest body of cavalry that the enemy has ever got together." He continued:

It is not the intention of this force to fight, unless compelled to do so. They go on a rail-ripping, horse-stealing expedition, and to "bring the horrors of war to our own doors"—as they express it. Once well on the wing and pursuit, as is always the case, will be well nigh useless. [The Army of the Potomac] *may well be depleted of its cavalry and fail to capture more than a few drunken stragglers.*

He concluded prophetically, "Stuart will doubtless move in a very few days, and the only way to effectually interfere with this dashing arrangement is to pitch into him where he is."[29]

By June 5, the Federal cavalry was growing antsy. The blue-clad horsemen spent the day drilling, racing their horses and listening to the rumbling of distant artillery. "Recd orders in the Evening to hold ourselves in readyness to march at any moment," recounted a member of the Eighth Illinois Cavalry in his diary that night.[30]

That day, Pleasonton notified Hooker that the enemy's cavalry pickets extended to Front Royal, nearly sixty miles west of Falmouth. Pleasonton then instructed Buford to "make a strong demonstration without delay upon the enemy in your front toward Culpeper, and push them as far as possible without jeopardizing your command." He also informed Buford that Confederate forces were in motion in front of Fredericksburg and that a portion of the enemy army had already moved toward Orange Court House.[31] Buford obeyed the order immediately and engaged the enemy troopers in skirmishing intended to flush out the size and disposition of the Confederate cavalry forces facing them.

The following day, a nervous Hooker cabled Buford that "[i]nformation has been communicated to me that three brigades of the enemy's cavalry are posted at Jefferson." Hooker further inquired how such a turn of events was possible and asked Buford if his pickets could shut down the Confederate lines of communication across the Rappahannock. Buford responded that Hooker's "information is incorrect about the number of cavalry at Jefferson" and that he would attempt to keep the Confederate lines of communication across the river closed. He concluded, "I have a large force in the neighborhood of Jefferson, reconnoitering."[32]

That same day, Hooker, nervous about the large concentration of Southern cavalry gathering in Culpeper County, asked Halleck whether Major General Julius D. Stahel's independent division of cavalry assigned to the defenses of Washington, D.C., could be sent to reinforce him. These reinforcements would not come. A few days earlier, Major John Singleton Mosby's guerrillas had captured a train on the Orange & Alexandria Railroad near Catlett's Station, creating great consternation in Washington. Consequently, Stahel's division could not be sent to reinforce Pleasonton because the Hungarian general's troopers were occupied with protecting the vital rail link. These additional horsemen—two large veteran brigades' worth—may well have made the difference at Brandy Station.[33]

On June 7, after collating all of the raw data from the field, Colonel Sharpe reported his conclusions to Hooker. Sharpe concluded that the Confederates intended to launch a massive cavalry raid, "the most important expedition ever attempted in this country." He estimated the size of Stuart's force at twelve to fifteen thousand saddle soldiers and announced, "There were strong indications that the enemy's entire Infantry will fall back upon Richmond and thence reinforce their armies in the west." Although Sharpe's conclusions about Stuart's ultimate objective were wrong, his analysis that there would be a large expedition into the North was absolutely correct.[34]

The uneasy Hooker proceeded cautiously. Pleasonton belayed the orders for Buford to pitch into the Confederate cavalry at Culpeper until further notice. Instead, Pleasonton instructed Buford to "[r]eport everything as it occurs."[35] Buford responded, "Your dispatch just received. I have sent to recall Colonel [Alfred N.] Duffié, who had your instructions to carry out. I fear he has gone too far."[36] That afternoon, Buford reported that Duffié had already crossed the Rappahannock at Sulphur Springs with twenty-five hundred men. He announced that "the information sent yesterday has been partly corroborated; none of it denied. Yesterday cannon firing was heard toward Culpeper. I suppose it was a salute, as I was told Stuart was to have had that day an inspection of his whole force." Buford noted that Major General John Bell Hood's Confederate infantry division was camped on the Rapidan at Raccoon Ford but that he could not determine whether any gray-clad infantry was stationed in the area north of the Rapidan. Ominously, Buford reported, "There is a very heavy cavalry force on the grazing grounds in Culpeper County."[37]

Now persuaded that Sharpe's estimates were correct, Hooker cabled President Abraham Lincoln of his "great desire to 'bust [Stuart's contemplated raid] up' before it got fairly under way."[38] The army commander began planning an expedition to do just that.

Chapter 2

ALFRED PLEASONTON AND THE UNION CAVALRY

In the wake of the defeat of the Army of the Potomac in the Battle of Chancellorsville, the commander of the Cavalry Corps, Major General George Stoneman, left the Army of the Potomac on May 15 to take medical leave. Stoneman suffered from a horrific case of hemorrhoids, making every moment spent in the saddle sheer agony. His senior division commander, Brigadier General Alfred Pleasonton, assumed temporary command of the Cavalry Corps while Stoneman sought relief for his piles.

Pleasonton was born in Washington, D.C., on July 7, 1824, the youngest of seven children of Stephen and Mary Pleasonton, and attended local schools. His father, a miserly government clerk during the War of 1812, had helped save the Declaration of Independence and other precious documents from the British torch and was promised a government education for his children as a reward. Alfred, therefore, was handed an appointment to West Point in 1840. He graduated seventh in the class of 1844 and was commissioned into the Second Dragoons. In 1846, he received a brevet to first lieutenant for gallantry in the Mexican War and then served on the Indian frontier and in Florida against the Seminoles. While serving in the West, Pleasonton met and befriended John Buford, who played a major role in the drama that unfolded in 1863. In 1861, while a captain, Pleasonton commanded several companies of his regiment on their march from Utah to Washington City in September and October. In February 1862, he was promoted to major.

During Major General George B. McClellan's spring Peninsula Campaign, Pleasonton and the (renamed) Second Cavalry were posted to army headquarters, and the major found himself nestled quite comfortably in the midst of the army's upper crust. In his element, Pleasonton stayed in McClellan's gaze and did all he could to make sure he was noticed. Even though his fallow horsemen were seeing little action, Pleasonton nevertheless transmitted a flurry of lengthy, vainglorious reports of his troopers' most mundane activities to headquarters. The cocksure Pleasonton made himself seem indispensable, and the gambit worked. In July, after the Seven Days' Battles, Little Mac bumped Pleasonton to brigadier general of volunteers. The promotion brought him field command of the Army of the Potomac's cavalry during the 1862 Maryland Campaign and at Fredericksburg.[39]

Many believed Pleasonton to be a conniver, a manipulator and a man desperate to advance his own cause—much like his father had been during his own political career. Active and energetic, he swaggered like a bantam rooster, exuding self-confidence. He was something of a dandy, preferring fancy uniforms, a straw hat, kid gloves and a cowhide riding stick. "Pleasonton is small, nervous, and full of dash," reported a war correspondent, "dark-haired and finely featured with gray-streaked hair."[10] After the war, tongue-in-cheek writers dubbed him the "Knight of Romance."

Pleasonton's courage in battle was suspect; he was "notorious" among those "who have served under him and seen him under fire."[11] Captain Adams, who possessed the acid pen of his great-grandfather John Adams, noted, "Pleasonton…is pure and simple a newspaper humbug…He does nothing save with a view to a newspaper paragraph."[12] Colonel Charles Russell Lowell, another Boston Brahmin who commanded the Second Massachusetts Cavalry, accused the cavalry chief of being a liar: "I don't call any cavalry officer good who can't see the truth and tell the truth… [I]t is the universal opinion that P[leasonton]'s own reputation and…his late promotions are bolstered up by systematic lying."[13] In spite of these unattractive personality traits, Alf Pleasonton had demonstrated competence in the field and in administration, and the Army of the Potomac's Cavalry Corps badly needed competence and experience.

When Pleasonton assumed command of the Cavalry Corps, Brigadier General John Buford took over command of the First Cavalry Division. John Buford Jr. was born near Versailles, Kentucky, on March 4, 1826. He was the first son of John and Anne Bannister Howe Watson Buford. Young John Buford came from a large family—he had two full brothers, as well as thirteen half brothers and sisters from the first marriages of both of his parents. His grandfather, Simeon Buford, had served under Colonel Henry "Light Horse Harry" Lee, father of General Robert E. Lee, in the Virginia cavalry during the Revolution, and his great-uncle, Colonel Abraham Buford, was a hero of the Battle of Waxhaws during the Revolution. John Buford's mother died in a cholera epidemic in 1835, and the family relocated to Rock Island, Illinois. As a youth, he was "a splendid horseman, an unerring rifle shot and a person of wonderful nerve and composure."[44]

Buford received an appointment to West Point in 1844. His performance there was solid, if unspectacular. He graduated sixteenth in the class of 1848. Upon graduation, and at his request, Buford was commissioned into the First Dragoons as a brevet second lieutenant. He only remained with the First Dragoons for a few months and transferred to the newly formed Second Dragoons in 1849. He served as quartermaster of the Second Dragoons from 1855 through the beginning of August 1858, fighting in several Indian battles along the way, including the Sioux Punitive Expedition, under the command of Brigadier General William S. Harney, which culminated in the Battle of Ash Hollow in 1856. Colonel Philip St. George Cooke, commanding officer of the Second Dragoons, cited Lieutenant Buford for his "good service" at Ash Hollow, as did Harney himself.

Buford participated in quelling the disturbances in Kansas during the mid-1850s and served on the Mormon Expedition to Utah during 1857. Buford won high praise from Cooke for his service during the arduous march west and served in Utah until the outbreak of the Civil War in 1861. Buford was torn between his loyalty to his native Kentucky and his loyalty to the government he had served for thirteen years. John Gibbon recalled:

> *One night after the arrival of the mail we were in his* [Buford's] *room, talking over the news…when Buford said in his slow and deliberate way, "I got a letter by the last mail from home with a message in it from the Governor of Kentucky. He sends me word to come to Kentucky at once and I shall have anything I want."*

Anxious, Gibbon asked, "What did you answer, John?" Gibbon was greatly relieved to hear Buford's reply: "I sent him word I was a captain in the United States Army and I intend to remain one."[45]

Reporting to Washington with his regiment, Buford requested, and received, an appointment as a major in the inspector general's office. He served in that position until June 1862. Major General John Pope, commanding the [Federal] Army of Virginia, knew of Buford's talent and special affinity for the enlisted man. Pope promoted Buford to brigadier general of volunteers and gave him command of a brigade of cavalry in the Army of Virginia. Buford served with great distinction during the Second Bull Run Campaign, providing superior scouting and intelligence services and also going toe-to-toe with the vaunted troopers of Jeb Stuart's Confederate cavalry on two different occasions. His men nearly captured both Stuart and Robert E. Lee at different points during the campaign, and his intelligence saved Pope's army from destruction shortly after the August 9, 1862 Battle of Cedar Mountain. Buford commanded the Union forces in a little-known but important phase of the Second Battle of Bull Run: the cavalry mêlée at Lewis Ford on August 30, 1862, where Buford enjoyed some success against Stuart's men and bought time for the beaten Army of Virginia's retreat. Buford himself was slightly wounded in this engagement, leading to his appointment as chief of cavalry under McClellan.[16]

When Stoneman took command of the newly formed Cavalry Corps in February 1863, Buford was serving on court-martial duty in Washington, D.C. He remained trapped on this unwelcome duty until the third week of March, despite repeated requests for his release. On February 9, Buford penned a revealing letter to his old friend Stoneman. "I have heard that all of the cavalry of the Army of the Potomac is to be massed under your command. I take it for granted that I am to have a command under you," he wrote candidly.

> *Being absent while you are making your organizations, I am a little afraid that the different brigade commanders being on the ground may succeed in getting the fighting regiments leaving me the less desirable ones. There is a great difference in the Reg'ts—some will stay while others will not under any circumstances. If I can have my choice I would prefer Western troops. If the Regulars are to be put together, I believe they would prefer me to either of the other cavalry commanders.[17]*

The Reserve Brigade of Regulars started out as an independent command but became a permanent part of the First Division after the Stoneman Raid. The First Division consisted of three brigades.

Thirty-one-year-old Colonel Benjamin Franklin "Grimes" Davis commanded the First Brigade. Born in Alabama and raised in Mississippi, Davis had five brothers and a sister. He was a cousin of Confederate president Jefferson Davis, who also hailed from Mississippi. Two of Davis's brothers served in the Eleventh Mississippi Infantry during the Civil War, and both were killed in battle before war's end. When young Benjamin's parents died, probably as a result of an outbreak of smallpox, he became a

Colonel Benjamin F. "Grimes" Davis of the Eighth New York Cavalry, a Mississippian who remained loyal to the Union. Davis was mortally wounded in the opening moments of the battle. *USAHEC.*

ward of a wealthy uncle who lived in Aberdeen, Mississippi. Another uncle was involved in politics and arranged an appointment to West Point for Davis, who entered the academy in 1850. "He was a youth of exceptional character and fine abilities, and…he had good size, pleasing appearance, strictly brave, and every way honorable." His academy mates nicknamed him "Grimes," and he served as captain of the cadets during his senior year. Davis graduated seventh in the class of 1854; Jeb Stuart was a classmate.[48]

Upon graduation, Davis joined the Fifth U.S. Infantry but transferred to the First Dragoons in 1855. In 1857, he suffered a wound while fighting Apache Indians on the Gila River Expedition. Davis spent most of his Regular Army career in the New Mexico Territory and California and was promoted to first lieutenant in January 1860. At the beginning of the war, he sought and obtained a commission as colonel of the First California Cavalry but deserted his unit to rejoin the Regulars when they marched east.[49] On July 31, he was promoted to captain of Company K of the First Dragoons, which had been redesignated as the First U.S. Cavalry. He first drew the attention of his superiors during the 1862 Peninsula Campaign, when, at the Battle of Williamsburg on May 2, his squadron charged a larger force of Confederate cavalry and routed it.[50]

In spite of his Southern roots, "Col. Davis was emphatically a son of the Union."[51] "He was a gallant man, an ambitious soldier, a courtly gentleman," recalled Wesley Merritt, who had a distinguished forty-three-year career in the Regular Army. "A Southerner…he stood firm by the flag under which he had received his qualifications and commission as an officer."[52]

As a result of his good service on the Peninsula, Davis received an appointment as colonel of the Eighth New York Cavalry in July 1862. Davis became famous in the aftermath of Jackson's capture of Harpers Ferry during the 1862 Maryland Campaign; refusing to surrender, he led fifteen hundred Union cavalry on a dangerous escape, capturing Major General James Longstreet's wagon train along the way. This feat led to his appointment to brigade command, and he served in that capacity with distinction.[53]

Davis was a veteran regular and was not afraid to lead men into a fight.[54] "When Colonel Davis found the rebels, he did not stop at anything, but went for them heavy," a member of the Eighth New York Cavalry reminisced. "I believe he liked to fight the rebels as well as he liked to eat."[55] The hard-fighting colonel was also a martinet. "Davis was a…proud tyrannical devil," recalled the regimental surgeon of the Third Indiana Cavalry.[56] Another Hoosier remembered Davis as "a strict disciplinarian. Prompt in the performance of his own duties and exacting of his inferiors. Brave and audacious. Much esteemed by his own regiment and respected by the whole command."[57] His veteran brigade consisted of the Eighth New York Cavalry, the Ninth New York Cavalry, the Eighth Illinois Cavalry and six companies of the Third Indiana Cavalry.

Colonel Thomas C. Devin of New York commanded Buford's Second Brigade. Following an education in the city's public schools, Devin formed a partnership with his brother, painting homes and selling varnish, paint and oils. Since his boyhood, Devin was enamored with the martial life and watched wide-eyed with other lads as local militia marched in parades and provided pomp for public ceremonies. When of age, Devin joined the neighborhood's company of militia cavalry, eventually rising through the ranks to command it as captain. An accomplished horseman, he garnered a reputation as an ideal cavalryman, even though he had, as yet, no practical battlefield experience. On March 4, 1861, Devin was promoted to lieutenant colonel and given command of the First New York State Militia Cavalry.

A staunch patriot, Devin wanted a part in the Civil War the moment it broke out. On July 12, 1861, Devin sought out strong-arm New York political boss Thurlow Weed. If anyone could get him into the action, Devin reasoned, it was Weed. He found Weed one evening on the steps of one of the city's landmarks, the Astor House, and although a stranger to the well-connected and powerful politico, Devin boldly stopped him. The episode

Colonel Thomas C. Devin of the Sixth New York Cavalry, commander of a brigade in Buford's First Division. Devin commanded the division that day because Buford was a wing commander. *USAHEC.*

made an impression on Weed, who later recalled that Devin "informed me that he desired to raise a company of cavalry, which, if he could obtain the authority, should be organized and ready to march in three days." Devin obviously had his own militia in mind, which was already outfitted and well drilled. "I was so favorably impressed with his bearing and manner that I immediately telegraphed Governor [Edwin] Morgan, earnestly asking his authority for Thos. C. Devin to organize a cavalry corps."

Devin was not satisfied to leave Weed's presence to await an answer, however. "[Devin] remained at my room until a favorable response from the Governor, two hours afterward, was received; and he was also faithful to his promise, for in three days, with a full company of men, he was on his way to the front." On July 19, 1861, Devin was mustered in for three months as captain of Devin's Independent Company of New York State Militia Cavalry. The one hundred mounted men from his former regiment preferred to call themselves the "Jackson Horse Guards" and took pride in the distinction of being the first unit of volunteer cavalry to arrive in Washington for service in the field.

Following a short stint on the staff of Brigadier General Isaac Stevens, Devin was commissioned colonel of the Sixth New York Cavalry, also known as the Second Ira Harris Guards, on November 18, 1861. The Sixth New York performed good service during the Antietam Campaign, and after the Battle of Fredericksburg, Devin assumed command of a brigade under Pleasonton, who regularly and fruitlessly urged his promotion to brigadier general.[58] Devin's "command was long known in the Army of the Potomac as one of the few cavalry regiments which in the earlier campaigns of that Army, could be deemed thoroughly reliable," observed an early historian of the Cavalry Corps. A healthy mutual respect and attachment developed between John Buford and Devin.[59]

"I can't teach Col. Devin anything about cavalry," Buford once said. "He knows more about the tactics than I do."[60] Another said of Devin that he was "of the school of Polonius, a little slow sometimes in entrance to a fight, but, being in, as slow to leave a point for which the enemy is trying."[61] Perhaps the finest accolade paid him was that "Colonel Devin knew how to take his men into action and also how to bring them out."[62] At forty, Devin was older than the other cavalry commanders, but he had experience and was always reliable under fire. "His blunt soldiership, sound judgment, his prompt and skillful dispositions for battle, his long period of active service, his bulldog tenacity, and his habitual reliability fully entitled him to the sobriquet among his officers and soldiers of the old 'war horse,' 'Sheridan's hard hitter,' and the like," observed one of Sheridan's staff officers after the end of the war.[63] Devin's brigade consisted of his Sixth New York, the Eighth Pennsylvania and the Seventeenth Pennsylvania.

Forty-seven-year-old Major Charles Jarvis Whiting of the Fifth U.S. Cavalry led the Reserve Brigade. Whiting, an outspoken abolitionist who was born in Massachusetts and raised in Maine, graduated fourth in the West Point class of 1835. He was commissioned as a brevet second lieutenant

Major Charles J. Whiting of the Fifth U.S. Cavalry, commander of the Reserve Brigade. His brigade bore the brunt of the fighting at Brandy Station. *Library of Congress.*

in the Second U.S. Artillery and served on engineering duty during the Seminole War in Florida. He resigned his commission on May 31, 1836, to become a railroad surveyor in the Florida panhandle. In 1838, he served as the assistant engineer for the survey of the Mississippi River delta. He then settled in Maine, where he established and served as headmaster of the Military and Classical Academy in Ellsworth, which a promising young student named Joshua Lawrence Chamberlain attended. After teaching for six years, Whiting surveyed the boundary between the United States and Mexico that was established by the Treaty of Guadalupe-Hidalgo. Whiting then settled in San Jose, California, where he farmed and surveyed. For the years 1850 and 1851, he served as surveyor general of California.[64]

When the size of the Regular Army was increased in 1855, a new regiment of light cavalry was formed. On March 3, 1855, Whiting was commissioned a captain in the newly formed Second U.S. Cavalry (which was redesignated as the Fifth U.S. Cavalry in 1861). He saw extensive action in the West, fighting against Comanche Indians on several occasions and earning praise for his valor in combat. The New Englander was known as an ambitious martinet who was eager to advance his own career.[65] The coming of the Civil War gave him that opportunity.

In March 1861, at the height of the secession crisis, Whiting was stationed at Fort Inge in Texas. When Texas left the Union, he and other loyal officers were stranded there. Whiting and Captains George Stoneman and James Oakes met to discuss how to escape. They pondered the possibility of trying to escape to the Jefferson Barracks via Indian country. However, they had insufficient supplies and no transportation, so they abandoned the plan.[66] Stoneman and Whiting eventually found their way back to Washington, D.C., on a steamboat. Whiting was assigned to teach new recruits basic cavalry tactics at the Carlisle Barracks in Pennsylvania.

A veteran officer like Whiting was needed at the front, and he was soon called to rejoin his regiment, which was assigned to the defenses of Washington and to Patterson's Valley Campaign of 1861. During that campaign, he demonstrated a personality trait that cost him dearly two years later. "It is said when he was ordered, at Falling Waters, to proceed with a squadron in search of a militia regiment which had become detached from the army, that he never ceased during the entire movement, to express his opinion of militia in general and of the politicians who were responsible for the war," duly recorded the historian of the Fifth U.S. Cavalry.[67]

Whiting then served in McClellan's Peninsula Campaign of 1862. He led the Fifth U.S. Cavalry in its ill-fated saber charge against Confederate infantry at Gaines Mill in June 1862 and was captured when his horse was shot out from under him.[68] After spending a month in Richmond's notorious Libby Prison, he was sent north to Washington under parole and then was exchanged for another captain and promoted to major. Whiting commanded the Fifth U.S. Cavalry throughout the fall and winter of 1862–63 and participated in the Maryland Campaign.

Although he was one of the oldest serving officers in the Regular Army cavalry, Whiting assumed command of the Reserve Brigade in June 1863 when Buford took command of the First Division.[69] His brigade consisted of the U.S. Army Regular cavalry units assigned to the Army of the Potomac, the First, Second, Fifth and Sixth U.S. Cavalry and the Sixth Pennsylvania Cavalry (also known as Rush's Lancers). His tenure in brigade command was brief.

Colonel Alfred Napoleon Alexander Duffié, of the First Rhode Island Cavalry, commanded the Second Cavalry Division. Born Napoleon Alexandre Duffié in Paris, France, on May 1, 1833, he carried the nickname "Nattie." His father was a well-to-do bourgeois French sugar refiner who distilled sugar from beets.[70] At age seventeen, Duffié enlisted in the French Sixth Regiment of Dragoons. Six months later, he was promoted to corporal

Colonel Alfred N. Duffié of the First Rhode Island Cavalry, commander of the Army of the Potomac's Second Cavalry Division. *Library of Congress.*

and received a second promotion, this time to sergeant, in March 1854. He served in French campaigns in Africa and in the Crimean War from May 1, 1854, to July 16, 1856. In 1854, the Sixth Regiment of Dragoons, along with two other mounted units, made a brilliant cavalry charge at the Battle of Kanghil, near the Black Sea port of Eupatoria in the Ukraine, earning Duffié two decorations for valor. In February 1858, he was made first sergeant in the Sixth Dragoons and then transferred to the Third Regiment of Hussars. Although he would have been eligible for discharge from the French army in 1859, Duffié signed on for another seven-year enlistment that spring after being graded "a strong man capable of becoming a good average officer."

On June 14, 1859, Duffié received a commission as second lieutenant in the Third Regiment of Hussars. Just two months later, Duffié tried to resign his commission, stating a desire to go into business. He had met thirty-two-year-old Mary Ann Pelton, a young American woman serving as a nurse in Europe's charnel houses. Duffié's regimental commander rejected the attempted letter of resignation, stating his "regrets that this officer so little appreciates the honor of recently having been promoted sous-lieutenant, and that he would prefer a commercial position to that honor."[71] When the French army refused to allow Duffié to resign, he deserted and fled to New York with Miss Pelton. Listed as absent without leave and court-martialed in 1860, he was sentenced to dismissal without benefits for desertion to a foreign country and stripped of his medals. On December 20, 1860, by decree of Emperor Napoleon III, Duffié was sentenced, in absentia, to serve five years in prison for desertion and was dishonorably discharged from the French army.[72]

After arriving in New York, he adopted the first name Alfred, perhaps to disguise his true identity from prying eyes. He married Miss Pelton, the daughter of a wealthy and influential New York family. Mary Ann Duffié's father was a dealer in boots, shoes and shoemakers' supplies and was "an energetic and successful businessman" who lived in an enclave of strong abolitionists on Staten Island.[73] When the Civil War broke out, Duffié received a commission as a captain in the Second New York Cavalry. He quickly rose to the rank of major and was appointed colonel of the First Rhode Island Cavalry in July 1862.[74]

Duffié took great pains to hide his military history and spun an elaborate web of lies, convincing all who cared to hear his story that he was the son of a French count and not a humble sugar refiner. He changed the reported date of his birth from 1833 to 1835. He claimed that he had attended the preparatory Military Academy at Vincennes, graduated from the prestigious military college of St. Cyr in 1854 and had served in Algiers and Senegal, Africa, as lieutenant of cavalry.[75]

He further claimed that he had been badly wounded at the Battle of Solferino in the War of Italian Independence in 1859, a conflict between the forces of Austria on one side and the allied forces of Piedmont, Sardinia and France on the other. Solferino was a huge and bloody affair, involving over 300,000 soldiers with nearly 40,000 casualties. However, his unit, the Third Hussars, was not part of the Army of Italy and did not fight at Solferino. Although Duffié boasted that he had received a total of eight wounds, his French military records do not suggest that he ever received so much as a scratch in combat. He even claimed to have received the Victoria Cross from Queen Victoria herself. Finally, he stated that he had come to the United States to take the waters at Saratoga Springs and not because he had deserted the French army and fled to America in the company of a woman who was not his wife. Perhaps the Peltons willingly massaged the myth of Alfred Duffié, French nobleman and war hero, to make their new son-in-law more palatable to their prominent social circles. His martial bearing no doubt helped to persuade both his superior officers and the men who served under him that he had noble roots and a superb military pedigree.[76]

"Confronting us, he presents the aspect of the beau ideal soldat…with his tall symmetrical form erect in saddle and severe facial expression emphasize[d] by a mustache and goatee of formal cut waxed to a point a la militaire," observed a war correspondent. "A Frenchman I judged him on sight, from his tout ensemble, and his first utterance, which launched without instant delay, proved my surmise correct."[77] Long before George Custer regaled the ranks with gaudy attire, Duffié wore an unusual uniform of his own design, knee boots and an ornately embroidered cap patterned after the French Chasseur design.[78]

Duffié spoke fractured English, which often cracked up his listeners. "His attempts were interlarded with curious and novel expletives, which were very amusing," admitted a fellow officer.[79] Upon assuming a new command, the Frenchman would sputter, "You no like me now. You like me bye and bye." He was right. Before long, they would follow him when he ordered a charge. "Once, in preparing to make a charge where the situation looked a little desperate," recalled a New Yorker, Duffié "encouraged his men, who were little more than boys, by saying, 'You all have got to die sometime anyway. If you die now you won't have to die again. Forward!' His charge was successful."[80]

Although the Gallic colonel got off to a rough start with his Rhode Islanders, he soon won them over. The men of his entire brigade grew to like him. "Duffié is in command of the Brigade. He is a Frenchman," observed Albinus Fell of the Sixth Ohio Cavalry. "He is a bully little cuss."[81] Another predicted that the Frenchman would quickly receive a promotion and leave the First Rhode Island. "He is a bully man," observed Sergeant Emmons D. Guild of the First Rhode Island Cavalry. "I tell you he will not stay long, so you will have to look out if you want to see him. His name is A.N. Duffié."[82] Despite his claims of martial grandeur, Duffié's experience showed, and he performed competently if not spectacularly. "Whatever may have been the faults of Colonel Duffié," recorded his regimental sergeant major, "there is no gainsaying the fact that he was probably the best regimental cavalry drill-master and tactician in the army."[83] When Hooker relieved Brigadier General William W. Averell of command of the Second Cavalry Division during the Battle of Chancellorsville, command of the division fell on Duffié as its senior subordinate. Duffié's tenure as a division commander was short; it quickly became apparent that command of such a large unit was beyond his abilities.

Colonel Luigi Palma di Cesnola commanded Duffié's First Brigade. Born to an ancient, ennobled Italian family, the thirty-year-old colonel had a glittering reputation. His father had fought for Napoleon. Cesnola was educated at the Royal Military Academy at Turin and entered the mounted arm of the Sardinian army. At age seventeen, the young count fought against powerful Austrian armies in Italy's war for independence. He also fought in the Crimean War in the late 1850s. Finally, in 1860, Cesnola immigrated to the United States and settled in New York. He married the daughter of an American naval officer and served as the director of a seven-hundred-student military school in New York.

With the coming of war, he offered his services to the Eleventh New York Infantry and received a commission as major as a result of his prior military service. He was promoted to lieutenant colonel in 1862, before accepting an appointment as colonel of the Fourth New York Cavalry.[84] The Fourth New York was a polyglot unit. "Other field officers included Americans and Germans, Frenchmen, Italians, Spaniards, Hungarians, and perhaps men of other countries. Most of them could speak only their own languages. They were sad rogues, and the regiment lacked cohesion and unity," claimed an officer of another regiment. "In some battles they fought very well, but generally they were not considered reliable, and there were scandals of frequent occurrence."[85] In February 1863, the dashing count was dismissed

Colonel J. Irvin Gregg of the Sixteenth Pennsylvania Cavalry commanded a brigade in Duffié's Second Cavalry Division. He was a first cousin of Brigadier General David M. Gregg. *USAHEC.*

from the service for allegedly stealing six pistols, but he was soon exonerated, reinstated and returned to his regiment.[86] He assumed command of Duffié's brigade when the Frenchman became division commander in May. Cesnola's tenure as a brigade commander would also be short.

Colonel John Irvin Gregg commanded Duffié's Second Brigade. Called "Long John" by his men, Gregg stood six feet, four inches tall. J. Irvin Gregg was born on July 26, 1826, at Bellefonte in Centre County, Pennsylvania, his family's home for nearly one hundred years. His grandfather, Andrew Gregg, served two terms in the United States Senate. He was a first cousin of Brevet Major General David McMurtrie Gregg, and both were first cousins of Pennsylvania's wartime governor, Andrew Gregg Curtin. He received a sound education in the academies of Centre and Union Counties. In December 1846, he volunteered as a private for the Mexican War, and upon reaching Jalapa, he received notice of his appointment as first lieutenant in the Eleventh U.S. Infantry, one of ten new Regular regiments. He was subsequently promoted to captain and recruiting officer, serving with honor to the close of the war, when the new Regular regiments were mustered out of the service. Gregg mustered out on August 14, 1848.[87]

Captain Gregg returned to Centre County, where he engaged in the manufacturing of iron in the family business, Irvin, Gregg & Co. He served in a local militia unit, the "Centre Guards," as first lieutenant, captain, major and lieutenant colonel. In November 1857, he married Clarissa A. Everhart, "a lady of rare amiability and beauty, whose early death was deeply and sincerely mourned." He later married again, to Harriett Marr, the daughter of a local Presbyterian minister. They had two sons, Irvin and Robert.[88]

At the outbreak of the Civil War, Gregg was first commissioned captain and then colonel of the Fifth Pennsylvania Reserves but was shortly thereafter appointed captain in his cousin Colonel David M. Gregg's regiment, the newly formed Sixth U.S. Cavalry. His duty in the field commenced with the Peninsula Campaign under Major General George B. McClellan, as commander of a squadron of Regular Army cavalry. He was present at the Battle of Williamsburg on May 5, 1862, and at Kent Courthouse on the ninth. On May 11, his troopers occupied White House Landing on the Pamunkey River. He was with the Union advance at Ellison's Mills on the twenty-first and at Hanover Courthouse on the twenty-seventh.[89]

In the preliminaries to the Seven Days' Battles, he skirmished with Rebel infantry and narrowly escaped capture, followed by long days and nights of weary marching as the Army of the Potomac fought its way to the James River. Captain Gregg did important service in the army's retirement from the Peninsula and in the campaigns of Second Bull Run and Antietam.[90]

In November 1862, he was selected to command the newly formed Sixteenth Pennsylvania Cavalry. Early in January 1863, his regiment joined the Army of the Potomac and was assigned to Brigadier General William W. Averell's cavalry brigade. During the remainder of the winter, he performed important outpost duty and acquired a reputation for efficiency that he never lost. The first and only battle in which Colonel Gregg participated as a regimental commander was at Kelly's Ford on March 17, 1863. After a long day of fighting, Averell withdrew from the battlefield and left the field in the possession of the Confederates. Even though Kelly's Ford cannot be considered a Union victory, it nevertheless marked a new era for the Army of the Potomac's mounted arm.[91]

"Throughout his entire term of service, [Colonel] Gregg displayed the best qualities of the intrepid soldier, and by his stubborn fighting on many fields fairly won the character of an heroic and reliable officer," wrote historian Samuel P. Bates, "one who was not afraid to face superior numbers, even under the most unfavorable circumstances, and who made his dispositions with so much coolness and self-possession as to reassure his own men and intimidate the foe."[92] Frederic C. Newhall, a staff officer serving with Cavalry Corps headquarters, described Gregg as "steadfast" and "cool as a clock."[93] His brigade consisted of the Third, Fourth and Sixteenth Pennsylvania Cavalry regiments.

Brigadier General David McMurtrie Gregg led the Third Cavalry Division. He was born in Huntingdon, Pennsylvania, on April 10, 1833, and was a first cousin of the wartime governor of Pennsylvania, Andrew Gregg Curtin. His paternal grandfather, Andrew Gregg, served in both the U.S. House of Representatives and the Senate from 1791 to 1813, so Gregg came from a family with a long history of public service. He was educated at various private schools and at Bucknell University. In 1851, he received an appointment to West Point and graduated in 1855. He was commissioned into the Second Dragoons and served in various posts in the West. In September 1855, he was promoted and transferred to the First Dragoons, serving in the campaigns against the Indians in Washington and Oregon from 1858 to 1860. He served out the balance of his antebellum career in California, working as regimental adjutant of the First Dragoons.[94]

On May 14, 1861, he was promoted to captain and transferred to the newly formed Third U.S. Cavalry, which was soon redesignated as the Sixth U.S. Cavalry. After commanding a company of Regulars assigned to the defenses of Washington, in January 1862 he was appointed colonel of the newly organized Eighth Pennsylvania Cavalry. His thorough training and active experience in Indian warfare had prepared him for the work of disciplining the new troopers under his charge. He served well on the Peninsula and in the Antietam Campaign. Accordingly, Gregg was promoted to brigadier general of volunteers on November 20, 1862.[95]

David Gregg was remembered fondly as

tall and spare, of notable activity, capable of the greatest exertion and exposure; gentle in manner but bold and resolute in action. Firm and just in discipline he was a favorite of his troopers and ever held, for he deserved, their affection and entire confidence.

Gregg knew the principles of war and was always ready and eager to apply them. Endowed

with a natural genius of high order, he [was] universally hailed as the finest type of cavalry leader. A man of unimpeachable personal character, in private life affable and genial but not demonstrative, he fulfilled with modesty and honor all the duties of the citizen and head of an interesting and devoted family.[96]

A former officer later commented that Gregg's

> *modesty kept him from the notoriety that many gained through the newspapers; but in the army the testimony of all officers who knew him was the same. Brave, prudent, dashing when occasion required dash, and firm as a rock, he was looked upon, both as a regimental commander and afterwards as Major-General, as a man in whose hands any troops were safe.*[97]

His men called him "Old Reliable."[98] No man commanded a division of cavalry in the Army of the Potomac longer than did David Gregg.

The commander of Gregg's First Brigade had only been out of the U.S. Military Academy for two years but had established a reputation for controversy. Hugh Judson Kilpatrick, a native of New Jersey, was born the son of a farmer on January 14, 1836. He had little education but still received an appointment to West Point in 1856 and graduated in the May class of 1861. Ever vigilant for opportunities for self-promotion, Kilpatrick realized that the fastest route for advancement lay in the volunteer service. With the assistance of Lieutenant Colonel Gouverneur K. Warren, one of Kilpatrick's instructors at West Point, Kilpatrick obtained a volunteer's commission as captain of Company H, Fifth New York Infantry, also known as Duryee's Zouaves. He was the first Regular Army officer wounded in combat at the 1861 Battle of Big Bethel. He returned to duty later that year as lieutenant colonel of the Second New York Cavalry and served capably during the campaigns of 1862. By December 1862, he was colonel of the regiment. He assumed command of one of Gregg's brigades during the spring of 1863.[99]

Later in 1863, Kilpatrick earned the unflattering moniker of "Kill Cavalry" for his penchant for using up men and horses. He had the reputation of being "flamboyant, reckless, tempestuous and even licentious."[100] An officer of the First Massachusetts Cavalry wrote, "Kilpatrick is a brave, injudicious boy, much given to blowing, and surely will come to grief."[101] Another Federal staff officer called Kilpatrick "a frothy braggart without brains."[102] He was one of those characters that men either loved or hated. There was no middle ground when it came to Judson Kilpatrick. His brigade consisted of the First Maine, Second New York and Tenth New York.

Colonel Sir Percy Wyndham, a rakish twenty-nine-year-old English soldier of fortune, led Gregg's Second Brigade. He was born on the ship *Arab* in the English Channel on February 5, 1833, while his parents were en route to Calcutta, India. Captain Charles Wyndham, his father, served in the British

Colonel Percy Wyndham of the First New Jersey Cavalry commanded a brigade in David Gregg's Third Division. Wyndham was badly wounded in the fighting for Fleetwood Hill. *Library of Congress.*

Fifth Light Cavalry. With that pedigree, the boy was destined to be a horse soldier. However, fifteen-year-old Percy Wyndham entered the French navy instead and served as a midshipman during the French Revolution of 1848. He then joined the Austrian army as a sublieutenant and left eight years later as a first lieutenant in the Austrian Lancers. He resigned his commission on May 1, 1860, to join the Italian army of liberation being formed by the famed guerrilla leader Giuseppe Garibaldi and received a battlefield promotion to major in the great Battle of Milazzo, Sicily, on July 20, 1860, where Garibaldi's army defeated the Neapolitans, consolidating the guerrillas' hold on the island. A grateful King Victor Emmanuel knighted the dashing cavalryman. With the conquest of Italy complete, the soldier of fortune went hunting for another opportunity and found one in the United States in 1861. Largely as a result of his reputation in Italy, Wyndham received an appointment as colonel of the First New Jersey Cavalry in February 1862.[103]

A Federal horseman recalled:

> *This officer was an Englishman, an alleged lord. But lord or son of a lord, his capacity as a cavalry officer was not great. He had been entrusted with one*

or two independent commands and was regarded as a dashing officer…He seemed bent on killing as many horses as possible, not to mention the men. The fact was the newspapers were in the habit of reporting that Colonel or General so-and-so had made a forced march of so many hours, and it is probable that "Sir Percy" was in search of some more of that kind of cheap renown.[104]

One Confederate trooper noticed that Sir Percy, who wore a spectacular mustache nearly two feet wide, was "a stalwart man…who strode along with the nonchalant air of one who had wooed Dame Fortune too long to be cast down by her frowns."[105] A Federal officer called Wyndham "a big bag of wind."[106] Another Northerner, remembering his first encounter with Wyndham, compared him to a bouquet of flowers, noting, "You poor little lillies [*sic*], you! You haven't the first [idea of] the glorious magnificence of his beauty. He's only been in Camp for two hours, and he now appears in his third suit of clothes!"[107] Wyndham's brigade included his own First New Jersey Cavalry, the Twelfth Illinois Cavalry, the First Pennsylvania Cavalry and the First Maryland Cavalry.

In addition, two brigades of horse artillery also served with the Cavalry Corps.[108] In the spring of 1863, the horse artillery "became a permanent fixture to the cavalry, which by this time had become greatly increased in numbers." There were nine Regular Army batteries, divided into two brigades. "When the cavalry moved a battery was generally assigned temporarily to each brigade," recalled a veteran Union horse artillerist.

When the duty was ended the batteries reunited and recuperating, prepared for the next move. The duty was necessarily arduous and exhausting to both men and horses. Days and nights of marching, in all kinds of weather and over the most difficult roads…the batteries always managed to pull through, and were equal at all times to their comrades of the cavalry in capability of overcoming difficulties.[109]

Each battery consisted of six three-inch rifled guns with an effective range of four thousand yards. These lightweight guns were highly accurate and lethal in the right hands.

Captain James M. Robertson commanded the first horse artillery brigade. The New Hampshire–born Robertson enlisted in the army in 1838 and served for ten years in Batteries F and H, Second U.S. Artillery. He served as quartermaster sergeant during the Mexican War and received a field commission to second lieutenant on June 28, 1848. He was promoted to first lieutenant in 1852. In May 1861, he finally received a promotion to captain and assumed command of Battery B, Second U.S. Artillery. His battery was combined with Battery L early in the war, and he led the combined batteries during the 1862 Peninsula Campaign. The grizzled veteran knew his business.[110]

Captain John C. Tidball, Buford's West Point classmate, commanded the second horse artillery brigade. The thirty-eight-year-old Tidball was born near Wheeling, Virginia, and grew up in eastern Ohio. After graduation, he was commissioned a lieutenant in the Third U.S. Artillery and spent his entire military career in the artillery service of the Regular Army. In the Seminole War, he proved himself a gifted artillerist. His battery was sent to Harpers Ferry in 1859 to help suppress the John Brown insurrection. With the coming of war, he was a section commander in the original "flying battery," Battery A, Second U.S. Artillery. When Captain William F. Barry was promoted, Tidball became captain and battery commander. Tidball led his battery in every significant campaign in the East, earning five brevets over the course of the Civil War. He was an extremely capable soldier who had a nearly fifty-year career in the United States Army.[111]

Robertson's First Brigade consisted of the Ninth Michigan Battery, commanded by Captain Jabez J. Daniels; the Sixth New York Battery, commanded by Captain Joseph W. Martin; the Second U.S. Artillery, Batteries B and L, commanded by Lieutenant Edward Heaton; the Second U.S. Artillery, Battery M, commanded by Lieutenant A.C.M. Pennington Jr.; and the Fourth U.S. Artillery, Battery E, commanded by Lieutenant Samuel S. Elder. Tidball's Second Brigade consisted of Battery E, First U.S. Artillery, commanded by Captain Alanson M. Randol; Battery G, First U.S. Artillery, commanded by Lieutenant Egbert W. Olcott; Battery K, First U.S. Artillery, commanded by Captain William M. Graham; Battery A, Second U.S. Artillery, commanded by Lieutenant John H. Calef; and Battery C, Third U.S. Artillery, commanded by Captain William D. Fuller.

As Pleasonton prepared his Cavalry Corps to fall on the large concentration of Confederate cavalry in Culpeper County, his command numbered about twelve thousand veteran horse soldiers, plus two brigades of veteran horse artillery, for a total force of about fourteen thousand men. Newly confident after their performance in the spring of 1863, these men were itching to make a difference in the conduct of the war. They were about to get their chance.

Chapter 3

JEB STUART AND HIS
CONFEDERATE CAVALIERS

In June 1863, Virginia-born James Ewell Brown Stuart was thirty years old. He was an 1854 graduate of West Point, where the commandant, Colonel Robert E. Lee, had befriended the young man. Stuart had always wanted to be a cavalryman; while a cadet, he wrote, "Had you not rather see your Cousin or even your brother a Bold Dragoon than a petty-fogger lawyer?"[112] He earned the unflattering nickname "Beauty" during his cadet years for his pronounced under bite and weak chin but was popular with his fellow cadets. Upon graduating, Stuart served with the First Cavalry on the Kansas frontier. The pious teetotaler married Flora Cooke, daughter of legendary cavalry commander Colonel Philip St. George Cooke. In October 1859, he served as a volunteer aide to Lee in the capture of John Brown at Harpers Ferry. When Virginia seceded in 1861, Stuart resigned his commission and became colonel of the First Virginia Cavalry. He became famous almost immediately, and the charge of the First Virginia helped to shatter the Union lines at First Bull Run in July 1861.

Stuart was promoted to brigadier general in September of that year and gained immortality for his so-called "Ride Around McClellan" during the 1862 Peninsula Campaign. He was promoted to major general on July 25, 1862, and assumed command of the Cavalry Division of the Army of Northern Virginia, a post he held for the rest of his life, with the exception of his brief stint in command of Jackson's corps at Chancellorsville. "He proved himself a premier intelligence officer, combining the highest skill and intrepidity," noted one biographer. Robert E. Lee often referred to Stuart

Major General James Ewell Brown "Jeb" Stuart, legendary commander of the Confederate cavalry. *Library of Congress.*

as "the eyes and ears of the army" and came to depend heavily on Stuart's accurate and timely intelligence reports.[113]

Stuart wanted—but did not receive—permanent command of Jackson's corps. Instead, Lee reorganized the Army of Northern Virginia from two infantry corps into three, promoted Richard S. Ewell and A.P. Hill to lieutenant general and assigned them to command the two newly formed corps. Stuart returned to command Lee's cavalry. Some historians have speculated that Stuart was desperate for his own promotion to lieutenant general and that he felt slighted by being passed over for promotion and corps command.[111] "It is rumored," reported Confederate general William Dorsey Pender in a letter to his wife, "that Stuart has tendered his resignation because they will not give him this corps, but I cannot think him so foolish."[115] Fortunately, this rumor was false. Stuart remained in command of the cavalry, but many have speculated that he was sulking about being passed over for permanent command of Jackson's corps.

Stuart was known for his flamboyant uniform and for his love of pomp and circumstance. John Esten Cooke, a novelist and cousin of Flora Stuart, served on Stuart's staff. He recalled seeing the cavalry chief

> *wearing a uniform brilliant with gold braid, golden spurs, and a hat looped up with a golden star and decorated with a black plume; going on marches at the head of his cavalry column with his banjo-player gaily thrumming behind him; leading his troops to battle with a camp song on his lips; here to-day and away to-morrow, riding, fighting, laughing, dancing.*

This description summed Stuart up well. At the same time, he took his military duties seriously and knew when to stop the clowning and do his job.[116]

In the wake of his superb performance at Chancellorsville, Stuart was at the zenith of his fame and power. He had already demonstrated a real gift for the traditional roles of cavalry: scouting, screening and reconnaissance. "Our sense of security against surprise [was] so confident with him in the saddle," noted one of Lieutenant General James Longstreet's staff officers.[117] Lieutenant Robert T. Hubard, an officer of the Third Virginia Cavalry, wrote that Stuart "made his cavalry more completely and thoroughly [to] be the 'eyes and ears' of the army than any other officer I ever knew."[118] Personally brave to a fault, Stuart welcomed a fight any time the opportunity presented itself. Perhaps the greatest compliment ever paid to Stuart came from the enemy. Major General John Sedgwick, commander of the Army of the Potomac's Sixth Corps, called Stuart "the greatest cavalry officer ever foaled in America."[119] A reputation like that was difficult to live up to, and Brandy Station helped to tarnish it.

In the days after the Battle of Chancellorsville, the Army of Northern Virginia's cavalry was at the height of its strength and effectiveness. Stuart's command consisted of five brigades of cavalry and two battalions of horse artillery.[120]

Stuart's favorite subordinate was twenty-six-year-old Brigadier General Fitzhugh Lee, nephew of Robert E. Lee. Short and prone to obesity, Fitz Lee, dubbed "the Laughing Cavalier" by Douglas Southall Freeman for his sense of fun, was a member of the West Point class of 1856. Fond of good food and fine whiskey, Fitz graduated near the bottom of his class (forty-fourth out of forty-nine) and was prone to accumulating demerits for pranks and other shenanigans. After graduation, Fitz was commissioned into the Second U.S. Cavalry (later redesignated as the Fifth U.S. Cavalry) and fought Comanche Indians in Texas. In 1859, while chasing Comanches in Kansas,

Brigadier General Fitzhugh Lee, nephew of General Robert E. Lee, commanded a brigade of cavalry in Stuart's Division. *USAHEC.*

Lee led his troopers in a dismounted attack and was shot and badly wounded by an arrow to his chest.[121] He eventually recovered from the serious wound and returned to duty in 1860. Again chasing Indians, Lee ended up in one-on-one hand-to-hand combat with a hostile brave. Using his ample bulk, Lee wrestled the Indian to the ground and then dispatched him with two shots of his revolver.[122]

When the Civil War broke out, Fitz Lee was teaching tactics at West Point. He resigned his commission in the U.S. Army and accepted a commission in the Provisional Army of the Confederate States of America, joining the staff of General Joseph E. Johnston. After the First Battle of Bull Run in July 1861, while serving on the staff of Brigadier General Richard S. Ewell, he was appointed lieutenant colonel of the First Virginia Cavalry, serving under Colonel Jeb Stuart's command. In April 1862, Lee was elected colonel of the First Virginia and then received a promotion to brigadier general three months later in recognition of his service during the Peninsula Campaign.[123]

Fitz's service to date was a mixed bag. He and Stuart were the closest of friends, sharing the same sense of humor and the same love of frivolity and pomp and circumstance. Lieutenant General James Longstreet felt that Lee "was anything but an efficient cavalryman," a sentiment shared by others.[121] Sometimes, such as at Chancellorsville, when his scouts discovered that the

Union flank was unprotected and vulnerable to attack, he was brilliant. Other times, he seemed slow and stupid, and he was plagued with the early stages of a terrible case of rheumatoid arthritis that kept him from actively participating in the Battle of Brandy Station.[125] His brigade consisted of five veteran regiments—the First, Second, Third, Fourth and Fifth Virginia Cavalry regiments.

In Fitz's absence, command of his brigade devolved to Colonel Thomas T. Munford of the Second Virginia Cavalry, a thirty-two-year-old graduate of the Virginia Military Institute (VMI). Munford was a member of Virginia's more prominent families and was well connected. After graduating from VMI in 1852, he worked on a railroad and as a gentleman planter. On May 8, 1861, he was commissioned lieutenant colonel of the Tenth Virginia Mounted Infantry, which was soon redesignated the Second Virginia Cavalry. His career as a cavalryman was "brilliant and notable." He was promoted to colonel of the Second Virginia on April 25, 1862, and led a brigade of cavalry during Stonewall Jackson's Valley Campaign, eventually assuming command of all of Jackson's mounted forces. After suffering several combat wounds at Second Bull Run, Munford temporarily commanded a brigade and periodically led a brigade and even a division. He took command of Fitz Lee's brigade just before the Battle of Brandy Station.[126]

Brigadier General William Henry Fitzhugh Lee, known to his friends as "Rooney" and to his family as "Fitzhugh," was the second son of Robert E. Lee. Very tall for a cavalryman at six feet, four inches and tending toward corpulence, Rooney was a big man. "Though carrying more weight than was suitable to the saddle and the quick movements of cavalry service, he was, nevertheless, a good horseman and an excellent judge of horses," recalled one of his officers. "So well and wisely, did he select them, that when mounted there seemed an admirable harmony between his own massive form and the heavy build and muscular power of his steed."[127]

Rooney Lee was not a West Pointer; his brother George Washington Custis Lee had graduated from the Military Academy, and War Department policy forbade two sons of the same family from getting a free education at the Military Academy. Instead, Rooney attended Harvard University, where he was a star oarsman. In 1857, after three years at Harvard, Rooney abandoned his academic career to accept a commission as a lieutenant in an infantry regiment of the United States Army. He served in the army for two years and then resigned his commission, determined to become a gentleman farmer at White House, a plantation on the Pamunkey River that he had inherited from the Custis family.[128]

After Virginia seceded, Lee was commissioned a captain in the Ninth Virginia Cavalry. In April 1862, he was elected colonel of the regiment and was promoted to brigadier general five months later. He was solid and competent, if not spectacular, and was well respected within the ranks of Stuart's cavalry. Stuart came to depend on his good judgment and unflappable demeanor.[129] Rooney Lee commanded a veteran brigade consisting of the Ninth, Tenth and Thirteenth Virginia Cavalry and the Second North Carolina Cavalry.

Forty-four-year-old Brigadier General Wade Hampton was one of the wealthiest men in the South. Tall, handsome and amiable, he stood about six feet tall and weighed more than two hundred solid pounds. The South Carolinian was enormously strong and seemingly tireless. According to an apocryphal tale, Hampton killed a bear with his bare hands while a teenager. The grandson of a U.S. Army general, Hampton had no formal military training. He graduated from South Carolina College (later the University of South Carolina) and took up the life of a planter and politician.[130]

Unlike so many men with wealth and intellect, Wade Hampton was modest and unpretentious, with a subtle self-deprecating sense of humor. He was a refined patrician with manners suited to his high position in society and was remembered by one who knew him well as "a prince among gentlemen."[131] Although he had opposed secession, when war came, he committed himself totally to the cause, personally raising and equipping at great expense the Hampton Legion, an outfit consisting of infantry, artillery and cavalry components.

On July 21, 1861, Hampton suffered the first of what would be several combat wounds while commanding infantry in the fighting at First Bull Run. His talents were recognized, and he was appointed a brigadier general on May 23, 1862, while commanding an infantry brigade. Eight days later, he suffered a second, more serious wound at Seven Pines (Fair Oaks). Once he recovered, he was confirmed as a brigadier and assumed command of a brigade of cavalry. In December 1862, just after the Battle of Fredericksburg, Hampton again was offered command of an infantry brigade but turned it down, preferring to remain with the cavalry.[132]

The big South Carolinian was known for his bravery, for leading charges and for personally killing thirteen men in combat during the Civil War. "Gen. Hampton always appeared to be unconscious of danger, with the fighting instinct ever uppermost, and to see a body of Yankees was to commence fighting and if possible to lead the charge," remembered a staff officer.[133]

For all of his virtues, Hampton and Stuart had a chilly relationship. Each man respected the other's abilities, but Hampton was much older than Stuart and thought little of Stuart's penchant for flamboyance and frivolity. Unlike Stuart, he viewed military service "from a sense of duty, and not from passion or to win renown."[134] He was also neither a Virginian nor a West Pointer, meaning that he was not part of Stuart's "in crowd" at headquarters, and he did not appreciate Stuart's obvious bias toward Virginians. Despite the chilly relationship, they still worked together well.[135] Hampton commanded a veteran brigade consisting of the Cobb's Legion Cavalry of Georgia, First South Carolina Cavalry, First North Carolina Cavalry, Jeff Davis Legion Cavalry of Georgia and Mississippi and the Second South Carolina Cavalry, which was originally the cavalry component of the Hampton Legion.

Brigadier General Beverly H. Robertson commanded a newly formed demi-brigade of two large, green regiments of North Carolina cavalry. An 1849 graduate of West Point, he spent his entire Regular Army career in the Second Dragoons on the western frontier. Robertson served under Turner Ashby in the Shenandoah Valley and took command of Ashby's brigade after

Brigadier General Beverly H. Robertson commanded a demi-brigade of two large but green regiments of North Carolina cavalry. *Library of Congress.*

the legendary cavalier was killed during Jackson's 1862 Valley Campaign. He did well in that position, besting John Buford in the final engagement at Second Bull Run, but Stuart relieved Robertson of command shortly thereafter. "Robertson has been relieved and sent to North Carolina," Stuart announced to his wife, Flora, in October 1862. "'Joy's mine.' My command is now okay."[136] Stuart once described Robertson as the "most troublesome man in the Army."[137] He thought that he had rid himself of Robertson by banishing him to North Carolina, where Robertson spent the next six months raising and training several new regiments of cavalry.

However, after receiving Lee's request for additional cavalry, Robertson and two regiments of his green brigade were given orders to travel to Virginia for the forthcoming invasion of the North. As a general statement, Robertson was an excellent organizer, trainer and administrator, but on the battlefield, he was cautious to a fault and undependable, and Stuart had no confidence at all in his abilities. Robertson's brigade, the smallest in Stuart's division, consisted of two very large but inexperienced regiments, the Fourth and Fifth North Carolina Cavalry, numbering 966 sabers.[138]

Brigadier General William Edmonson "Grumble" Jones, a member of the West Point class of 1848 (he was Buford's classmate), commanded a fine veteran brigade consisting entirely of Virginia horsemen from the Shenandoah Valley. Jones, described by one of his men as "that stern old warrior," richly deserved his nickname.[139] Jones "was an eccentric officer, who seemed to take pleasure in self-torture, as if doing penance," observed a Kentucky horse soldier who served under Jones after the end of the Gettysburg Campaign. "He was a small man, beyond middle life, exceedingly plain in dress, brave to a fault, cool and imperturbable."[140]

The thirty-nine-year-old Jones graduated from Emory and Henry College in Virginia in 1844 and then matriculated at West Point, graduating twelfth out of forty-eight. Jones spent his entire Regular Army career in the mounted arm, serving on the frontier in the Regiment of Mounted Rifles until his resignation in 1857. He spent much of his career fighting Indians and serving garrison duty in the Pacific Northwest. After resigning his commission, he spent the next several years as a reclusive farmer, living a lonely and bitter life. He had not always been so short-tempered. His young wife was washed from his arms in a shipwreck shortly after their marriage, and Jones never recovered from the loss. He grew "embittered, complaining and suspicious" as a result, frequently quarreling with his fellow officers.[141]

At the outbreak of the Civil War, Jones formed a cavalry company and was elected its captain, serving under Jeb Stuart in the First Manassas (Bull Run) Campaign. He became colonel of the First and later the Seventh Virginia Cavalry and was promoted to brigadier general on September 19, 1862. Shortly thereafter, Jones assumed command of Robertson's former brigade. Jones was a plain dresser with a legendary gift for profanity. He was a martinet who was "brave as a lion and…was known as a hard fighter. He was a man, however, of high temper, morose and fretful," as a fellow Confederate general described him. "He held the fighting qualities of the enemy in great contempt, and never would admit the possibility of defeat where the odds against him were not much over two to one."[142]

Unfortunately, Jones and Stuart, with markedly opposite personalities, constantly clashed. In the fall of 1862, when Jones came up for promotion, Stuart wrote to Flora, "I hope he will be assigned to the Infantry, I don't want him in the Cavalry, and I have made a formal statement to that effect."[143] More formally, Stuart wrote to the Confederate War Department:

> *I have the honor to state further that I do not regard Brigadier General Jones as deserving this command or as a fit person to command a Brigade of Cavalry. I say this from a thorough acquaintance with him in every grade from Lieutenant up…With Brigadier General Jones I feel sure of opposition, insubordination, and inefficiency to an extent that would in a short time ruin discipline and subvert authority in that brigade.*[144]

Interestingly, Jones was assigned to command the same brigade from which Robertson had just been relieved. Jones returned the sentiment, usually referring to Stuart as "that young whippersnapper."[145]

When Stuart learned that Jones's brigade would be joining his cavalry division, he asked that Jones be assigned to command an infantry brigade. General Lee responded, "I am perfectly willing to transfer him…if he desires it; but if he does not I know of no act of his to justify my doing so."[146] Jones responded by writing to Secretary of War Seddon:

> *I most especially tender my resignation as Brigadier General in the* [Provisional Army of the Confederate States]. *My reason for doing so is my conviction that where I am now ordered my services cannot be serviceable to my country. Other reasons not necessary to mention exist. Being of conscript age, I will not escape service.*

Seddon did not act on the request, meaning that the two officers would be forced to serve together whether they wanted to do so or not.[117]

Although Stuart personally disliked Jones, he respected his abilities, praising his "marked courage and determination" and referring to him as "the best outpost officer in the army."[118] Jones's veteran command, consisting entirely of Shenandoah Valley men, was, like its leader, always itching for a fight. His fine veteran brigade consisted of the Sixth, Seventh, Eleventh and Twelfth Virginia Cavalry Regiments and the Thirty-fifth Battalion of Virginia Cavalry.[119]

Major Robert F. Beckham commanded the famous Stuart Horse Artillery Battalion. Beckham, a twenty-six-year-old native of Culpeper, came from a prominent and wealthy family. He grew up a privileged child in a handsome farmhouse called Auburn, which played a major role in the drama that would unfold at Brandy Station. Beckham was a member of the West Point class of 1859, graduating sixth out of twenty-two. As befit someone with his high class rank, he was commissioned into the topographical engineers, serving under the command of Captain George G. Meade. With the coming of war in 1861, he resigned his commission in the United States Army and was appointed an artillery officer in the Provisional Army of the Confederate States. He fought in the First Battle of Bull Run with his battery in July

Major Robert F. Beckham, commander of the Stuart Horse Artillery. Beckham's men performed superbly that day. *USAHEC.*

1861 and then served on the staff of Major General Gustavus W. Smith. He was commissioned major of ordnance on August 16, 1862.[150]

About a week after Major John Pelham, the dashing commander of Stuart's horse artillery, was mortally wounded during the March 17, 1863 Battle of Kelly's Ford, Beckham was appointed commander of the horse artillery at Stuart's specific request.[151] Until then, specific batteries had been assigned to serve with specific brigades of cavalry. However, after assuming command, Beckham reorganized the horse artillery into an organized battalion and prepared his gunners for the coming campaign. Recognizing his good service, on May 21, with Robert E. Lee's endorsement, Stuart wrote to General Samuel Cooper, the Confederate adjutant general, requesting that Beckham be promoted to lieutenant colonel.[152] Beckham was competent, and his steady performance at the Battle of Brandy Station helped to save Stuart's horse soldiers from suffering a catastrophic defeat.[153] Beckham's battalion consisted of Captain James F. Hart's South Carolina battery, which was originally part of the Hampton Legion; Captain Roger P. Chew's Virginia battery; Captain James Breathed's Virginia battery; Captain Marcellus Moorman's Virginia battery; and Captain William N. McGregor's Virginia battery. Beckham had twenty-two guns in five batteries at his disposal.

For the first two years of the war, the Confederate cavalry had rather literally ridden rings around its Union counterparts and was openly contemptuous of them. "The truth was, no doubt, that their cavalry was afraid of us, for up to that time [the fall of 1862] our superiority in that arm of the service was unquestioned, and they seldom ventured within our reach, and whenever they did they invariably came to grief," noted one of Stuart's staff officers.[154] However, the formation of the Army of the Potomac's Cavalry Corps in the spring of 1863 began to shift that balance. The Federal horsemen had demonstrated a real feisty streak during the spring—first at the Battle of Kelly's Ford on March 17 and then during the Stoneman Raid—and the Confederates were beginning to change the way they looked at their blue-clad adversaries.[155]

Thus, Stuart's division mounted about ten thousand horsemen and horse artillerists during the Battle of Brandy Station. They had their hands full that day.

Chapter 4

THE CONFEDERATE GRAND REVIEWS

THE SECOND GRAND REVIEW, JUNE 5, 1863

Buford was correct—the Confederates were up to something. Stuart had just staged the second grand review of his cavalry in a two-week period on June 5. The first review occurred on May 22, amid much pomp and circumstance. "We are having a grand review tomorrow at Brandy Station of all of Stewart's [*sic*] Cavalry," reported an officer of the Twelfth Virginia Cavalry on June 4.

> *I reckon it will be an imposing sight. We are to have a sham fight and charge artillery loaded with blank cartridges. Divisions of infantry are making their appearance in these parts. We know nothing in reality but the general impression is that there will be a forward move.*[156]

That night, in anticipation of the next day's pageantry, Stuart and his dashing cavaliers romanced the local belles at a grand ball, dubbed the "Sabers and Roses Ball," held in the nearby Culpeper County Courthouse.

"A fine & very imposing affair—8000 men mounted," correctly observed a lieutenant colonel of one of Fitz Lee's regiments.[157] Senator Louis T. Wigfall of Texas, whose son Halsey was an officer in Breathed's battery, attended the review as a guest of honor. Former Confederate secretary of war George Randolph attended as Stuart's special guest, and current secretary of war

James A. Seddon attended the second review, along with a large entourage of local ladies. The field selected for the review site was "admirably suited to the purpose, a hill in the centre affording a reviewing stand from which the twelve thousand men present could be seen to great advantage."[158] As Stuart's adjutant, Major Henry B. McClellan, described it:

> *Eight thousand cavalry passed under the eye of their commander, in column of squadrons, first at a walk, and then at the charge, while the guns of the artillery battalion, on the hill opposite the stand, gave forth fire and smoke, and seemed almost to convert the pageant into real warfare. It was a brilliant day, and the thirst for the "pomp and circumstance" of war was fully satisfied.*[159]

A trooper of the Twelfth Virginia Cavalry observed, "The officers & men were exceedingly well mounted & dressed."[160] Another said, "It made quite a formidable display and will strike terror to Stoneman & Co."[161]

Wade Hampton's Tar Heels of the First North Carolina Cavalry "rode with a military primness and were mounted on steeds of delicately-shaped limbs with glistening eyes full of fire and motion," noted one observer.[162] One of Robertson's North Carolinians recalled that the artillery fire and "the yelling of the men and rising clouds of dust gave every appearance of a real battle."[163] However, many of the men had more than just martial glory on their minds that day.

"Many were the sly glances cast by the soldier boys at the country lassies, as they passed along their front in the columns of review," recalled an officer of the Sixth Virginia Cavalry.[164] "The effect was thrilling, even to us, while the ladies clasped their hands and sank into the arms, sometimes, of their escorts in a swoon, if the escorts were handy, but if not, they did not," one of Stuart's staff officers recorded.[165]

"It was observed that General Stuart's personal charms never showed to better advantage than on that day," noted a Southern horse soldier.

> *Young, gay, and handsome, dressed out in his newest uniform, his polished sword flashing in the sunlight, mounted on his favorite bay mare in gaudiest trappings, his long black plume waving in response to the kisses of the summer breeze, he was superb in every movement, and the personification of grace and gallantry combined.*[166]

Stuart, dressed in a "short grey jacket, wide-brimmed whitish hat with long white plume," bowed low from the saddle and waved to the adoring crowd.[167] Not all shared that view. "Of course, many ladies were present to whom Genl. S. was familiarly polite," wrote a horse artillerist. "Such days do not present him in his best light."[168]

A horse artillerist left an excellent description of the sham battle. "The cavalry is charging across the field; the artillery is opening," he recorded. "The scene is beautiful beyond description…We commenced firing blank cartridges; fired eleven rounds while the cavalry were charging. The scene is magnificent," he concluded. The grand review ended on that breathtaking note.[169]

When the grand review was over, Stuart held another ball, the second in three weeks, much to the delight of the young ladies of Culpeper County. "The day wound up with a ball; but as the night was fine, we danced in the open air on a piece of turf near our headquarters, and by the light of enormous woodfires," recalled Stuart's aide, Major Heros von Borcke, "the ruddy glare of which gave the whole scene a wild and romantic effect."[170]

The spectacle of the grand review did not enthrall all of the Southern horsemen. "Reviews are very nice things for lookers on but far from pleasant for those concerned especially if the weather be hot and dusty," noted an officer of the Stuart Horse Artillery.[171] Brigadier General William E. "Grumble" Jones's brigade had only arrived at Brandy Station on June 3 and 4 after completing a long and taxing raid in western Virginia, and his men and horses were tired and tattered. "Many…grumbled about the useless waste of energy, especially that of the horses; and when it was announced a few days afterward that there was to be another grand review on the 8th, the grumblers were even more numerous and outspoken." Nearly all of the grumbling ceased, however, when Stuart announced that Robert E. Lee had ordered another review for June 8 and that he planned to attend in person.[172]

That review would be held on the sprawling estate of John Minor Botts. An ardent Unionist and former congressman, Botts had been deeply persecuted in Richmond, where he resided in 1861, including being incarcerated. He had fled to Culpeper County to escape the abuse, to "seek retirement and obscurity, to get out of the way of the world, and to follow for the balance of my life the peaceful pursuits of agriculture."[173] Before long, he was also deeply unpopular with most of his neighbors in Culpeper and with the Confederate high command. He had acquired his twenty-two-hundred-acre farm, Auburn, from John Grigsby Beckham, the father of Major Robert F. Beckham, the commander of Stuart's horse artillery battalion. Some claimed that Botts swindled Beckham out of the property by taking advantage of Beckham's mental instability, but Botts staunchly

Auburn, the handsome plantation home owned by ardent Unionist John Minor Botts. The grand reviews of the Confederate cavalry were held on the grounds of Botts's farm. *Library of Congress.*

claimed that he had purchased it at auction by paying the outstanding property taxes on the farm.[174] "He is a hale and hearty gentleman, loyal and true," noted a Northern newspaper of Botts, "has many friends in the South, and is rather too much for his enemies," perhaps explaining why his farm was chosen as the site of the grand review.[175] While Stuart's cavalry occupied Culpeper County in May and early June 1863, "daily and hourly I was subjected to all sorts of vexatious annoyances," he wrote after the war. "I had neither peace nor rest, day or night, from the time this cavalry force came upon me until the arrival of the Federal army under General Meade in the month of September."[176]

Stuart had conducted his review on Botts's farm, and Botts was livid at the damage to his crops. He rode immediately to Stuart's headquarters to protest and demand compensation for the damages. "Mr. Botts ripped and rarred and snorted," noted a servant, "but Genrul Stuart warn't put out none at all." After failing to calm his angry caller, Stuart simply dismissed him with a laugh and a wave. Perhaps Stuart knew that his chief of horse artillery had grown up there, and perhaps he had heard the whispers about how Botts had acquired the farm and was determined to exact a measure of retribution.[177]

The Confederate troopers began preparing their equipment and horses, wanting to look their best for the critical eye of their beloved commander in chief. Their attention distracted, the Southerners seemed unaware of Buford's presence in the area.

THE FEDERAL CAVALRY PREPARES ITS RESPONSE

As a result of his accurate report of the Confederate activities, Pleasonton ordered Buford to send all of his transportation, excepting his pack mules and one wagon per regiment, to the supply depot at Potomac Creek, a sure sign that a major movement by the Union cavalry loomed. Buford dispatched part of his force toward the concentration of Confederate cavalry at Culpeper. He remained at Warrenton Junction, readying the balance of his command for a meeting with their unsuspecting foes at Brandy Station.[178]

Vigilant Union horsemen probed Stuart's pickets, attempting to ascertain the precise whereabouts and intentions of the Rebel cavalry. Buford sent Duffié's division into northern Culpeper County. The Frenchman reported that he marched south, came within four and a half miles of Culpeper, taking no casualties, and that the Confederates seemed to be avoiding a fight. At 3:00 a.m. on June 7, Buford forwarded this intelligence to Pleasonton, who was on his way to Warrenton Junction to assume field command of the Cavalry Corps.[179]

Pleasonton passed this information on to Hooker with a note of caution. "Colonel Duffié only reconnoitered the road from Sulphur Springs toward Culpeper," wrote the cavalry chief. "Does not know what cavalry is on the Brandy Station or Stevensburg roads. It is on those roads the bulk of the enemy's cavalry are reported." He continued, "Let us act soon, and please telegraph my instructions. My people are all ready to pitch in. Let me have discretion to cross at the best positions as determined by latest information."[180]

After a long, hot, dusty day of marching, the Army of the Potomac's Cavalry concentrated at Catlett's Station on the Orange & Alexandria Railroad. It made its preparations to pitch into the vast concentration of Confederate cavalry, eager to show what Northern steel could do.[181]

THE THIRD GRAND REVIEW, JUNE 8, 1863

While the Union troopers prepared to attack, Stuart's unsuspecting troopers held another grand review, this time in front of Robert E. Lee himself. Lieutenant Generals James Longstreet and Richard S. Ewell, along with a number of other generals and staff officers, also attended. Fitz Lee invited Major General John Bell Hood, a former cavalryman who commanded a hard-fighting infantry division in Longstreet's Corps, to attend the review and "to bring any of his friends." Hood appeared with his entire division, announcing that these were "all his friends" and that he thought he should bring them along.[182] "You invited me and my people," Hood told his old friend Fitz Lee, "and you see I've brought them."

"Well, don't let them holler, 'Here's your mule!'" declared Lee in response.

"If they do," warned Wade Hampton, "we'll charge you." Hood's infantrymen settled in to watch the spectacle unfold in front of them.[183] "Their presence only increased the ambition of the troopers to do their best," observed a horse artillerist. "The infantry, at that stage of the war considered it a mere bagatelle to belong to the cavalry."[184]

When one of Major Beckham's artillerists showed up to the review riding an especially long-eared mule, Stuart had him shooed from the field in a big hurry before he could attract the attention of Hood's sharp-eyed foot soldiers, who would have had a great time hooting and hollering about it. "I cared very little about the matter, but the mule looked a little bit surprised, and, I think, felt ashamed of himself and his waving ears, which cost him his prominent position in the grand spectacle," wrote the artillerist, his tongue planted firmly in his cheek.[185]

"This was a business affair, the spectators being all soldiers," observed one of Stuart's staff officers.

> *Many men from Hood's Division were present who enjoyed it immensely. During the charges past the reviewing stand the hats and caps of the charging column would sometimes blow off, and then, just as the charging squadron passed and before the owners could come back, Hood's men would have a race for them and bear them off in triumph.*[186]

"Marshaled on the plain were one hundred and five squadrons of cavalry, six light field batteries, ambulances with their trained corps of field attendants, etc.," observed a North Carolina horse soldier. "At no time during the history of the war was this branch of service in such fine condition. Its members, discipline, and equipments were good enough to create within the mind of our great commander the utmost satisfaction."[187] Stuart's command was "at its zenith of power and efficiency," as Captain William W. Blackford, Stuart's engineering officer, correctly put it, and his troopers proudly primped for General Lee.[188]

However, when the review began, Grumble Jones and his brigade were not present. Stuart dispatched Lieutenant Frank Robertson of his staff to go to Jones's camp to find out why the Virginian and his command were absent and to order them to report to the review field. Robertson found Jones and his staff lounging on the grass. Aware of the antipathy between the two officers, Robertson "never changed General Stuart's messages, and several times received violent language in return—a sort of cushion between the two generals in communications." When Robertson related Stuart's order, Jones "blazed all sorts of language at me, and I rode from the thunder with no answer as a return message." However, Jones, although unhappy with having to participate in something he viewed as useless frivolity, had his buglers blow "Boots and Saddles," and within minutes, his whole brigade was in the saddle; they were in line with the rest of Stuart's cavalry by the time General Lee reached the reviewing.[189]

General Lee well knew his cavalry chief's propensity for pomp and circumstance. He watched as the local ladies adorned Stuart and his horse with garlands of flowers. Covered with blossoms, Stuart presented himself to the commanding general. Lee surveyed his cavalier from head to foot and quietly warned, "Do you know General that Burnside left Washington in like trim for the first battle of Manassas. I hope that your fate may not be like his." In spite of Lee's understated warning, Stuart faced a rude surprise the next day.[190]

The twenty-two regiments of Confederate cavalry arrayed themselves along either side of a straight furrow plowed into the rich farm fields of Botts's farm. Their lines extended for nearly three full miles, all the way to Jonas Run, which bisected the road to Brandy Station. Stuart's famed horse artillery crowned nearby Fleetwood Hill, bristling with sixteen guns of four batteries of fine artillery. Captain Daniel Grimsley of the Sixth Virginia Cavalry noted:

> *It was a splendid military parade; Stuart's eyes gleamed with peculiar brightness as he glanced along this line of cavalry in battle array, with men and horses groomed their best, and the command arrayed with military*

precision, with colors flying, bugles sounding, bands playing, and with regimental and brigade officers in proper positions. [191]

General Lee sat watching the glorious spectacle atop a low rise near the railroad bed. The sight of the Southern commander impressed all who saw him. "It was my first sight of the great chieftain," proudly recalled William L. Wilson of the Twelfth Virginia Cavalry. "Even his personal appearance indicates great mental endowment and nobility of soul." Wilson noted that the review passed quietly and with "less éclat than that of last Friday." [192] An awed horse artillerist noted in his diary, "Went out again on review with the cavalry and our artillery. This time, however, before the greatest living man in the world, Robert E. Lee." [193]

Confederate general William Pendleton recalled that Lee and his staff "had a ride of it, some six miles at full run for our horses, down the line and up again, and then had to sit our horses in the dust half the day for the squadrons to march in display backward and forward near us." [194] Captain Charles T. O'Ferrall of the Twelfth Virginia Cavalry recalled "the appearance of General Lee as he rode in review with General Stuart, with Stuart's black plume waving like the white plume of Henry of Navarre, aroused the enthusiasm of the corps to the highest pitch." [195] In an effort to conserve ammunition, Lee ordered that no artillery rounds be fired in this review. [196] The Southern commander and his staff rode rapidly along the entire line, inspecting the proud gray troopers as they went.

Then, Lee resumed his position, and

at the sound of the bugle, taken up and repeated along the line, the corps of horsemen broke by right wheel into columns of squadron, and moving south for a short distance, the head of the column was turned to the left, and again to the left, moving in this new direction, whence it passed immediately in front of the commanding general. It was a splendid military pageant, and an inspiring scene…as this long line of horsemen, in columns of squadron, with nearly ten thousand sabers flashing in the sun light…passed in review before the greatest soldier of modern times. [The column advanced at a walk] until it came within some fifty or one hundred paces of the position occupied by the reviewing general, when squadron by squadron would take up first the trot, then the gallop, until they had passed some distance beyond, when again they would pull down to the walk. After passing in review, the several brigades were brought again to the position which they occupied in the line, whence they were dismissed, one by one, to their respective camps. [197]

Stuart's impressive martial display lasted several exhausting hours.

"It was a magnificent day, befitting the superb body of cavalry that, under Stuart, marched rapidly in review for the Commander-in-Chief," observed one of Lieutenant General James Longstreet's staff officers. "A sight it was not soon to be forgotten. The utmost order prevailed. There could be no doubt that the cavalry was as ready for the work before us as was our matchless infantry." [198]

Hood's infantrymen greatly enjoyed the pageant that played out in front of them. Every time one of the galloping horsemen lost a hat, the Texans broke ranks and raced out to snatch the trophy. However, as Stuart's engineering officer, Captain William W. Blackford, noted, "This was the last of our frolics for a long time, for on the morrow we were to begin the fighting which was kept up almost daily until two weeks after the Battle of Gettysburg, and we were to begin it in a severe action." [199]

At the end of the pageant, Stuart pointed out a significant problem to General Lee. The saddles and carbines manufactured in Richmond for the Army of Northern Virginia had proved themselves defective and inadequate. That night, Lee wrote to Colonel Josiah Gorgas, the Confederacy's talented chief of ordnance. "My attention was thus called to a subject which I have previously brought to your notice, viz., the saddles and carbines manufactured in Richmond," stated the army commander. The general noted that he had not inspected these items himself but had been assured that the saddles ruined the backs of horses and that the carbines were so defective as to be demoralizing.

I am aware of the difficulties attending the manufacture of arms and equipments, but I suggest that you have the matter inquired into by your ordnance officers, and see if they cannot rectify the evils complained of. It would be better, I think, to make fewer articles, and have them serviceable.

This problem continued to plague the Army of Northern Virginia Cavalry Division for the balance of the war. [200]

"I reviewed the cavalry in this section yesterday," noted Robert E. Lee in a letter to his wife. "It was a splendid sight. The men and horses looked well… Stuart was in all his glory. Your sons and nephew were well and flourishing."

He noted that his nephew Fitz sat on the ground, watching his men pass in review. A severe case of rheumatism prevented him from climbing into the saddle, so Fitz sat with "some pretty girls in a carriage," cheering his men. Fitz's disability meant that Colonel Thomas T. Munford of the Second Virginia Cavalry had temporary command of his brigade and that Fitz would miss the great cavalry battle that loomed. The general's son Rooney, very tall for a cavalryman at six feet, three inches, presented a handsome sight as he put his proud black charger through its paces. As Lee penned this letter on the morning of June 9, little did the Southern commander realize that things were about to change dramatically.[201]

Grumble Jones, described by one of his men as "that stern old warrior," was most unhappy with the show—he felt it a foolhardy waste of resources.[202] "No doubt," muttered Jones,

> the Yankees, who have two divisions of cavalry on the other side of the river, have witnessed from their signal stations, this show in which Stuart has exposed to view his strength and aroused their curiosity. They will want to know what is going on and if I am not mistaken, will be over early in the morning to investigate.[203]

Jones's estimate of the Yankee intentions proved right on target.

Sergeant Alonzo West of the First Maryland Cavalry served in Sir Percy Wyndham's brigade of Gregg's division. Gregg's division had marched at two o'clock that afternoon. "Halted once on the road and could see large clouds of dust rising from the opposite side of the Rappahannock," noted West in his diary. "It looked as though there was a large force on a rapid march."[204] There *was* a large force on a rapid march: the entire Confederate cavalry force, going through its paces for Robert E. Lee.

As luck would have it, Jones's brigade drew picket duty that night. Consequently, his brigade's horses remained saddled and bridled all night so that they could move at a moment's notice. "We all laid down that night by our saddled and bridled horses, with our boots on, and sabers and pistols buckled around us and our carbines at our sides, with nothing to do in case we were called up but to strap our blankets on our saddles, mount our horses, and fall into mind," recalled a member of the Twelfth Virginia Cavalry.[205] Luckily for Jeb Stuart, Jones and his intrepid troopers would be ready to meet the threat that awaited them the next morning.

Thus, the stage was set for the great drama that would play out on the hills and dales of Culpeper County.

Chapter 5

PLEASONTON'S PLAN

When he arrived at Warrenton Junction, Alfred Pleasonton knew only of the great concentration of enemy cavalry near Culpeper. He did not know that Confederate infantry was also camped there. Pleasonton and Hooker did not know that Stuart's cavalry had gone to Brandy Station to cover the northward march of the infantry corps of Lieutenant Generals Richard S. Ewell and James Longstreet. Lee had ordered that the march north resume on June 10.[206] Pleasonton worried about the whereabouts of the Southern foot soldiers and requested infantry support for his cavalry.

Responding, Hooker notified Pleasonton that two brigades of hand-picked infantry under the command of Brigadier Generals David A. Russell and Adelbert Ames would report to Pleasonton at Kelly's Ford. Each brigade consisted of fifteen hundred selected foot soldiers. "The command was to be one well-disciplined and drilled, capable of marching rapidly and with endurance, with officers noted for energy and efficiency," as a member of the Third Wisconsin Infantry recalled.[207] Each regiment culled out those who could not be relied on for a forced march, further streamlining the infantry force.[208] These regiments came from all of the corps of the Army of the Potomac and represented the best marching and some of the best fighting regiments of the army. "The infantry force selected challenged particular admiration," reported a newspaper correspondent. "The regiments were small, but they were *reliable*—such for instance as the Second, Third, and Seventh Wisconsin, Second and Thirty-third Massachusetts, Sixth Maine,

Eighty-sixth and One Hundred and Twenty-Fourth New York, and one or two others of like character."[209]

Disregarding Pleasonton's note of caution about the extent of Duffié's reconnaissance, Hooker fired off instructions that would send the Federal horsemen directly into the area where Pleasonton believed the bulk of the Southern cavalry lay waiting. "From the most reliable information at these headquarters, it is recommended that you cross the Rappahannock at Beverley and Kelly's Fords, and march directly on Culpeper," instructed Hooker. "For this you will divide your cavalry force as you think proper, to carry into execution the object in view, which is to disperse and destroy the Rebel force assembled in the vicinity of Culpeper, and to destroy his trains and supplies of all description to the utmost of your ability." The army commander continued:

> *Shortly after crossing the two fords, the routes you will be likely to take intersect, and the major-general commanding suggests that you keep your infantry force together, as in that condition it will afford you a moving point of d'appui to rally on at all times, which no cavalry force can be able to shake.*

He concluded, "It is believed that the enemy has no infantry. Should you find this to be the case, by keeping your troops well in hand, you will be able to head in any direction." If the strike succeeded and the Confederates were routed, Hooker wanted Pleasonton to vigorously pursue the Southern cavalry and use all available means to destroy Stuart's corps once and for all.[210]

If Pleasonton had correctly assessed the whereabouts of the Confederate cavalry, Hooker's plan would carry the Northern saddle soldiers right at them. Nevertheless, orders were orders, and Hooker had been very specific in his instructions to Pleasonton. The cavalry chief set about planning his expedition.

Gregg's division spent June 7 preparing for the coming expedition. "Haversacks were stored, cartridge-boxes filled, horses shod, the sick sent back, and all the usual preparations for active campaigning gone through with," recalled a member of the First Pennsylvania Cavalry.

> *Then commenced the irksome and wearying delays incident to the moving of troops. Momentarily expecting the order to move, hour after hour passed, and still we were not yet off. Evening came and night passed, and reveille awoke us to another day's expectancy.*[211]

On June 8, Pleasonton ordered Duffié to march his division to Kelly's Ford, where he would join Gregg's command for the crossing. The Frenchman had to move from the far right, near Warrenton, down to Kelly's Ford, an impractical move for the division that was supposed to lead the way on the left. "Slowly pursuing our way through the heat and clouds of dust raised by the march of a division of cavalry over parched and arid fields, we at length reached the vicinity of the river, and at nine p.m., bivouacked for the night about a mile from Kelly's Ford," continued the Pennsylvania horse soldier.[212] Thus, the pieces fell into place for the great cavalry battle at Brandy Station. Nine thousand Union cavalrymen and three thousand infantrymen were prepared to pounce on the unsuspecting Confederates the next morning.[213]

Pleasonton formulated an excellent plan for his foray across the river. Buford would command the right wing of the operation, including the First Division and Ames's brigade of selected infantry regiments. In addition, several batteries of Federal horse artillery would also accompany the columns, adding firepower to the already potent Union force. Gregg would command the left wing, which included Russell's infantry brigade, Gregg's Second Division and Duffié's Third Division.

Under Pleasonton's plan, Buford's men would cross the Rappahannock at Beverly Ford and ride to Brandy Station, where they would rendezvous with Gregg's Second Division. Gregg's division would cross the Rappahannock at Kelly's Ford. Duffié's small division would also cross at Kelly's Ford and would proceed to the small town of Stevensburg to secure the flank east of Culpeper. Buford and Gregg would then push for Culpeper, where they would fall on Stuart's unsuspecting forces and destroy them. In case there was Confederate infantry in the area, the Federal infantry would support the attacks. Pleasonton had his men pack three days' rations because he intended to chase the routed Confederates. Careful timing would be required to pull off the attack as planned.[214]

The problem was that the plan was based on flawed intelligence. Instead of being back in the vicinity of Culpeper, two brigades of Stuart's troopers and all of his horse artillery were just across the Rappahannock River at Beverly Ford. Stuart had positioned his units to cover the river fords. Fitz Lee's brigade was at Stark's Ford, Rooney Lee's brigade covered Welford's Ford, Grumble Jones's men guarded Beverly Ford, Beverly Robertson's men held Kelly's Ford and Wade Hampton's brigade was camped between Brandy Station and Stevensburg. Stuart's dispositions meant that instead of regrouping on the south side of the river, Pleasonton would not be able to control or coordinate the movements of his two columns. They would be destined to operate independently, devoid of any communication or coordination.

The rolling terrain around Brandy Station featured mostly fields and woods. Its well-defined road network lent itself to rapid movement by large bodies of mounted troopers. The Beverly Ford Road, which crossed the Rappahannock two miles north of St. James Church, was a major artery for commerce. The Carolina Road, which was the main north–south route of commerce through the commonwealth of Virginia, crossed the crest of Fleetwood Hill. "The country was open and level, and presented, on the whole, the best field for a cavalry battle in Virginia," noted a Union officer.[215] A long north–south ridge called Fleetwood Hill rose above the railroad station that gave the settlement its name. "Fleetwood Heights is a beautiful location," observed an officer of the Sixth Virginia Cavalry. "Being an elevated ridge…it commands the country and roads leading north and south from Brandy Station."[216] Stuart's headquarters crowned this prominence overlooking the area around Brandy Station, the plumed cavalier's personal guidon fluttering in the gentle breezes. One of Stuart's staff officers described the area: "The country is open for miles—almost level without fences or ditches and the finest country for cavalry fighting I ever saw."[217]

The Northern horse soldiers did not have much faith in their new commander. "Stuart is in our front with a big force of cavalry," observed a member of the Sixth U.S. Cavalry on the night of June 8. "I only wish Stoneman was here. I have no confidence in Pleasonton."[218] Pleasonton's plan assumed that the Confederate cavalry was concentrated at Culpeper, five miles from Brandy Station. A rude surprise awaited the Federals the next day, when they discovered that the Rebel cavalry lay just across the Rappahannock.

Chapter 6

Buford's Assault and the Death of Grimes Davis

The infantry was the first to march, as it had the more difficult march. The Second Massachusetts Infantry had to cover thirty-one miles to reach the rendezvous point.[219] The foot soldiers set off at a brisk pace. "This was adventure," recalled one. "In fine health, excellent spirits, with fresh, cool air, we stepped off sixteen miles and went into bivouac at eleven." Along the way, they passed their brethren in the cavalry, who had drawn up by the road to clear the way for the infantry. "A merry bandying of jokes, as we passed this seemingly vast array of horsemen, showed the light-hearted humor of brave soldiers. The boys chaffed the cavalry because they could not keep up with us and had to turn out and let us pass."[220] One member of a cavalry detachment called out, "What's your hurry, boys? Where are you going?"

"We're going to Richmond," responded a Massachusetts man. "Saddle up, you cowards, and come along!"[221]

The entire Union Cavalry Corps marched on the afternoon of June 8, arriving at the Rappahannock fords about midnight.[222] "Received orders at Noon from Col. Davis to have 3 days rations & 20 pounds of Forage & prepare for a big march," a member of the Eighth Illinois Cavalry recorded in his diary. Davis's command marched fifteen miles that day, passing Bealeton Station and then heading up the Rappahannock River to Beverly Ford. His troopers bivouacked after midnight, preparing for the next day's adventure.[223]

Buford's men camped on the north side of the Rappahannock, just above Beverly Ford. High bluffs overlooking the river protected them from the prying eyes of the enemy on the other side. One of his troopers later recalled, "We marched that night to within a mile or two of the fords, and awaited the approach of dawn."[221]

"Late in the night we arrive behind the wood nearest the river, and bivouac for the night. No fires are allowed, and we make our supper on cold ham and hard tack, spread our saddle-blankets on the ground, and with saddles for pillows, prepare for a night's rest," recalled the chaplain of the Sixth Pennsylvania Cavalry. "Our minds are full of the coming battle on the morrow, and various speculations are indulged in regard to our prospects of success."[225]

The sight of Buford's horse soldiers as they prepared to go into battle left a lasting impression on Captain Daniel Oakey of the Second Massachusetts Infantry. "Buford's whole column was now concealed in the woods," he recalled.

> *The cheerful clank and jingle of the cavalry was, by some means, suppressed; there was no merry bugle breaking upon the still hours of the night; and, as the moon threw deep shadows across the quiet country road, there seemed no trace of "grim-visaged war."*[226]

The Yankee horsemen fully understood that they would face combat the next day:

> *Our men are confident of success, and eager for the fray. A group of officers are eating their cold supper, perhaps the last they shall all take together. The morrow will soon break upon us, full of danger and death. Messages are committed to friends to be transmitted to distant loved ones, "in case anything should occur." And after solemn and earnest prayer we are all sleeping soundly.*[227]

Even though he served on Pleasonton's staff, Captain Custer was nervous but excited. "I never was in better spirits than I am at this moment," he proclaimed. In case "something happens to me," he told his sister in a letter penned about 2:00 a.m. that night, he had arranged for his chest and personal effects to be shipped to her in Monroe, Michigan. "If such an event occurs, I want my letters burned."[228]

At two o'clock in the morning, the Federal troopers awakened to hushed orders; the command "to horse" was whispered instead of blared by the division's buglers. Buford's troopers quietly mounted and moved stealthily toward Beverly Ford, arriving at 4:30 a.m. That night a thick fog had settled across the river, and a ghostly haze covered the approach of the Union troopers, making it difficult to discern shapes across the river in the cool and pleasant dawn.[229] Trooper Sidney Davis of the Sixth U.S. recalled that "[t]he dull gray dawn gave a weird shadowy appearance to the landscape and those morning figures."[230] Captain Frederic C. Newhall of the Sixth Pennsylvania, who served on Pleasonton's staff, could see a cluster of officers standing by the riverbank through the ghostly fog. One among them, John Buford, acknowledged the passage of his command "with his usual smile. He rode a gray horse, at a slow walk…and smoked a pipe…[and] it was always reassuring to see him in the saddle when there was any chance of a fight."[231]

The water at Beverly Ford was three and a half feet deep, with narrow openings atop the steep riverbanks, meaning that the Union troopers had to cross the river in columns of four. Grimes Davis's brigade led the way, with Pleasonton and his staff sitting on the riverbank, watching them pass. One of Davis's staff officers sat at the ford, and as each company commander passed by, he received the whispered order, "Draw sabers!" Davis's horse soldiers waded the Rappahannock, his Eighth New York in the lead, followed by the Eighth Illinois and the Third Indiana.[232] Once across the river, Buford ordered Davis to push any enemy vedettes back from the ford a mile or so.[233] "We dashed rapidly across, the foremost squadrons receiving a sharp fire from the enemy's rifle pits," reported a member of the Eighth New York.[234]

Private Robert N. Shipley, a twenty-one-year-old from Wayne County, New York, served in Company C of the Eighth New York Cavalry. "We had most of the regiment across, when we were fired upon by the rebel's pickets which immediately fell back to a large tract of timber, two miles or more square," he recounted. "Col. Davis ordered our regiment to charge which we did, not thinking that there was more than a company or so that guarded the ford."[235]

A company of Jones's Sixth Virginia Cavalry picketed the area, and the sudden appearance of Davis's soldiers surprised it. Unbeknownst to the Federals, Jones's men had constructed a stout barricade of rails across the river and along the edge of a wood.[236] After participating in the grand review, John W. Peake and a friend had stood picket duty at Beverly Ford until 2:00 a.m. After being relieved, the two weary troopers made their way back to the picket reserve and tried to get some sleep. About daylight, the rattling of carbines shook them from slumber. They scrambled for their horses, with the pickets and Yankee troopers following them in a great hurry. Peake and his friend used a cedar brush fence for a crude breastwork and opened fire on the blue-clad horsemen. Their fire slowed the Federals long enough for Gibson to bring the rest of his company forward. "Keep cool, men, and shoot to kill," he calmly told his men.[237]

"Captain Gibson, who was a brave and prudent officer, had already blockaded the road as best he could with the material at hand, and waited patiently to receive them," recalled a Virginia horse soldier.

> When at close range the captain gave the word and a sheet of fire flashed in their faces and the shower of lead poured into their ranks, emptied many saddles and caused the advance to recoil, but the head of the main body advancing rapidly to the support of their advance, Capt. Gibson was compelled to fall back, the Yankees pressing close on his rear.[238]

Lieutenant Henry Clay Cutler, the twenty-three-year-old commander of Company B of the Eighth New York Cavalry, was struck in the neck by the first volley by Gibson's pickets and fell dead, the first of many casualties that day. Enraged, the New Yorkers charged Gibson's pickets; the Rebels fled, hanging onto the necks of their horses for dear life.[239] Gibson lost two dead and several men wounded in this opening action.[240]

Trooper Luther W. Hopkins of the Sixth Virginia looked behind, called to the captain and told Gibson that the pursuing Yankees were closing in on them. Just as Hopkins spoke, two bullets hissed by his head. Gibson yelled to his men to move forward, and bending low on the necks of their horses, Hopkins and Gibson dashed away to safety.[241] A member of Breathed's battery of horse artillery recalled that Gibson's men "fought like demons" in resisting the Federal advance.[242]

"I hitched my horse, and, wrapped in a blanket, lay down to sleep," recalled an exhausted member of the Sixth Virginia Cavalry. "But I was soon rudely awakened by the watchman, who shouted that the enemy was crossing the river. We all jumped up and mounted our horses."[243] Day was breaking, and the gray-clad pickets scurried up from the banks of the river in every direction, firing their pistols to raise the alarm.

Many of the Confederates were either still asleep or cooking their breakfasts when Davis's onslaught caught them. "The Company was surprised, yet contended for every foot of ground between them and the camp of Jones's and W.H.F. Lee's brigades, near St. James Church, with the battalion of horse artillery," recalled a member of the Sixth Virginia.

The 6th Regiment, which was out on the road, got off first; the 7th Regiment next, just as the Federals were getting up into our midst. Many of our men had not finished their breakfast and had to mount their horses bareback and rush into the fight. [244]

As Davis's horsemen closed in on their camps, Confederate officers quickly turned out their commands and ordered them "to horse." [245] A New Yorker recounted:

We had not gone a quarter of a mile when suddenly a heavy fire was poured into our ranks by their skirmishers who filled the woods on each side of us. At the same time a strong force of cavalry appeared coming down the road in front of us, and a battery of artillery could be seen through an opening, ready to open fire as soon as we should advance a little further. It was rather a tight place, for it was almost impossible to form in line of battle under such circumstances. [246]

"There were lively times for a few minutes," observed a Regular. [247]

Gibson's company retired slowly, their retreat protected by ditches in the low ground on either side of the narrow Beverly Ford Road, thereby preventing the Union troopers from flanking them and limiting their attack to the Sixth Virginia's front. "The enemy came pouring up from the river, and we opened fire on them, checking them for the moment," recalled Luther W. Hopkins of the Sixth Virginia Cavalry. "Two of our men were killed, several wounded, and two horses killed." [248]

Gibson's delaying action permitted twenty-two-year-old Major Cabell E. Flournoy, the temporary regimental commander, to scrape together a force of 150 men with which to blunt the Union onslaught. The sleepy Southern troopers sprang to horse after being awakened by the crack of gunfire coming from the vicinity of the ford. "There being no information or apprehension of an attack, our men had, carelessly, turned their horses out to graze." Only forty horses were haltered and ready for action, so the camp soon became a beehive of activity. [249] Flournoy led a hasty countercharge, many of his men dashing off without their coats or saddles. [250]

The two forces collided in the road, and a brief but savage saber fight occurred, as sabers clanged and pistols echoed. "The fight was at close quarters, and for a short time was fierce and bloody," recalled a member of the Sixth Virginia. [251] "It seemed as if the whole air was alive with rebel bullets," recounted a member of the Eighth Illinois. [252] "The roar of the

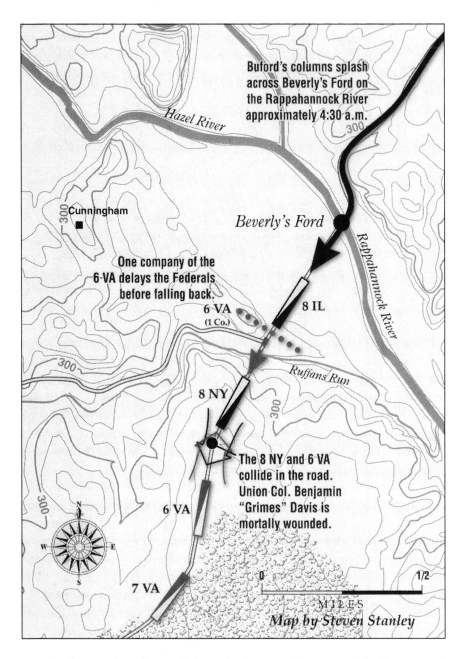

guns in the woods at that early hour in the morning was terrific," concurred a Virginian.[253] During this altercation, the Sixth Virginia sustained thirty casualties, or 20 percent of the total force engaged. Flournoy yielded to the sheer weight of numbers. Nevertheless, Flournoy's stand "was of great value," for it permitted the Confederate horse artillery to withdraw to safety on the high ridge where St. James Church sat. "Flournoy's Sixth was all that was between the four Confederate batteries and Buford's column."[254] The stout resistance by the Virginians prompted one of Buford's Regulars to grudgingly admit, "The rebs contested every inch of ground manfully, and the fight grew beautifully larger & larger."[255]

However, Lieutenant Robert Owen Allen, of Company D of the Sixth Virginia, riding at the rear of Flournoy's retreating column, spotted Grimes Davis, alone and about seventy-five yards ahead of the rest of his column. Seeing an opportunity, Allen dashed up to Davis, who was facing his men, urging them on. Davis's last words were "Stand firm, Eighth New York!" Even as he yelled this, Davis evidently sensed that he was in danger, for he turned upon Allen with a swing of his saber. Allen ducked this blow by throwing himself on the side of his horse. At the same time, Allen fired his pistol, killing Davis instantly with a bullet to his head. Sergeant John Stone of Company D, Sixth Virginia, rode forward to Allen's assistance. Enraged by the loss of their beloved commander, the Union troopers charged Stone and, mistaking him for Davis's killer, attacked him ferociously. A savage saber blow split Stone's skull "midway between eyes and chin," killing him instantly.[256]

The loss of Davis hit the Union troopers hard. "The success was dearly bought, for among the noble and brave ones who fell was Col. B.F. Davis, 8th N.Y. Cav. He died in the front giving examples of heroism and courage to all who were to follow," lamented Buford. "He was a thorough soldier, free from politics and intrigue, a patriot in its true sense, an ornament to his country and a bright star in his profession."[257] Wesley Merritt, who had a long and nearly unparalleled career in the United States Army, wrote years later that Davis "was dearly beloved throughout the [Reserve Brigade], and many a veteran of the First, Second, and Fifth drew his chin more grimly to his breast and with clenched teeth awaited the shock of battle, anxious to avenge the death of this hero."[258]

Panicked couriers dashed to Stuart's headquarters atop Fleetwood Hill, bearing news of the Yankee advance. "Yankees in our headquarters!" they cried. Hearing the commotion, Stuart and his staff mounted and galloped to the sound of the guns, prompting Captain William Farley, a volunteer aide and Stuart's favorite scout, to declare, "Hurrah! We're going to have a fight!"[259] Along the way, Stuart and his aides dodged the panicked teamsters of the Confederate wagon trains hurrying away from the fighting:

The wagon trains came first and went thundering to the rear mid clouds of dust—then came the cavalry regiments at a trot with here and there a battery of artillery—all hurrying to the front with the greatest possible speed.[260]

Stuart galloped toward the wooden St. James Episcopal Church to assume personal command of the fight.

St. James Church sat atop a high ridge about two miles from Beverly Ford. The church itself was about two hundred yards to the west of the Beverly Ford Road. Opposite it sat the brick house of Emily Gee, which occupied a small knoll that commanded both sides of the road for a distance of about five hundred yards. The Confederates were fortunate to have such a strong position to fall back to, and they made the most of their good fortune that day.

As Stuart and his aide, Major Heros von Borcke, approached St. James Church, they encountered Confederate stragglers from Jones's brigade who shouted, "The Yankees are in our rear! Everything back there is lost!"[261] While Stuart tried to bring order to the fight at St. James Church, Rooney Lee's brigade also rushed to the sounds of the guns from its camp at a nearby estate called Welford, just west of Yew Ridge, a small ridge running north and south and resting to the northeast of the northern end of Fleetwood Hill. Lee formed his command into line of battle near the Greene farmhouse and then dismounted his men behind a stone wall on the Cunningham farm. Jones's hard-pressed command received crucial reinforcements at a critical moment.

The Confederate cavalry chief and his staffers joined the charge. "I saw General Stuart that day riding out on the field where shot and shell were raining around, and he didn't seem to bat an eye," recalled a sergeant of a Virginia cavalry regiment.[262] "With his characteristic energy, he ordered the mischief-makers attacked from all sides, and stability was soon achieved," recounted Captain Justus Scheibert, a Prussian engineering officer traveling with Stuart's command as an observer.[263]

Lieutenant Chiswell Dabney, one of Stuart's staff officers, chased a lone Yankee trooper, emptying his pistol as he ran down the fugitive. He finally trapped the bluecoat when the Yank's horse failed to jump a watery ditch at the base of a hill. The Federal disengaged himself from his horse, which had fallen into the water, crawled up on the other bank and began fumbling with his carbine. Dabney leveled his pistol at the man, playing "a bluff game, ordering him to drop his gun or I would blow his head off. Fortunately, he did not know my pistol was empty," recalled Dabney. "I made him wade over. The bullets were flying pretty thick and he said, 'Don't keep me here or I will be shot by my own men,' so I sent him running to the rear where he was picked up by the provost guard."[264] Stuart's presence helped to stabilize the situation.

The Eighth New York lost its way in the woods and pulled back to regroup. "For the first half hour we were in the woods it was awful," admitted Private Shipley.

> *The balls flew like hail stones, and sabers glistening above our heads. Wherever we turned it seemed certain death, and no escape from it. How so many of us did escape without a scratch is a mystery, though I thought but very little about being killed.*

Shipley saw men with grievous wounds and never flinched. "It is a singular feeling that takes possession of a man in time of battle," he concluded.[265]

"The 8th New York Cav. crossed ahead and went about a mile when the rebels charged them. They broke and ran like a flock of sheep, and we, being close in their rear, now found ourselves among the rebels, who thought they were just doing it, and true enough, they were," observed a member of the Eighth Illinois Cavalry. "But it was played out when they met us…the frightened New Yorkers came rushing on and we were obliged to draw our sabres and threaten to split their heads, to bring them back to their senses."[266]

Major William S. McClure of the Third Indiana Cavalry assumed command of Davis's brigade after Grimes Davis fell with his mortal wound. *USAHEC.*

The Eighth Illinois, next in the Union column, held off the Confederate counterattack, permitting the rest of the column to regroup and prepare to resume the charge. "We charged off as the left drove the enemy through the woods 1 mile, killed 8 wounded [?] took a few prisoners," recorded an Illini trooper. "The enemy fell back & opened artillery on us, shelled the Woods in every direction."[267] Command of the brigade devolved upon twenty-six-year-old Major William S. McClure, a merchant from Madison, Indiana, temporarily commanding the Third Indiana in the absence of Lieutenant Colonel George H. Chapman, the regiment's ranking officer.

When the sad news of Davis's fall reached me, I crossed and pushed to the front to examine the country and to find out how matters stood. I then threw the 1st Division on the left of the road leading to Brandy Station with its left extending toward the R[ail] Road.

Responding, Buford dispatched the Third Indiana to rescue the New Yorkers, and the Hoosiers drove the Confederates back. McClure's men then joined the running battle. The fully roused Confederate cavalry and horse artillery pressed McClure's troopers hard as they attempted to form lines of battle. Sabers "gleamed and flashed in the morning sun" for just a moment before the Federal horsemen fell back into the cover of the woods.[268] Buford also brought up Ames's infantry brigade and posted the Reserve Brigade on the right, all connecting from right to left.[269]

The Sixth Pennsylvania Cavalry of the Reserve Brigade was coming up as a rough litter bearing a wounded officer came down the Beverly Ford Road. "Who is that, boys?" inquired Chaplain Samuel L. Gracey.

"Colonel Davis, sir," came the response.

"Is it possible? Noble fellow! Is he wounded badly?"

"A Minié ball through his head, sir."

Gracey paused a moment to pray for Davis. "He is insensible, his hair matted and clotted with blood," recalled the chaplain. "God have mercy on the brave, noble, patriot-soldier, the hero of Harpers Ferry!"[270]

At the same time, the Seventh Virginia Cavalry, under the command of Lieutenant Colonel Thomas Marshall, arrived and joined the Sixth Virginia's counterattack. The Seventh Virginia, which was acting as the grand guard for the Confederate cavalry that day, galloped to meet the threat, crashing into the blue-clad troopers. "On this ground I think it may justly be said that Col. Marshall with his Seventh done did the best and bravest fighting of the day," recounted a Southerner.[271]

Confederate troopers surrounded and nearly captured three full companies of the Eighth Illinois. "To the right a large party of the enemy tried to force our cavalry back," recalled an Illini trooper,

> *and actually got possession of the road in our rear, but the part of the Eighth Illinois regiment not engaged in the fight here had an opportunity to display their courage, and the conflict was severe, but the enemy were forced to yield the ground, after a bloody encounter.*[272]

In the end, the Rebels gave way after buying precious time for the rest of the gray-clad horsemen to react.

Captain Alpheus Clark, commander of the Eighth Illinois, engaged Flournoy in a pistol duel that ended when Flournoy wounded Clark in the hand. This seemingly inconsequential wound proved fatal when Clark contracted lead poisoning and died. Captain George Forsyth, the next ranking officer, was also badly wounded in the leg during this fighting.[273] The regiment's next senior captain, Elon J. Farnsworth, took command of the Eighth Illinois and led it for the rest of the day, earning praise from both Buford and Pleasonton. The corps commander marked the talented and ambitious young man for advancement.

Captain Alpheus Clark of the Eighth Illinois Cavalry received a mortal wound at Brandy Station. *USAHEC.*

Captain George A. Custer came across the river with Davis's horsemen and charged with them. Although at least one of Custer's biographers claims that Custer assumed command of Davis's brigade and rallied it after Davis fell, those claims are unfounded. However, the dashing young man earned Pleasonton's praise for his courage. He was knocked from his saddle when his horse could not clear a stone wall. Later that day, he delivered the captured headquarters flag of the Twelfth Virginia Cavalry to Hooker's headquarters. When he wrote his report of the battle, Pleasonton stated that Custer was "conspicuous for gallantry throughout the fight."[274]

After making his way back to report Davis's death, Custer spent the rest of the day at the Cavalry Corps commander's side. "The time was coming and very near at hand," noted one of Custer's many biographers, "though he knew it not, for him to win his star, and emerge from the inconspicuous position of a staff officer to one in which he could command public attention." And so it was.[275]

Although the surprise of the original Union assaults nearly bagged four batteries of Confederate horse artillery, quick thinking by Captain James F. Hart of the Washington (South Carolina) Artillery saved them. Hart, as described by a Tar Heel horse soldier of Hampton's Brigade, "was a brave man and good officer. You could depend on him being on time always."[276] He now faced a crisis. "As the men rubbed their eyes open, they saw the Confederate cavalry pickets dash by our guns and scurry back along the road towards their camps, closely followed by the Federal cavalry." Responding, Hart hastily placed two of his guns in the Beverly Ford Road. As soon as the head of the Federal cavalry column appeared in his front, Hart opened on it with his guns, stopping the enemy's advance dead in its tracks, as the Yankee horsemen deployed into line of battle while the rest of the Confederate batteries fell back to safety on a prominent ridge nearly two miles to their rear. Alone, the artillerists stood by their guns, armed only with their rammers. Desperately fighting to try to save their guns, the gunners used their rammers to unhorse a couple of Yankees who dared to come too close.[277] Once Jones's troopers came up to support them, the two guns eventually fell back, firing and retreating by prolonge, and they joined the main line at St. James Church.[278] This action slowed the Yankee approach long enough for Grumble Jones to deploy his entire brigade in line of battle to protect the guns from the Union attack.[279]

"Our cavalry checked them long enough for our battery to harness up, which was done in double quick time, but so close were the enemy on us that one of our horses was killed before we could move out," noted a gunner of Captain Marcellus Moorman's battery. "We fell back half a mile on the first hill and took position where we kept the enemy in check in our front."[280]

"Our camp…was in the edge of a woods, and this morning at daylight, just as we were rounding up the last sweet snooze for the night, bullets fresh from Yankee sharpshooters came from the depths of the woods and zipped across our blanket beds, and then such a getting up of horse artillerymen I never saw before," recalled Sergeant George M. Neese of Captain Roger P. Chew's fine battery of horse artillery. "Blankets were fluttering and being rolled up in double-quick time in every direction, and in less than twenty minutes we were ready to man our guns, and all our effects safely on the way to the rear. Before I got out of bed I saw a twig clipped from a bush by a Yankee bullet not more than two feet above my head."[281] Another Southern gunner recalled:

> *We were aroused about daylight from our dreams of home, wives and sweethearts by the firing of our pickets a few hundred yards from us and the whizzing of musket balls all around us. The enemy had made a sudden dash across the ford and were driving our pickets back into our camp, where they were met by our cavalry and our battalion and checked for the time.*[282]

The steady, accurate fire of Beckham's gunners forced the Federal horse soldiers to take cover and wait for the arrival of their artillery, breaking up the momentum of the Union assault. The Southern artillerists, fighting largely alone, held Buford's determined assault at bay, having lost only Major Beckham's field desk, which fell out of his headquarters wagon as it jostled away. Beckham and his men performed gallantly on that long, hard morning.[283]

The rattling of gunfire awoke Jones, and he dashed off at the head of his troops without his coat or boots.[284] "All right, Captain, we will take care of them, we'll give them Hell!" he cried as he galloped past Hart's guns. Jones realized that a moment of crisis faced his command. "As the batteries were neither ready for action or movement," he wrote, "it was a matter of the utmost importance to gain time."[285] The gunners did what they could to limber up their guns and had hardly hitched their horses to their guns when Jones came flying back faster than he went. "He said nothing when he came up to us but wheeled to the right between the gun and the woods and went down the road very rapidly." Major Beckham rode up and ordered Hart to remain where he was until the rest of the

Brigadier General William E. "Grumble" Jones commanded an excellent brigade of Confederate cavalry. The irascible Jones and his troopers bore the brunt of the fighting at Brandy Station. *Library of Congress.*

battalion could pull back and then to retreat by pieces at intervals of seventy-five yards.[286]

The sounds of gunfire also roused the men of the Twelfth Virginia Cavalry. "Instantly our regimental bugle sounded the call to mount," recalled an officer of the Twelfth Virginia, "the men sprang out of their blankets, and I am sure in less than ten minutes the regiment was in line awaiting orders." One trooper drolly observed "that such an early rising was not good for a man's liver, but we would knock the livers out of the disturbers of our rest as soon as we could get at them." They would not have long to wait.[287]

Once safely out of range of the stalled Yankees, Stuart's batteries unlimbered again east of St. James Church, about a mile and a half from Beverly Ford, defending a ridge that they held for much of the morning's fight. These Confederate batteries kept up a steady fire, helping to repulse repeated Union attacks on the St. James Church position.[288] One of the Confederate gunners noted, "It was a close call and brilliant dash on the part of the enemy."[289]

The Eighth Illinois charged into the Sixth and Seventh Virginia, driving them back. As one Confederate trooper succinctly put it, "Quicker than some of us came we went."[290] Colonel Thomas C. Devin's Second Brigade was close behind the Eighth Illinois, coming up to join the action. "As Colonel Devin approached the skirmish line, he at once became the target for the Rebel sharpshooters and, the way the minie balls were whizzing around him, it was the next thing to a miracle that he was not killed," recalled a member of the Seventeenth Pennsylvania Cavalry. "One of the skirmishers hailed him and said, 'Colonel, this is no place for you.' He replied by saying, 'Those fellows across the ravine could not hit an elephant if they would try.'" Moments later, a Confederate sharpshooter shot Devin's horse out from under him.[291]

Seeing the approaching Union troopers and recognizing the extreme danger facing his lone brigade, Grumble Jones committed the last of his reserves to the fight. "The men, worn out by the military foppery and display of the previous day's review, were yet under their blankets," recalled Captain Frank Myers of the Thirty-fifth Battalion of Virginia Cavalry, which later became known as White's Comanches.[292] In an effort to secure his flanks and rear, Jones sent the Eleventh and Twelfth Virginia regiments, along with the Comanches, to join the battle line centered at St. James Church.[293] Jones ordered the Thirty-fifth to charge the approaching Yankees before the Comanches could even form a line of battle as the blue-clad horsemen repulsed the charge of the Twelfth Virginia. A member of the Twelfth Virginia described the charging Yankees "as thick as angry bees from a hive."[294]

The Thirty-fifth Battalion of Virginia Cavalry slammed into the lead elements of the Federal charge near the Emily Mary Gee house, staggering them. After a brief mêlée, the Virginians drove the Union troopers back into the woods, where they received reinforcements. Rallying, the Union troopers again charged and this time shoved the Thirty-fifth back into the woods from which they came. In the meantime, the Twelfth Virginia was also heavily engaged. One member of Company H of the Twelfth Virginia exclaimed, "It was then warm work, hand to hand, shooting and cutting each other in desperate fury, all mixed through one another, killing, wounding, and taking prisoners promiscuously." This stalemate lasted a while, with each charge being met by a countercharge. Another member of the Twelfth Virginia recalled, "For hours this seesawing was kept up. Finally, after we had driven them the fourth or fifth time to their rallying point [the nearby woods], they showed no disposition to charge again, and we fell back to the hill."[295]

Captain Charles T. O'Ferrall of the Twelfth Virginia Cavalry deployed his squadron into line of battle and advanced until they found enemy cavalry in the woods ahead. Colonel Asher Harman told O'Ferrall he would support his advance with the rest of the regiment, so O'Ferrall's two companies moved out, skirmishers leading the way. The Federals held their fire until the Virginians reached the woods and then unleashed a galling fire, checking O'Ferrall's advance and inflicting casualties on his command. The Federals then charged the isolated Virginians. Harman led the rest of the Twelfth Virginia forward, and the "fight became close, fast and furious." Outnumbered, the Virginians fell back to a hill in the field, where reinforcements came up. The Virginians then charged again. "Several times was this repeated," recalled O'Ferrall. "We would drive them into the woods and then they would rally and drive us to the hill." They kept up this seesawing for several hours, with both sides taking heavy losses in this intense fighting.[296]

Brigadier General Wade Hampton's brigade also responded to the threat. Hampton rousted his command and got his men in their saddles quickly. "As soon as the firing was heard, 'boots and saddles' was sounded, and our brigade hurried forward and in a very short time engaged the enemy," recounted a member of the Georgia Hussars of the Cobb Legion Cavalry. "Never for a moment were we (our brigade) repulsed, but we drove the enemy before us like a flock of sheep."[297] Hampton deployed about one hundred dismounted men as sharpshooters down the Beverly Ford Road, while dismounting his other three available regiments and forming a line of battle.[298]

Lieutenant Colonel Will Delony served in the Cobb Legion Cavalry. He had a bird's-eye view of Hampton's charge. "They charged the Yankees and drove them through the woods for 300 or 400 yards into a point where our men were very much exposed both to the fire of their Infantry and a cavalry charge," he reported to his wife.

> *By this time our men had expended nearly all their ammunition and many of them were completely exhausted—Capts* [Barrington S.] *King and* [Jeremiah E.] *Ritch then ordered their men to fall back—Ritch telling them that he was too much exhausted to go with them—King led them back & the enemy advanced slowly on them until our ammunition was entirely gone and the enemy captured five of Ritch's men and two of King's were captured.*

Captain Ritch refused to surrender, fighting alone until he had emptied both of his pistols and was finally taken prisoner. "His gallantry was conspicuous to the entire brigade—as it was done in our sight, but we could not get up in time to relieve them," concluded Delony.[299]

In the meantime, as the foes traded saber licks, the Reserve Brigade, commanded by Major Charles J. Whiting, a stodgy old Regular, crossed the Rappahannock and rode toward the sound of the firing. Advancing, the

Regulars met little resistance for the first mile of their approach. Near an old farmhouse, Trooper Sidney Davis of the Sixth U.S. and his companions spotted "partially covered by an army blanket, lying prone on his back…the dead body of one of our officers, from whose death wound the warm blood of life still dripped over his dark blue uniform." The sight of Grimes Davis's corpse chilled the Regulars, causing many of them to pray for safety in the coming battle.[300]

At 7:40 a.m., surprised by the stout resistance of the Confederates, Pleasonton decided to ride to the front. He took a few minutes to scrawl a dispatch to Washington before heading for the ford. "The enemy is in strong cavalry force here," he wrote. "We have had a severe fight. They were aware of our movement, and were prepared." Things did not bode well for the success of Pleasonton's ambitious expedition.[301]

Chapter 7

THE FIGHT FOR THE GUNS AT ST. JAMES CHURCH

Brigadier General John Buford did not know the size or strength of the force guarding the Confederate guns at St. James Church. He deployed the guns of Lieutenant Samuel S. Elder's battery of horse artillery. Buford sent a messenger to Major Robert Morris Jr., the commander of the Sixth Pennsylvania Cavalry. "General Buford sends his compliments to Major Morris," panted the courier, "and directs him to clear the woods in his front."[302] The Lancers stared across a field nearly half a mile wide, intersected by four ditches. The ground rose steadily to the woods, and upon the ridge sat a small house that became the Confederate headquarters, as well as the Southern artillery.[303]

Without hesitation, Morris formed up his five companies and began moving forward. It was no small task to hold a steady line while moving around trees and other obstacles under fire, but each trooper and horse handled this maneuver with the skill of a Regular. Nearing the edge of the wood, the command "Draw!" echoed down the lines, followed by "Sabers!" The exhilarating metallic clang of hundreds of blades being drawn from scabbards and carried to shoulder rang out.

A few Confederate skirmishers, still deployed in the field far in advance of the main Rebel line, spotted the bright morning sunlight flashing off the Yankees' blades. They wasted little time retreating back up the hill to the safety of their lines. The Southern gunners on the ridge had also seen the flashes and paused to see what would develop. This sudden halt in firing caused an unnerving quiet to drift over the battlefield.

Major Robert Morris Jr., commander of the Sixth Pennsylvania Cavalry, was captured during the charge on the Confederate guns at St. James Church. *USAHEC.*

Confederate eyes and ears strained to gain a sense of what was happening in the wood. The sounds of tramping hoofs, snapping twigs, rattling scabbards and stretching leather broke the silence and then grew louder. These sounds could mean only one thing: the movement of massed cavalry into position.

As the Pennsylvania horse soldiers emerged from the tree line, they closed up boot-to-boot and redressed their lines. Major Morris, great-grandson of the financier of the Revolutionary War, stiffened with resolute pride as he watched his battalion step out onto the field. Seeing this, the Confederate cannoneers resumed firing, large plumes of smoke rising from the ridgeline across the field. Lead whistled a deadly tune as bullet and canister found their marks on men and horses. Major Morris could see that the once thin lines of gray had been reinforced. His Philadelphians now faced a large force of enemy carbines blasting away at his flanks while bursts of canister from Beckham's guns rent great gaps in his front rank as it dashed across the field.

The popping of Southern carbines increased in intensity as Major Morris gave the command: "Forward, guide right, march!" The two waves

The Fight for the Guns at St. James Church

A depiction of the charge of the Sixth Pennsylvania Cavalry at St. James Church drawn by renowned Civil War artist Alfred Waud, who witnessed the attack and then spent several hours walking the battlefield after the action shifted. The terrain is accurately portrayed. The Gee house appears on the left of the Beverly Ford Road. *Harper's Weekly*.

of blue lines moved out in concert with each other. After advancing some twenty paces, Morris shouted, "Trot, march!" Sod flew from the horses' hooves. Some sixty paces later, the major called out, "Gallop, march!" Buglers echoed the command above the ever-increasing din of battle. As the pace of the horse soldiers quickened, so did the pace of canister that blasted in their faces. Now closing quickly on Beckham's cannons, Major Morris pointed his saber and yelled, "Charge!"[304] Union bugles sounded, his men raised their sabers and a resounding cheer rivaling that of the Rebel yell carried along the lines as the Sixth Pennsylvania put spurs to horse. For a moment, the grand charge transfixed the Southern artillerists, but they were hardened veterans and soon grabbed whatever weapons they could find and prepared to defend their guns. Samuel L. Gracey, chaplain of the Sixth Pennsylvania, later wrote, "The Philadelphia men rode hard across the open field toward their date with destiny, their company guidons snapping in the warm spring breeze."[305]

The Sixth Pennsylvania made a "dash of conspicuous gallantry" across the wide meadow, directly into the teeth of sixteen pieces of Confederate horse artillery at St. James Church.[306] Indeed, the performance of the Sixth

Pennsylvania that day so impressed John Buford that he henceforth called them "my Seventh Regulars."[307]

The Sixth Pennsylvania "charged the enemy home, riding almost up to the mouths of his cannon," nearly capturing two of the Confederate guns.[308] "Shells burst over us, under us, and alongside," breathlessly recounted a survivor of the charge, "and bullets were singing through the air like a hornet's nest."[309]

"Shell and shrapnel shot tore gaps in their ranks, but still they advanced, now at a charge to capture the battery," noted an admiring gunner of Hart's battery.

> *When within two hundred yards of us and the guns about to use canister, Lt. Col. Elijah V. White, commanding a small detachment of Virginia cavalry, led his force between our guns and the enemy, and gallantly charged into them. Our fire ceased instantly, and with nothing else in their way, the charging column rolled back White's little force as if it was a wisp of straw and thundered on. When within twenty yards of the guns, double shotted with canister, we delivered their last fire into the mass of Federals and Virginians alike, but it was now too late to stop them.*

He noted that in spite of the threat posed by the charging Lancers, the gunners stayed at their posts, manning their guns with great discipline and courage. He concluded that the charge of the Lancers was "one of the most daring charges the cavalry on either side had attempted up to this time. It deserved better success."[310]

"The Sixth fell upon these with great gallantry," reported a Northern correspondent who witnessed their valiant dash, "and regardless of the chances of flank attacks from the other battalions, drove them, fighting hand to hand, through the brigade in reserve, and then wheeling about, passed round the battalion on the right and resumed position for another charge."[311]

"We dashed at them, squadron front with drawn sabres, and as we flew along—our men yelling like demons—grape and cannister [sic] were poured into our left flank and a storm of rifle bullets on our front," recalled Major Henry C. Whelan of the Sixth Pennsylvania.

> *We had to leap three wide deep ditches, and many of our horses and men piled up in a writhing mass in those ditches and were ridden over. It was here that Maj. Morris's horse fell badly with him, and broke away from him when he got up, thus leaving him dismounted and*

Captain Ulric Dahlgren, of Hooker's staff, was sent by Hooker to observe the cavalry expedition. Dahlgren rallied the Sixth Pennsylvania Cavalry after Major Morris went down. *USAHEC.*

bruised by the fall. I didn't know that Morris was not with us, and we dashed on, driving the Rebels into and through the woods, our men fighting with the sabre alone, whilst they used principally pistols. Our brave fellows cut them out of the saddle and fought like tigers, until I discovered they were on both flanks, pouring a cross fire of carbines and pistols on us, and then tried to rally my men and make them return the fire with their carbines.[312]

When the Lancers charged, Captain Ulric Dahlgren joined them. On June 7, Hooker had sent Dahlgren to carry his orders for the raid to Pleasonton. The ambitious and daring young captain, who was a member of Hooker's staff, remained with the Cavalry Corps to observe and report on the actions of the horse soldiers. The aggressive youth was unable to resist pitching into the fray. He rode alongside Major Morris and reported, "Just as we were jumping a ditch, some canister came along, and I saw his horse fall over him, but could not tell whether he was killed or not, for at the same instant my horse was shot in three places." The wounded horse fell, throwing Dahlgren. "Just then the column turned to go back—finding that the enemy had surrounded us. I saw the rear passing me, and about to leave me behind, so I gave my horse a tremendous kick and got him on his legs again. Finding he could still move, I mounted and made after the rest—just escaping being taken. I got a heavy blow over the arm from the back of a saber, which bruised me somewhat, and nearly unhorsed me," recounted Dahlgren. The young man rallied the Lancers and led them to safety. The wounded horse had to be put down.[313]

A newspaper correspondent reported, "Captain Dahlgren, of General Hooker's staff, a model of cool and dauntless bravery, charged with the regiment, and his horse was shot in two places."[314] Pleasonton informed Hooker that Dahlgren had "been baptized in fire" and that the young man was a "capital aid."[315] Dahlgren found another mount after the battle and rode back to Hooker's headquarters to report on the day's activities. He had had a very long and trying day and was flushed with exuberance. Impressed, Hooker marked Dahlgren for advancement. Assigned to Cavalry Corps headquarters in the days following Brandy Station, the courageous captain performed magnificently in the coming weeks.[316]

As the Lancers reached the Confederate artillery, it opened up, raking the Union line. "Never rode troopers more gallantly than those steady Regulars, as under a fire of shell and shrapnel, and finally of canister, they dashed up to the very muzzles," recalled Captain James F. Hart of the Washington, South Carolina Artillery, "then through and beyond our guns, passing between Hampton's left and Jones's right."[317]

"There are few instances recorded of a similar charge upon so strong a line of artillery," observed the historian of the Army of Northern Virginia's artillery branch. He noted that the Light Brigade's "charge at Balaclava was no more daring than the one which [the Federals made] at Saint James Church, the latter possessing the additional feature that it was premeditated and not the result of accident." Left with no alternatives, Beckham's desperate gunners redoubled their efforts.[318]

"We gave them fifty rounds," recalled an artillerist caught in the whirling maelstrom raging among the guns.

> Our cavalry are charging desperately. We ceased firing for a few moments but have commenced firing again and have several shells in their column. The fight has become heavy, and we are surrounded on three sides. The Yanks are facing on our front, right, and rear. The shell are bursting above

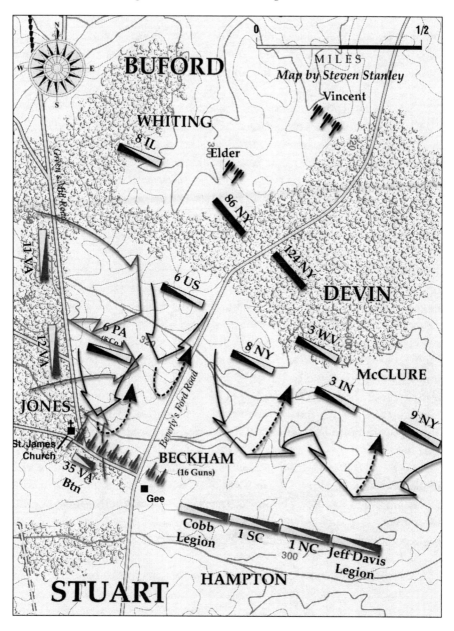

and around us thick…This is fearful hard work. Part of the time we had no support. This is now getting at close range.[319]

"What an awful fire! So close that we are almost in the smoke of the battery. Many of our saddles are emptied, and the horses, freed from the restraint of their riders, dash wildly away; and at the same moment, hundreds of carbines fend their charges of death into our never-wavering ranks," recalled a member of the Sixth Pennsylvania.

Our color sergeant reels, and falls from his horse; another sergeant catches the colors before they reach the ground; and on through the storm of death our weakened lines advance until they meet the enemy, and hand to hand the conflict rages. Though we are outnumbered two to one, we break their ranks, and pursue them into the woods. Now the enemy on our right begin to close upon us: our commander has fallen. Major Whelan assuming command, attempts to withdraw us from our terrible position. But how are we to retreat? The enemy have completely surrounded us—all is lost![320]

Spotting the predicament facing the Sixth Pennsylvania, four squadrons of the Sixth U.S. charged in support of the gallant Lancers, who were engaged in "a race for life."[321] Lieutenants Louis H. Carpenter and Andrew Stoll led their squadrons out of the woods. Carpenter called for the charge, and away they went. As they charged, Carpenter watched the Lancers break and scatter. "As we went along at headlong speed, cheering and shouting it seemed to me, that the air was perfectly filled with bullets and pieces of shell, shells burst over us, under us, and alongside," recounted Carpenter. The Regulars crossed a wide ditch and continued on. The Virginians retreated to the cover of the woods, where they opened a heavy carbine fire.[322]

The Regulars arrived just as the Confederates were about to fall on the bloodied Pennsylvanians. Horse soldiers of both sides merged into a wild mêlée among the guns. "The warlike scene was fascinatingly grand beyond description, and such as can be produced and acted only by an actual and real combat," recalled Confederate gunner Neese.

Hundreds of glittering sabres instantly leaped from their scabbards, gleamed and flashed in the morning sun, then clashed with metallic ring, searching for human blood, while hundreds of little puffs of white smoke gracefully rose through the balmy June air from discharging firearms all over the field in front of our batteries...the artillerymen stood in silent awe gazing on the struggling mass in our immediate front.[323]

"This is a wide contrast from yesterdays <u>sham battle</u>," succinctly noted another Confederate artillerist with a chill.[324]

Another survivor of the charge remembered "a mingled mass fighting and struggling with pistol and saber like maddened savages."[325] The lines of battle ebbed and flowed like the waves of the ocean, prompting an officer of the Twelfth Virginia Cavalry to write, "These charges and countercharges continued until noon, without any decisive advantage to either side, but with considerable loss to both, in men and horses."[326]

The men of Carpenter's and Stoll's squadrons laid down a heavy fire with their pistols and carbines for several minutes until their position became untenable and the Regulars retired. "As we turned, a rebel made a dash close to me; I cut at him twice and missed him," recounted Lieutenant Carpenter. "As he passed he threw his saber at me. One of my men almost thrust his carbine against the breast of the rebel and shot him dead."[327] The Lancers and the Regulars retreated across the same fields toward the main Union line. They withstood heavy Confederate artillery fire, sometimes from a range as short as fifty yards. Both the Lancers and the Regulars demonstrated superb leadership at the company and squadron levels, and their officers did a fine job of regaining control of their scattered commands, which remained effective combat units.

The air whistling with the sounds of shrapnel and Minié balls, the beleaguered Federal horse soldiers clung to the necks of their horses as they dashed across the fields toward friendly lines in the woods. As the Sixth U.S. attempted to re-form in the woods, "the timber on the left was so dense that, but for the coolness of the officers and men, the formation of squadron would have been an impossibility."[328] "The Rebel Battery then advanced and opened on my position and for two hours rained a storm of shot, shell, grape, and canister through the woods," recalled Colonel Devin.[329]

Buford ordered Elder's battery to open on the Confederate artillery. Firing from a range of fifteen hundred yards, Elder found that the terrain protected the Confederate batteries and that his efforts at counter-battery fire were futile. Instead, Elder opened on the Confederate cavalry, occupying the Confederate battery by sending an occasional shot arching toward the Confederate gunners. The weight of the Yankee cavalry charges soon drove off the Southern guns, and Elder moved forward to better support the attacking cavalrymen. Elder later wrote, "In my frequent changes of position, [I] was never alone, nor did my support flinch, although compelled to sit in their saddles under the most severe artillery fire."[330]

Buford had wanted the Second U.S. Cavalry to support the charges of the Sixth Pennsylvania and Sixth U.S. However, the Second U.S., under

Merritt's command, received different orders from the Reserve Brigade commander, Major Whiting, and did not join the charge. While the valiant charges of the Lancers and the Sixth U.S. relieved the pressure on Buford's left, which had been pressed by Jones's counterattack, they exposed the Kentuckian's right flank. Seeing an opportunity, Jones pressed Buford's right. Shifting the Seventeenth Pennsylvania and Sixth New York of Devin's brigade, as well as a section of Captain William M. Graham's battery of horse artillery, forward to relieve the pressure, Buford drove the Confederates from his right flank. He anchored his right flank along a tributary of the Rappahannock called Hazel River and the left flank along the Rappahannock, spread across the Cunningham farm. He now occupied a solid and defensible position.

Recognizing that he was about to be overrun, and hoping that Stuart would arrive with reinforcements, Jones sent the Thirty-fifth Battalion and the Eleventh Virginia charging into the midst of the Federal attackers. McClure's bluecoats faltered in the face of the determined charge and fell back through the woods onto the oncoming columns of Devin's Second Brigade. McClure's troopers eventually retired all the way to the Rappahannock before regrouping. The charge of the Thirty-fifth Battalion also drove Devin's supporting troopers one hundred yards back into the woods.[331]

Devin's brigade rallied and formed a dismounted line of battle in the woods. Charging the Virginians on foot, Devin's men drove the gray cavalry back toward St. James Church. The fight in the woods around St. James Church was severe and hand-to-hand in many places. One of Devin's staff officers, Lieutenant Henry E. Dana of the Eighth Illinois, engaged two Rebel troopers in a hand-to-hand fight. "After discharging the contents of their pistols they used them as clubs. The lieutenant finally threw his at one of his antagonists, striking him in the face and inflicting a severe wound; then, warding off the other's blow with his arm, escaped with no further injury than a lame arm and a face well powder-burned."[332] The Comanches of the Thirty-fifth Battalion captured and sent more than twenty-five Union officers and enlisted to the rear. The fight proved much tougher than any of the Union officers could have anticipated, and Buford was surprised to learn that Brigadier General Wade Hampton's command had come onto the field.[333]

Seeing the fierce combat whirling around Beckham's guns, Stuart took charge of the fight and ordered Hampton's men into the line of battle, at the Gee house on the right of Jones, facing north. To flush the Federal cavalry from the woods, Hampton dismounted some of his horse soldiers and sent them forward as skirmishers. Before long, several hundred of Hampton's command were fighting against Devin's dismounted troopers. "Our regiment, the 1st North Carolina, along with the Jeff Davis Legion were deployed for two hours in the wood, dismounted, fighting the enemy with good success, driving them back on their reserves," noted one of Hampton's Tar Heels. "Here we were charged by the Federal cavalry who were in turn charged by the Cobb Legion when they fled to the woods."[334] A Georgian of the Cobb Legion observed, "Never for a moment were we (our brigade) repulsed, but we drove the enemy before us like a flock of sheep."[335]

Captain Rufus Barringer of the First North Carolina Cavalry, a forty-one-year-old lawyer who was acting as major that day, was seriously wounded while placing some of his troopers in position as sharpshooters to protect Beckham's guns. Barringer was knocked off his horse, shot through the right cheek by a Federal sharpshooter. The bullet exited his mouth, taking several teeth with it and causing serious injury, which kept him out of service for five months. Barringer eventually recovered and was promoted to brigadier general about a year later.[336]

"By 12 o'clock we had almost forced him in our front across the river; in fact, I believe that they were crossing," noted one of Hampton's Georgians.[337] Hampton tried to outflank Devin's position, shifting steadily to the New Yorker's left. Thus stymied, Devin remained locked in position along the Union right, anchoring the flank, for much of the afternoon.[338]

Chapter 8

THE ACTION SHIFTS

R ooney Lee's command fell into line to the left of Jones, extending to the north. His men could hear the fighting raging at St. James Church, imbuing a sense of urgency in their movements. "The impression among the men was that we were going up into [Rappahannock County]," recounted a private of the Ninth Virginia Cavalry, "but on marching two or three miles we were attracted by the Roar of Artillery near Brandy station, 5 miles below Culpeper C.H., which taught every man to know where he was going."[339] Lee's Virginians galloped over a mile to reach their assigned position: a stone wall that offered a strong defensive position and ran parallel to Lee's position. The wall, following the lay of the land, was L-shaped.

Dismounted sharpshooters advanced against the strong Union position in the woods. A vicious firefight broke out. "After advancing in the woods about ½ mile the fire became general & for about 3 miles along the line there was an incessant roar of small arms which lasted all day. During the fight Charles Ward of our Company was struck in the head by a Minnie [*sic*] ball & killed instantly. Emmett Lipscomb & Pilkinton were wounded, the latter mortally and the former slightly," reported a private of the Ninth Virginia Cavalry. "In all there were about 50 killed in the woods. We finally succeeded in driving the enemy out of the woods with great loss on their side." The Southerner likened it to bird hunting, with both sides hiding behind tree stumps and any other nearby cover.

After driving Buford's men off, Lee posted dismounted troopers along the wall and others along a ridge directly behind and above the wall. These

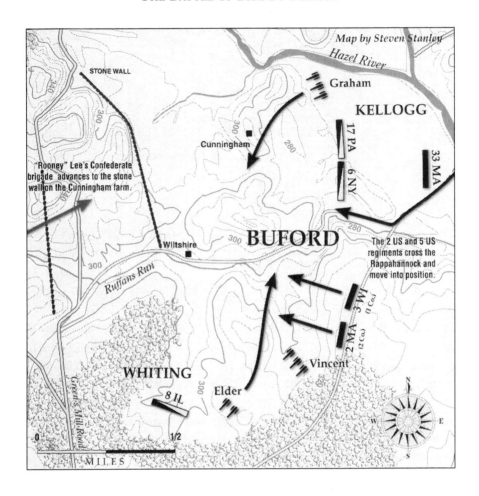

defensive positions offered excellent fields of fire, affording Lee's men an opportunity to enfilade the flank and rear of the Union position. The determined Confederates awaited the next attack with some of their best troops on line.[310]

Utilizing this strong defensive position, Lee fended off a number of uncoordinated, piecemeal attacks by Buford's cavalry. The Fifth U.S. made the first assault, trying to drive Lee's men from the stone wall. The Fifth, under Captain James E. Harrison, had only three small squadrons that day and was under strength. Keeping one squadron to support a section of Graham's battery, thirty-one-year-old Harrison, a native Virginian who remained loyal to the Union, dismounted his remaining two squadrons and pushed them forward as skirmishers. Their Sharps carbines blazing, the Regulars seized and held a portion of the wall, fending off a number of ferocious Confederate counterattacks. They remained in place until the Regulars completely exhausted their ammunition. Finally, these two hard-pressed squadrons were relieved, and Harrison's men retired to support Graham's battery. The Fifth U.S. sustained thirty-eight casualties, including four killed and three mortally wounded—a high percentage of their small force involved in the fighting, demonstrating the intensity of the fighting for the stone wall.[341]

Emboldened by Harrison's limited success, Buford decided to commit the rest of the Reserve Brigade. He ordered the Regulars forward, supported by Elder's battery and Ames's infantry brigade. Buford deployed the dismounted Regulars in line of battle alongside McClure's and Devin's brigades, with the infantry regiments protecting the flanks. While the fresh troops were being organized, Buford called up his artillery.

A vigorous artillery duel erupted between Beckham's and Elder's guns. Beckham's guns soon found the range of Elder's battery and disabled several pieces manned by Batteries B and L, Second U.S. Artillery. The counter-battery fire kept the Confederate artillery occupied, making an assault easier. Now protected by artillery fire, Buford's lines surged forward, supported by the deadly fire of the longer-range rifled-muskets of Ames's infantry. They attacked the wall, but the steady fire of Lee's dismounted troopers drove them back. A lull settled across the battlefield as the two sides regrouped.

At 11:30 a.m., Pleasonton, who had finally arrived on the battlefield, wired Hooker: "All the enemy's force are engaged with me. I am holding them until Gregg can come up. Gregg's guns are being heard in the enemy's rear."[342] Buford's tired horse soldiers had been fighting constantly since dawn. Although Gregg's attack was supposed to have been coordinated with Buford's, Buford had fought alone for nearly six hours.

Nobody had expected a battle of such magnitude, but neither side was willing to quit. Both Stuart and Buford used the lull to redeploy and to recover dead and wounded comrades. At that moment, as Stuart prepared for a full-scale counterattack, the sound of fighting to his rear shifted his attention away from Buford. Finally, about 11:30 a.m., as one member of the Eighth New York recorded in his diary, Buford's men "heard the booming of distant cannon which told us that Gen. Graig [sic] had arrived from Kelly's Ford and was engaging the enemy."[343]

Hearing Gregg's guns barking near Fleetwood Hill, Buford "resolved to go to him if possible." With that goal in mind, Buford took all of his force, except for the Fifth U.S., which anchored the right and supported Graham's battery.[344]

The men of the 124th New York marched to the sound of the guns. "As we moved forward, wounded men began to straggle back past us," recalled a New York infantryman.

Some of these were on horseback, others with pale faces and blood-stained garments came staggering along on foot, and occasionally one was borne hurriedly by on a stretcher, or in the arms of, apparently tender-hearted, but really cowardly, comrades. A little farther on we began to pass over, and saw lying on either side of us, lifeless bodies of men, dressed, some in grey and some in blue, which told unmistakably that the tide of battle was with the Union line.

Steeled, the New York infantrymen formed a line of battle and prepared to meet the enemy.[345]

The New Yorkers found themselves in a band of thick woods. They received orders to defend the position at the tree line but to stay concealed if they could, meaning that the Orange Blossoms formed into a single rank with a gap between each man. The men received orders to conceal themselves behind the nearest tree that could provide them with cover. The New Yorkers watched as a body of dismounted Confederate sharpshooters approached through the open field to their front. The Rebels entered a ravine just before the New Yorkers received orders to open fire, forcing the Empire Staters to wait, their weapons raised and at the ready, until the gray-clad sharpshooters emerged from the ravine. Instead, the Confederates continued on down the ravine to a position where they could enfilade the Federal infantry.[346]

After working their way around the Federal flank, the Southern sharpshooters opened on the surprised New Yorkers and then charged toward them. Concealed by the dense woods and hanging powder smoke, the men of the 124th New York shifted their positions and returned fire, opening "an almost hand to hand Indian fight," as an Orange Blossom recalled. The two sides blasted away at each other from a distance of a few feet until the arrival of a company of the 86th New York drove the gray-clad sharpshooters off. The Confederates heard shouted orders for a regiment of cavalry to charge through the trees, which helped to hasten their withdrawal. They hastily retreated, leaving several dead behind them. The "cavalry" turned out to be Colonel Augustus Van Horne Ellis, the regimental commander, accompanied by a couple of staff officers and a few couriers, all mounted on horseback. The 124th New York lost two men killed and several men wounded in this action.[347]

Colonel Augustus Van Horne Ellis, commander of the 124th New York Infantry. His command was heavily engaged with Wade Hampton's cavalry along the Beverly Ford Road. *Library of Congress.*

Brigadier General Adelbert Ames commanded the ad hoc infantry brigade assigned to Buford's right wing. *Library of Congress.*

Ames advanced several companies of the Third Wisconsin and Second Massachusetts Infantry as skirmishers, while the rest of the Third Wisconsin went to support Devin. They crossed the river on the run, formed a line and drove the Confederate cavalry back. "They won considerable praise for the steadiness and accuracy of their fire," observed a member of the Thirty-third Massachusetts.[348] "Soon the infantry were at business, and it was much relief to the cavalry," noted a Badger. "The woods were full of wounded horses, limping around on three legs, with that look of pleading in their great, expressive eyes that appealed strongly to sympathy as did the sufferings of the wounded men."[349] A captain of the Third Wisconsin recounted that his company suffered five men seriously wounded out of twenty during what he described as "a lively fight" before driving the Southerners back.[350] A Bay Stater observed that the Confederate horse soldiers "were deceived as to the number of our rifles, and showed no inclination to expose men and horses to the deadly fire of experienced infantry skirmishers."[351]

The infantrymen had a bird's-eye view of the fighting roiling in their front. "It is one of the most exciting scenes in war to see," recalled a member of the Third Wisconsin Infantry,

> as we saw on that soft, June morning, some of the squadrons of Buford and those of Stuart come together, at topmost speed, with a rush, a thunder of advancing squadrons, the loud shouts, the sabers flashing and swinging in the air, then the clash, the hewing strokes, the indescribable jumble and melee, the rearing of horses, the snapping of pistol shots, the huddling together, horses overthrown, riders unhorsed and trodden under foot of the wrestling squadron, and constantly dropping out of the crush the riderless horse, quivering with excitement, galloping a little to the rear and then turning instinctively to rejoin the troop; and from both sides the wounded men limp in the saddle with drooping head, reeling in faintness, their sabers hanging to the wrist and dangling from a sword-arm palsied with the weakness of wounds or the languor of death.[352]

Ames ordered the Thirty-third Massachusetts to cross. The Bay Staters forded the Rappahannock, moved through the stand of woods to the left, passing "plenty of dead cavalrymen, blue and gray," and formed a line under heavy artillery fire. The Massachusetts men shook out skirmishers, supported by the Second Massachusetts. "The skirmishers so annoyed a rebel battery at the edge of the woods beyond, that it paid them the rare compliment of opening on them with round shot," recalled the historian of the Thirty-third Massachusetts. Not even the presence of a large force of Confederate cavalry on their flank bothered the blue-clad infantry, which continued to advance the skirmish line cautiously against the heavy artillery fire.[353]

Stuart responded to the infantry threat. He decided to hold the infantry in place with sharpshooters carefully selected from his cavalry and with his horse artillery. He sent the dismounted sharpshooters forward and ordered Beckham to open with his guns. He also ordered Rooney Lee to shift his brigade to a position where he could operate on the flank of the sharpshooters, but Buford's cavalry prevented the Virginians from pressing the Federal infantry.[354]

"Both parties fought earnestly and up to 12 o'clock the enemy held his position," observed one of Buford's Hoosiers, "but after that hour saw fit to fall back."[355] Late in the morning, Alfred Pleasonton finally came across the Rappahannock River and established his headquarters in Mary Emily Gee's large brick house near St. James Church, and he put a leash on the aggressive Buford, preventing the Kentuckian from pressing Lee's troopers further.[356] "The rebels were between two fires and so fell back to escape being cut in two," reported a Bay State infantryman.[357] A second front was about to break out. The brute force of Gregg's attack on Fleetwood Hill was about to crash into Stuart's headquarters with the savage power of a tidal wave.

Chapter 9

GREGG'S COMMAND ARRIVES

B rigadier General David M. Gregg had not had an easy time of it. Because of the long march from near Warrenton, Alfred Duffié's division stopped to rest for a while and then pushed on. The Frenchman then turned onto the wrong road to Kelly's Ford, a poor decision for an officer who had spent time in the area. His division was nearly three hours late in arriving at Kelly's Ford, and Gregg sat and waited impatiently. Gregg gave orders that his men were not to light fires and that rations would have to be eaten cold. The horses were not to be unbridled or unsaddled, and each man was to sleep with his horse's reins looped over his arm.[358] "The unusual precaution taken to prevent all unnecessary noise, betokened that we were in the neighborhood of the enemy, and might soon expect an encounter," noted an officer of the First Pennsylvania Cavalry.

> *In pursuance of previous orders, we were roused from our slumbers at three o'clock the next morning, and before we had finished our hasty breakfast, the thunder of Buford's cannon, borne on the calm morning air from Beverly Ford, where he had already commenced crossing his division, brought us to the saddle, and soon we were drawn up on the river bank, around Kelly's Ford, awaiting our time to cross.*[359]

While the men of Kilpatrick's brigade napped or waited to cross, Kilpatrick summoned his officers to his bivouac. "General Kilpatrick loved a good, social time almost as well as he did a fight," observed an officer of the

Brigadier General David M. Gregg, commander of the Third Cavalry Division, Army of the Potomac's Cavalry Corps. Gregg commanded the left wing at Brandy Station. *Library of Congress.*

First Maine Cavalry. Kilpatrick had prepared a whiskey punch. "Speeches, songs and toasts followed and a very pleasant hour passed quickly (so did the whiskey punch), and the officers returned to their respective regiments, for good hours were kept that night." Kilpatrick called upon an officer of the First Maine to make a parting toast. "Here's hoping we will do as well at Brandy Station tomorrow as we are doing at whisky tonight," he declared. "Good, blamed good!" responded Kilpatrick. "Best thing I have heard tonight!" About 3:00 a.m., the men were awakened, and with the first pale fingers of dawn, they moved out.[360]

In the meantime, Russell's infantrymen had marched to Kelly's Ford, where they bivouacked in a meadow near a creek that was a tributary of the Rappahannock River. A detail of fourteen men of the Fifth New Hampshire Infantry received orders to cross the river, with uncapped guns, in the advance and to set up several pontoon boats to assist the troops with wading the stream. A second detachment from the Eighty-first Pennsylvania followed. Under cover of darkness, the New Hampshire men rushed across the river, scrambled up the steep bank and traded a few shots with the Confederate pickets, who mounted and fled to spread the word that a force of Union

Brigadier General David A. Russell, commander of the ad hoc brigade of infantry assigned to serve with the left wing. *Library of Congress.*

infantry was operating in the area. The foot soldiers secured the crossing and made it ready for Gregg's cavalry to cross.[361]

After securing the crossing, Russell's foot soldiers were pretty much done for the day. "The infantry of this expedition were not engaged in the fight and none were killed or wounded," noted the historian of the Fifth New Hampshire. "They were in a very good view of the battle between the two cavalry forces." The infantry remained in place, keeping Kelly's Ford open for the returning cavalry.[362]

Finally, sometime between 5:00 and 6:00 a.m., Duffié appeared, after taking nearly five hours to cover five miles. The crossing at Kelly's Ford had not gone well. Gregg's crossing was to have coincided with Buford's. However, Duffié's division was late to the rendezvous, delaying the entire crossing for several hours. Finally, about 5:00 a.m., Captain P. Jones Yorke led his squadron of the First New Jersey Cavalry across Kelly's Ford, the sounds of their crossing muffled by a nearby milldam. The Jerseymen captured a number of Robertson's pickets to prevent them from sending up the alarm.

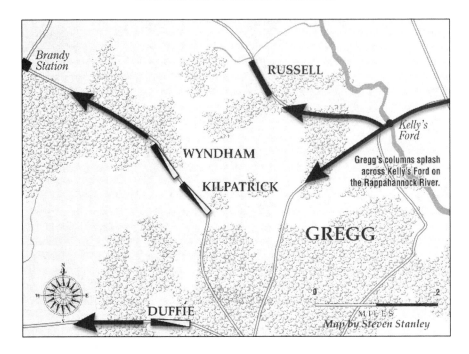

Like Buford, Gregg was surprised to find Confederate resistance at the ford; Pleasonton's faulty intelligence also failed to disclose the presence of Rebel pickets at Kelly's Ford. Gregg's men captured the Southern vedettes before they could spread word of the Yankee approach, and the Pennsylvanian's column finally splashed across the Rappahannock. He left the Fourth New York behind to guard the ford.[363]

By the time they returned to give the "all clear" and the rest of the column could begin crossing, it was 6:00 a.m., and Gregg was way behind schedule.[364] It took nearly three hours for the two divisions to make their way across the river, with Judson Kilpatrick's brigade bringing up the rear. By then, Buford's command had already been engaged in combat for nearly five hours.[365]

A member of the First Maine Cavalry remembered that he could hear Buford's guns booming as they approached Kelly's Ford to cross.[366] The sound of the fight raging at St. James Church chilled Gregg's troopers. "Many a man tightened the girth of his saddle, and examined his carbine, and tried the edge of his sabre on the ball of his thumb," recalled one.[367] The Federal troopers grimly prepared to go into battle.

The green North Carolina brigade of Brigadier General Beverly H. Robertson picketed the ford. This brigade, made up of two large but completely inexperienced regiments, patrolled the area immediately surrounding Kelly's Ford. Captain William White commanded Robertson's pickets. When advance elements of the First New Jersey splashed across the river at Kelly's Ford, White reported the Federal advance to Robertson, who in turn reported the news to Stuart. Stuart ordered Robertson to go to Kelly's Ford instead of Beverly Ford and further instructed Robertson to hold the Federals in check and protect the Confederate right flank. Near John Kelly's mill, Robertson encountered White's pickets as they fell back in the face of the Union advance. Union infantry appeared from behind a line of trees, prompting Robertson to dismount part of his command and advance them as skirmishers.[368]

Robertson sent scouts to his right, hoping to ascertain the strength of the Union force. He learned that Gregg's Third Division had already passed around his right flank and was headed toward Brandy Station on the Brandy Station Road. He immediately sent Captain William N. Worthington of his staff to Stuart to report the Yankee advance. His scouts then informed him that Duffié's Second Division had also passed around their right flank, heading toward Stevensburg along the Willis Maddens Road. Robertson sent Lieutenant W.P. Holcombe to Stuart with this unwelcome news.[369] Robertson later claimed that Stuart ordered him to retreat from Kelly's Ford to Fleetwood Hill, leaving the road to Brandy Station open for the Yankee advance.[370] Stuart then countermanded the order to retreat and directed Robertson to march his command back to the Kelly's Mill Road position to block the Union route of advance. "Just then the enemy's line of skirmishers emerged from the woods," claimed Robertson, "and I at once dismounted a large portion of my command, and made such disposition of my entire force as seemed best calculated to retard their progress."[371]

Under Pleasonton's original scheme, David Russell's infantry was to take the direct route to Brandy Station from Kelly's Ford, but the men found their way blocked by Robertson's Tar Heels. "I therefore determined to hold the ground in my front should the infantry attempt to advance upon the railroad, and placed my skirmishers behind an embankment, to protect them from the artillery, which had been opened from the woods," proclaimed Robertson in defense of his actions.[372] The North Carolinians traded shots with the blue-clad infantry for several hours until Russell brought up a battery, which quickly drove off the butternut horsemen. "They ran away after a little skirmish," sniffed a sergeant of the First Maryland Cavalry of Wyndham's brigade.[373] Robertson did little else to check the Yankee advance, which proceeded largely unhindered. "Brigadier-General Robertson kept the enemy in check on the Kelly's ford road but did not conform to the movement of the enemy to the right, of which he was cognizant," wrote Stuart, "so as to hold him in check or thwart him by a corresponding move of a portion of his command in the same direction. He was too far off for me to give him orders to do so in time."[371]

Robertson claimed that he failed to hinder Gregg's advance because he was trying to check Russell's infantry. He further alleged that his small brigade was an insufficient force to prevent the Yankee advance, so he did not even try to block Gregg's march. His North Carolinians spent the balance of the day jousting with Russell's infantry near Kelly's Ford. Although Robertson eventually received orders to join the main body of Stuart's force at Fleetwood Hill, he did not arrive until after the fighting had ended and Gregg had begun to withdraw from the battlefield. Thus, the green Tar Heels played no role at all in the great cavalry battle raging just a few miles behind them. Their casualties that day totaled four horses killed.[375]

Robertson's failure exposed the Confederate flank to attack and left Fleetwood Hill completely uncovered. After marching together for about four and a half miles, Duffié's division turned southward, headed for the rear of Stuart's supposed position at Culpeper, while Gregg's command headed north and took the direct route to Brandy Station. Unbothered by the North Carolinians, Gregg's Federals enjoyed a pleasant, though longer, march to Fleetwood Hill. "We galloped through the woods over a road so dusty that we could hardly recognize each other as we rode along," recalled a Maine horseman.[376] While Gregg could plainly hear Buford's guns roaring at St. James Church, he took a longer, more roundabout route instead of brushing Robertson out of his way and marching immediately to the guns over the shortest overland route, permitting Stuart to concentrate the fury of his entire command on Buford. Instead of heading straight for Brandy Station, Gregg turned his division onto the Fredericksburg Plank Road, meaning that he took a route nine miles long, instead of a more direct route that would have covered only six miles.[377] As Gregg marched, Pleasonton sent a galloper to him, informing the Pennsylvanian "of the severity of the fight on the right and of the largely superior force of the enemy." After scribbling a note to Duffié to hurry to Brandy Station, Gregg finally raced off toward the sound of the guns.[378]

Each of his brigades was formed in three columns by squadron. Wyndham's brigade led Gregg's advance on the left, followed by Kilpatrick's brigade just behind and to the right. The First Maryland Cavalry of Wyndham's brigade was sent to move on the train depot, while the rest of his brigade formed and prepared to attack Fleetwood Hill.[379]

The ground between Kelly's Ford and Brandy Station was "rolling, interspersed with clumps of trees, and not the most desirable for cavalry operations, nevertheless the men of the different regiments succeeded in keeping in excellent order," noted a correspondent of the *New York Times*.[380] Upon reaching a stand of woods about three-quarters of a mile from Brandy Station, Gregg had his division draw up into squadron fronts in preparation of attacking.[381] Sometime around 11:00 a.m., nearly seven hours after Buford's initial attack, Wyndham's command finally reached the tracks of the Orange & Alexandria Railroad a half mile from the depot when it spotted a single enemy gun atop Fleetwood Hill and headed straight for it. The Carolina Road, an important route of north–south commerce, ran across the crest of Fleetwood Hill. If Gregg could capture and hold the hill, his position would dominate the line at St. James Church, and Stuart's force would have to abandon its strong position there. He would also interdict Stuart's primary route of retreat to Culpeper.

Grumble Jones somehow learned of the Yankee advance, perhaps via one of Robertson's couriers, and sent a messenger to Stuart with this information. Stuart snorted when he heard the courier's report and responded, "Tell Gen. Jones to attend to the Yankees in his front, and I'll watch the flanks." The courier returned to Jones and repeated what Stuart had said. It was Jones's turn to snort. He retorted, "So he thinks they ain't coming, does he? Well, let him alone; he'll damned well soon see for himself."[382] This prediction proved correct soon enough.

Chapter 10

THE FIGHT FOR FLEETWOOD HILL

S tuart's personal tent fly still fluttered above Fleetwood Hill as the Yankee tidal wave bore down on it. Two regiments, the Second South Carolina and Fourth Virginia, had picketed the hill, but Hampton sent these two regiments to Stevensburg to block Duffié's advance. Other than a few miscellaneous staff officers and orderlies, the dominant topographical feature of the area lay unprotected. However, one artillery piece, a twelve-pound Napoleon of Captain Roger P. Chew's Battery of horse artillery and commanded by Lieutenant John W. "Tuck" Carter, happened to be present. Carter used almost all of his ammunition in the whirling mêlée at St. James Church and pulled back to Fleetwood Hill to refill his limber. Major Henry B. McClellan, Stuart's capable adjutant, was the highest-ranking officer in the area.

Major McClellan was a transplanted Philadelphian, a first cousin of General George B. McClellan and had only recently joined Stuart's staff. He was a gifted staff officer who found himself in the right place at the right time this day. Just a few minutes after one of Robertson's couriers had informed him that the Yankees were advancing in force on his exposed position, the head of Wyndham's column came into view. Seeing the urgency of the situation, McClellan sent a series of orderlies off to warn Stuart. Realizing that if he did not take charge, nobody would, the major sprang into action.

"They were pressing steadily toward the railroad station, which must in a few moments be in their possession. How could they be prevented from also occupying the Fleetwood Hill, the key to the whole position? Matters looked serious!" recalled McClellan.

Major Henry B. McClellan, Jeb Stuart's able adjutant general, was one of the saviors of Fleetwood Hill. *Williams College.*

But good results can sometimes be accomplished with the smallest means. Lieutenant Carter's howitzer was brought up, and boldly pushed beyond the crest of the hill; a few imperfect shells and some round shot were found in the limber chest; a slow fire was at once opened upon the marching column, and courier after courier was dispatched to General Stuart to inform him of the peril.[383]

The few shots lobbed by Carter's gun caused confusion in the Federal ranks, and they hesitated a moment to evaluate the threat. Carter's stand caused Wyndham and Gregg to conclude that Fleetwood Hill was more formidable than it really was.[384]

This pause made all of the difference for Gregg's assault. "There was not one man upon the hill besides those belonging to Carter's howitzer and myself, for I had sent away even my last courier, with an urgent appeal for speedy help," observed McClellan.

Could General Gregg have known the true state of affairs he would, of course, have sent forward a squadron to take possession; but appearances demanded a more serious attack, and while this was being organized three rifled guns were unlimbered, and a fierce cannonade was opened on the hill.[385]

122

McClellan's couriers found Stuart directing the fighting at St. James Church. "Ride back there and see what all that foolishness is about," incredulously responded Stuart to the messenger. Just then a second courier sent by McClellan reined in. "General," cried the desperate courier, "the Yankees are at Brandy!"[386] The repeated urgency of McClellan's messages combined with the sound of cannonading finally prompted Stuart to pull two of Jones's regiments, the Twelfth Virginia Cavalry and the Thirty-fifth Battalion of Virginia Cavalry, from the St. James Church line and send them to Fleetwood. "Then it was that the 12th Virginia wheeled about, and almost alone, in a broken and disordered column of 'fours,' galloped to the rescue, and threw itself with headlong impetuosity against the stately squadrons of Gregg—advancing with drawn swords and within fifty yards of the Fleetwood flag," recalled a Tar Heel trooper.[387]

"The regiment, in the great haste with which it repaired, to the point designated, became much scattered and lengthened out," recalled a captain of the Twelfth Virginia.[388] Captain Charles T. O'Ferrall of the Twelfth Virginia saw a Confederate officer sitting on his horse by a piece of artillery on elevated ground, waving them on. The Virginians quickened their already rapid pace and soon reached the mounted officer, who was probably McClellan. The officer pointed out two regiments of cavalry drawn up in columns of squadrons, awaiting them after seeing their cross-country approach. Forming into line, the Virginians put spurs to their horses, unleashed the Rebel yell and charged. The Federals also charged, and the two forces met, "sabers flashed, crossed, and clashed, pistols rang."[389] Another member of the same regiment observed, "The enemy gained our rear beautifully but our brigade cleaned them out nicely."[390] The Twelfth Virginia arrived just as Carter ran out of ammunition and was retiring his gun. The surging Federals were a mere fifty yards from the crest of Fleetwood Hill when the Virginians arrived.[391]

Stuart, now fully aware of the crisis he faced, told one of his staff officers, Lieutenant Frank S. Robertson, "Go for Hampton. Tell him to come. For God's sake, bring Hampton."[392] With the Cobb Legion Cavalry in the lead, Hampton and his brigade galloped across country, headed straight for Stuart's tent fly. Hampton threw off his coat in order to free up his sword arm and tossed the coat to his son, Preston, who acted as Hampton's orderly. Preston dropped the coat to the ground, declaring, "I came here to fight, not carry coats!" He put spurs to his mount and rode into battle alongside his father.[393]

Captain Justus Scheibert, a Prussian engineer attached to Stuart's command as an observer, had a clear view of the situation. "We had been surrounded by 10,000 men while seven regiments of infantry were holding too strongly the attention of our commander at the front," he wrote.

> *If the enemy had now launched a strong and boldly resolute attack on the astounded brigades, without letting the leaders come to their senses, and had vigorously exploited the surprise, there would probably have been nothing left for the startled troops to do but to fight their way out of the battle individually.*

However, Stuart's quick thinking and prompt response saved his command from that fate. He left the sharpshooters to keep the Federal infantry tied down and also left Rooney Lee's brigade to occupy Buford. The rest of his command dashed toward Fleetwood Hill.[391]

The veterans of the First New Jersey Cavalry led Gregg's advance. "As is usual in times of danger, we were in the advance," proudly declared Major Hugh Janeway. The Jerseymen headed straight for Fleetwood House.[395] "With a ringing cheer," the First New Jersey, with Lieutenant Colonel Virgil Brodrick at their head, "rode up the gentle ascent that led to Stuart's headquarters, the men gripping hard their sabers, and the horses taking ravines and ditches in their stride."[396]

Wyndham's lead regiment, the First New Jersey, briefly took possession of the hill, but the Confederate onslaught crashed into them, driving the Jerseymen back. "The two forces met with a crash that could have been heard miles away," recalled a Confederate horse artillerist. "Back and forth they swayed across the slope of Fleetwood Hill. While this movement was going on the Federal cavalry were reinforced heavily."[397] Major Myron Beaumont of the First New Jersey Cavalry noted:

> *The enemy had withdrawn behind the crest of the hill, and it was not until we were within a hundred yards of the top that they advanced to meet us. They were armed, principally, with pistols and carbines, our men using generally the saber. Then began the most spirited and hardest fought cavalry fight ever known in this country.*[398]

It took a few precious minutes for the Confederate reinforcements to reach the hill. "All things considered, it was the speediest all round movement I ever remember," recalled one of Hampton's troopers.[399] As the head of the small Confederate column reached Fleetwood, it met Carter's withdrawing gun, now entirely out of ammunition. The vanguard of Wyndham's attacking column was just fifty yards from the crest of the hill. The two forces crashed together with tremendous force.[400] "No more brilliant spectacle was ever witnessed than the brave Hampton leading on his gallant Carolinians, as with flashing sabers they plunged into the masses of Gregg's troopers and scattered them far and wide," recorded one of Stuart's staff officers.[401] As Captain William W. Blackford, of Stuart's staff, recorded, "There now

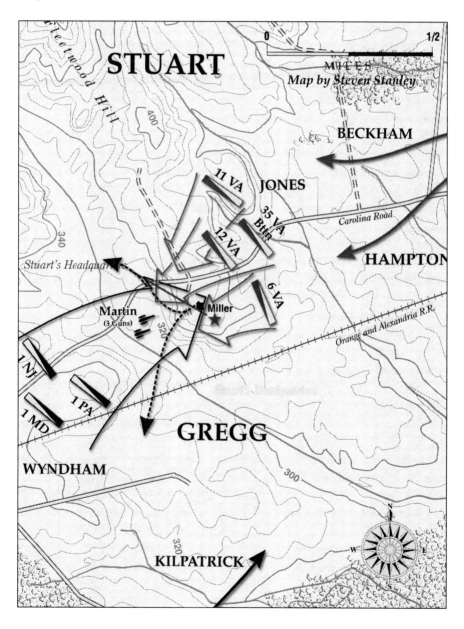

followed a passage of arms filled with romantic interest and splendor to a degree unequaled by anything our war produced."[102]

As Gregg approached, he could see the fight raging in the distance. The roar of the artillery grew louder as he rode. The Pennsylvanian ordered his troopers to draw sabers, and "their willing blades leaped from their scabbards, and with one wild, exultant shout they dashed across the field, on, over the railroad, and, with Wyndham at their head, rode over and through the headquarters of Stuart, the rebel chief."[103] The swarming Federals presented quite a spectacle. "The heights of Brandy and the spot where our headquarters had been were perfectly swarming with Yankees," recalled Stuart's aide, von Borcke, "while the men of one of our brigades were scattered wide over the plateau, chased in all directions by their enemies."[104]

Stuart sent the rest of Jones's brigade and the balance of Hampton's brigade and Hart's battery to McClellan's aid at Fleetwood, and the Confederate chieftain rode to the sound of the fighting himself, arriving just behind the Twelfth Virginia, with White's Thirty-fifth Battalion in tow close behind. As the artillery crested the hill, Captain Hart saw the drama playing out in front of him: "As we came near Fleetwood Hill, its summit, as also the whole plateau east of the hill and beyond the railroad, was covered with Federal cavalry."[105] Hart's gunners deployed and "opened a rapid and well-directed fire of shell and shrapnel on the enemy's masses." Their shells whizzed over the heads of the Confederate horsemen.[106]

A wild mêlée broke out. "Round and round it went; we would break their line on one side, and they would break ours on the other," recalled a trooper of the Twelfth Virginia. "Here it was pell mell, helter skelter—a yankee and there a rebel—killing, wounding, and taking prisoners."

"Here we had a general fight," noted another member of the Twelfth Virginia Cavalry, "all mixed up and every man for himself."[107] Another Virginian observed, "On each side, in front, behind, everywhere on the top of the hill the Yankees closed in upon us. We fought them single-handed, by twos, fours, and by squads, just as the circumstances permitted."[108] Solo combat raged everywhere. "My saber took him just in the neck," recalled a Jerseyman, "and the blood gushed out in a black-looking stream."[109] Another member of the Twelfth Virginia noted that he was captured twice and escaped twice during the frenzied fighting for Fleetwood Hill.[110]

White led one charging column while Major George M. Ferneyhough led another. "I ordered 20 men to continue the pursuit from which I was thus reluctantly forced to desist," reported White, "and returned with the remainder of my command to renew the contest for the possession of the hill."[411] Ferneyhough's column likewise slugged it out with the Jerseymen atop Fleetwood Hill, saber blades glinting in the bright sun. The Jerseymen began shoving the Comanches back down the hill. "Stuart's headquarters were in our hands," proclaimed a victorious member of the First New Jersey, "and his favorite regiments in flight before us."[412]

Seeing Ferneyhough's men falling back, Colonel Asher W. Harman of the Twelfth Virginia tried to provide a rallying point for them at the eastern base of Fleetwood Hill. Meanwhile, elements of the First Pennsylvania Cavalry arrived and joined the New Jersey horsemen in the mêlée. "For God's sake, form! For my sake form!" Harman bellowed as the fighting whirled around him.[413] His men rallied, and Ferneyhough's retreating troopers joined them. Harman was wounded in the mêlée. They then charged back up the hill, where Flournoy's Sixth Virginia, just arriving, joined them in the counterattack.

The First New Jersey had already repulsed two charges of the Confederate cavalry, and casualties thinned their ranks. They lost all unit cohesion and were "no longer in line of battle, fighting hand to hand with small parties of the enemy, and with many a wounded horse sinking to the earth." Trying to open a route of retreat, a large portion of the regiment charged the Confederate guns that had unlimbered near the Barbour house, also known as Beauregard.[414]

Elements of the First New Jersey Cavalry still occupied a spur of Fleetwood Hill and, pressed by Jones's cavalry, had no route of retreat available to them. The Jerseymen had to hack their way through the Confederate guns in a scene reminiscent of the fight at St. James Church. "The unexpected suddenness of this movement seemed to paralyze us all," recalled one of McGregor's section commanders, "friend and foe alike, for the enemy passed at a walk, accelerated to a trot, and did not design to fire upon or charge us, or attempt to make us surrender." As soon as their shock wore off, one of the gunners cried out, "Boys, let's die over the guns!"[415] One of McGregor's men knocked a New Jersey trooper from the saddle with a vicious blow with his sponge staff.[416]

"Hart's men beat them with their gun sticks," recalled an officer of the Cobb Legion Cavalry.[417] "Scarcely had our artillery opened on the retreating enemy from this new position than a part of the 1st New Jersey Cavalry, which formed the extreme Federal left, came thundering down the narrow ridge, striking McGregor's and Hart's unsupported batteries in the flank," recalled Captain Hart,

and riding through between guns and caissons from right to left, but met by a determined hand to hand contest from the cannoneers with pistols, sponge staffs,

Brigadier General Wade Hampton of South Carolina commanded a veteran brigade of Georgia, Mississippi and South Carolina cavalry. *Library of Congress.*

and whatever else came handy to fight with. Lieutenant-Colonel Brodrick, commanding the regiment, was killed in this charge, as also the second in command, Major J.H. Shelmire, who fell from a pistol ball, while gallantly attempting to cut his way through these batteries. The charge was repulsed by the artillerists alone, not a solitary friendly trooper being within reach of us.[118]

The Jerseymen charged three times against an enemy force four times larger. "The fighting was hand to hand and of the most desperate kind," recounted Lieutenant Thomas L. Cox of the First New Jersey.

Col. Brodrick fought like a lion. Wherever the fight was the fiercest his voice could be heard cheering on his men, and his revolver and sabre dealing death to the enemy around him. His bravery and daring conduct is the admiration and praise of everyone in the division. His horse was killed in the first charge, but he immediately mounted another and was soon leading his regiment.

The stout Confederate counterattack drove off the Jerseymen, who had to leave their mortally wounded colonel behind. He died a few days later while in Confederate hands.[119]

Lieutenant Colonel Virgil Brodrick of the First New Jersey Cavalry. Brodrick was mortally wounded in the fighting for Fleetwood Hill. *USAHEC.*

Three different times during this mêlée the enemy captured the guidon of Company E of the First New Jersey, and twice the Jerseymen retook it. "The third time, when all seemed desperate, a little troop of the First Pennsylvania cut through the enemy and brought off the flag in safety." As the Jerseymen retreated, the Confederates charged their rear guard, but the next unit in line checked their assault, saving the rear of the blue-clad column.[120] Wyndham fell, badly wounded in the leg. "He kept the field for some time after being hit," noted Major Hugh Janeway of the First New Jersey Cavalry, "but was finally obliged to give up."[121] The Jerseymen withdrew with 150 prisoners in tow.[122] With that, the determined Confederates regained possession of Fleetwood Hill.

Thirty-four-year-old Captain Henry W. Sawyer commanded Company K of the First New Jersey Cavalry. Sawyer received two serious wounds in the fighting for Fleetwood Hill, one of which passed clear through his thigh, and the other struck his right cheek and then passed out the back of his neck on the left side of his spine. Despite these two serious wounds, Sawyer remained in the saddle until his horse was shot. The mortally wounded beast sprang into the air and fell dead, throwing Sawyer with so much force that it knocked him senseless. When he recovered consciousness, Captain Sawyer saw Lieutenant Colonel Brodrick lying near and crawled up to him, but on examination he found that Brodrick was dead. A short distance farther on he saw Major John H. Shellmire, also dead, while all around him were men of his own or other companies, either killed or wounded. While by the side of Colonel Brodrick, Captain Sawyer was seen by two Rebel soldiers, who took him prisoner and, after washing the blood from his face with water from a neighboring ditch, conveyed him to the rear.[123]

The regimental historian of the First New Jersey Cavalry pointed out that "men and horses had been fighting for over three hours and were now utterly exhausted…there were not a dozen horses that could charge—not a man who could shout above a whisper." The Jerseymen went into battle with 280 officers and enlisted men and, in a span of three hours, lost 56, including their regimental commander and his second in command. They hung on gamely, nursing the fading hope that Duffié's men would come up from Stevensburg to tip the balance in the fight for Fleetwood Hill.[124]

The First Pennsylvania Cavalry, also of Wyndham's brigade, joined the action. Its troopers charged about a mile and a half from the railroad, to the left of the First New Jersey. "Scarcely half the regiment had gotten into position, when the enemy opened a battery, at point blank range, from the eminence of the Barbour house, hurling with great rapidity shot and shell into our ranks," recalled an officer of the First Pennsylvania. "When we moved forward it was to storm the position, and, if possible, to capture the battery. As we marched straight toward the smoking cannons' mounts, they first saluted us with spherical case, and as the distance grew less, hurled grape and canister into our faces."[125]

The Pennsylvanians formed themselves at the base of Fleetwood Hill, all the while drawing heavy fire, and half the regiment, led by Colonel Owen Taylor, moved on the house from the front, while the other half, led by Lieutenant Colonel David Gardner, swung around to the left and rear. The two wings charged and cleared the enemy from its front.[126]

An officer of the First Pennsylvania Cavalry remembered, "At one time the dust was so thick we could not tell friend from foe."[127] Lieutenant Thomas B. Lucas of the First Pennsylvania Cavalry received a vicious saber slash to his head during the chaos. Lucas's high-spirited mount bolted, and when it hit a muddy spot, Lucas pitched off the horse. The dismounted lieutenant found himself surrounded by enemy cavalrymen. "Kill the Yankee!" demanded one, crashing his saber down on Lucas's skull. Fortunately, the blade turned broadside just enough for it to glance off the lieutenant's skull instead of cleaving it. A few of his men spotted his peril and rescued him with a savage charge, leaving a grateful Lucas with a painful but not serious wound.[128]

After pulling out of the St. James Church line, Hampton's men also pitched into the mêlée. They quickly formed up and galloped cross country, headed for Stuart's headquarters. David Gregg saw the neatly aligned columns cutting across the fields, headed for Fleetwood Hill, and mistook them for John Buford's command. Their arrival quickly disabused him of this notion.[129]

"The whole plain was covered with men and horses, charging in all directions, closed in hand to hand encounters, with banners flying, sabers glittering, and the fierce flash of firearms, amid the din, dust, and smoke of battle," recalled a member of the First North Carolina. "Such scenes cannot last beyond a few fearful minutes. And so here."[130] One of Hampton's Georgians noted:

> *Thousands of flashing sabers streamed in the sunlight; the rattle of carbines and pistols mingled with the roar of cannon; armed men wearing the blue and the gray became mixed in promiscuous confusion; the surging ranks swayed up and down the sides of Fleetwood Hill, and dense clouds of smoke and dust rose as a curtain to cover the tumultuous and bloody scene.*[131]

Lieutenant Chiswell Dabney, one of Stuart's staffers, recalled that there was an icehouse atop Fleetwood Hill. "The top was gone and so hardly pressed were the enemy at this point by Hampton that the Color Bearer of

A depiction of the hand-to-hand mêlée for possession of Fleetwood Hill. *Moore,* Kilpatrick and Our Cavalry.

131

one of Gregg's regiments went headlong into the hole as he fled and was killed as well as his horse by the fall," remembered Dabney. "The colors became one of the trophies of the fight."[132] There were plenty of trophies for the men of both sides that day.

While the fighting raged, Captain Joseph Martin's Sixth New York Independent Battery had joined Gregg's assaulting column, deploying across Flat Run near the base of the southwest slope of Fleetwood Hill. The Empire State gunners opened, drawing the attention of the Confederate cavalry. Major Flournoy ordered his Virginians to charge the guns. They drew sabers and charged down the slope into the teeth of canister belched by Martin's guns. Lieutenant Robert O. Allen, who had bested Grimes Davis in the morning duel on the Beverly Ford Road, was severely wounded in the shoulder by a canister ball. The Sixth Virginia dashed among the guns, forcing the gunners to defend themselves with pistols and rammers.[133] "I must say that they were the bravest cannoneers that ever followed a gun," admired one of the Virginians. "As we shot their men and horses down, they would fight us with their swabs, with but few of them left."[134] Pressed by countercharges by the Federal cavalry, the Sixth Virginians retreated back up Fleetwood Hill in a rout.

The mêlée spread and grew general in the fields in and around Fleetwood Hill. "First came the dead heavy crash of the meeting columns, and next the clash of sabers," recounted a member of the First Pennsylvania, "the rattle of pistol and carbine, mingling with the frenzied imprecation, the wild shriek that follows the death blow, the demand to surrender, and the appeal for mercy, forming the horrid din of battle."[135] A Marylander noted that the Confederates "met us hand to hand but the Rebs used their pistols while we only used our sabers, which the Prisoners say they can't stand before." The spectacle impressed him. "It was what I have long wished to see," he continued. "It was charge after charge from both sides so long as we were in the field, which was an hour and a half."[136]

One of the Confederate horse artillerists had a bird's-eye view of the titanic struggle playing out in front of Fleetwood Hill. "So stubbornly was this contest fought that the brigades of Jones and Hampton charged time and time again across its summit before they finally succeeded in getting a foothold," he recalled.[137]

"The scene now became terrific, grand, and ludicrous," recalled a member of the First Maryland (Union) Cavalry.

The choking dust was so thick that we could not tell "t'other from which."
Horses, wild beyond the control of their riders, were charging away through

the lines of the enemy and back again. Many of our men were captured and escaped because their clothes were so covered with dust that they looked like graybacks.[138]

Indeed, the heavy dust worked to the advantage of the Federal troopers. Sergeant Charles U. Embrey of Company I of the First Maryland was captured but made good use of his brown shirt—Embrey pretended to be an orderly to a Confederate colonel for a few minutes until he escaped. Sergeant Philip L. Hiteshaw of the same company was captured and escaped because he wore gray trousers.

Perhaps, though, the best story pertains to Major Charles H. Russell of the First Maryland. Major Russell found himself cut off from the main body of Gregg's division, but he rallied fifteen men and went to work. He hid his little command in the woods, and every time a group of the enemy came by, the major dashed at it with three or four men and, when close upon it, turned and called out to an imaginary officer to bring up his supporting squadrons from the woods. Then he fell back, always bringing a few prisoners with him. At one time, he had garnered as many as forty or fifty prisoners using this ruse. Finally, the gray-clad cavalry charged his position and retook all but fourteen of the prisoners. "The major turned, fired his pistol into their faces, and again called upon that imaginary officer to bring up those imaginary squadrons." The Rebels halted to re-form for the charge, and while they were forming, Russell and his little column slipped away to rejoin their regiment. Russell lost his hat in the mêlée and now wore a captured Rebel cap. "He looked like a Reb. When he returned through the two divisions of Rebel cavalry, he had so many prisoners and so few men that they doubtless mistook him and his party for their own men moving out to reconnoiter."[139]

Soon the whole plain in front of Brandy became a whirling blur of saber-swinging duels, with the two sides mixed promiscuously. "The fighting spun out more and more from all sides, moving on the entire periphery of a circle with a diameter of about a thousand paces," recalled Captain Scheibert, the Prussian observer attached to Stuart's headquarters. "Dust clouds rolled rapidly toward the forest (signs of pursuit), and many floated up, giving news of an unsuccessful attack." He continued:

It is impossible to present the individual scenes of this twelve hour battle, particularly since a man could see and hear only what was happening right around and before him. Shrapnel, case shot, and pistol balls hissed through the air from all sides. Excited, riderless horses were running about like scalded cats, and

Lieutenant Colonel Elijah V. White, commander of the Thirty-fifth Battalion of Virginia Cavalry of Grumble Jones's brigade. His unit saw heavy fighting all day at Brandy Station. *Library of Congress.*

Negroes in mortal terror ran from one side to the other with their masters' horses, not finding protection anywhere against enemy shells. Ambulances assembled in the center in a thick mass. Men who were running away toppled over one another without sense or reason. Lost soldiers asked about their regiments, and couriers sought Stuart out to request speedy reinforcement. In short, it was chaos.[110]

With complete victory nearly within his grasp, the taciturn David Gregg caught the spirit of the moment. A staff officer noted that the Pennsylvanian "showed an enthusiasm that I had never noticed before. He started his horse on a gallop…swinging his gauntlets over his head and hurrahing."[111]

Major James M. Gaston of the First Pennsylvania Cavalry served on Gregg's staff. At some point during the whirling mêlée, Gaston was captured, and his captors, while leading him to the rear, began drawing lots for his clothing and equipment. The major recognized that the Confederates were distracted by their potential booty and saw an opportunity. His horse, a fast walker, got a little ahead of the distracted captors, prompting the major to wheel about, bid them adieu and gallop off to safety.[112]

As the chaotic fighting whirled around them, the remaining gunners of Martin's battery greatly annoyed the Confederates, taking a toll on the unsupported Confederate troopers using the crest of Fleetwood Hill as their base of operations. "The gallant fellows at the battery hurled a perfect storm of grape upon the Comanches" of the Thirty-fifth Battalion of Virginia Cavalry.[443] Consequently, Martin's battery "became a serious bone of contention."[444]

Finally growing weary of the annoying Yankee artillery, Lieutenant Colonel Elijah V. White, commanding the Thirty-fifth Battalion, ordered his men to charge the battery, making their way through a perfect storm of shot and shell. The unit's historian recorded:

> *With never a halt or a falter the battalion dashed on, scattering the supports and capturing the battery after a desperate fight, in which the artillerymen fought like heroes, with small arms, long after their guns were silenced. There was no demand for a surrender, nor any offer to do so, until nearly all the men at the battery, with many of their horses, were killed and wounded.*[445]

Martin later reported, "Never did men act with more coolness and bravery, and show more of a stern purpose to do their duty unflinchingly, and, above all, to save their guns." He added:

> *Of the 36 men that I took into the engagement, but 6 came out safely, and of these 30, 21 are either killed, wounded, or missing, and scarcely one of the them will but carry the honorable mark of the saber or bullet to his grave.*[446]

White and a few of the Comanches attempted to turn Martin's guns on the Yankees, but they received no support, and a Federal counterattack loomed. Captain Hampton S. Thomas of the First Pennsylvania Cavalry, one of Gregg's staff officers, found two companies of the First Maryland Cavalry and led them forward to rescue the guns. Joined by other nearby Federals, the Marylanders charged down the hill.[447] Seeing a wall of blue descending on him, White pulled back, leaving the guns for the Yankees. The guns, however, were largely useless. One gun tube had burst, and the other was rendered useless by having a ball rammed down it without powder. In addition, nearly all of the battery's horses had been killed by enemy fire, meaning that the guns would have to be dragged away by hand.[448]

Meanwhile, parts of McGregor's and Chew's batteries arrived on Fleetwood Hill, near the Carolina Road. Stuart, having no more men to throw into the breach, sent the artillerists into battle. The guns quickly unlimbered and opened a severe and effective fire. "We have been fighting for the last hour more fiercely than ever. It is fearful," recorded one of

Colonel Judson Kilpatrick of the Second New York Cavalry commanded a brigade in David Gregg's Third Cavalry Division. *Library of Congress.*

Chew's men. "Shells are bursting around us thick. We have made it so warm for their cavalry, they brought two batteries to play on us. If my face is as black, dirty, and powder stained as most I see, I am a beauty."[119]

That night, Captain James M. Robertson, commander of the horse artillery battalion that accompanied the Cavalry Corps to Brandy Station, asked a prisoner which battery had done such effective work on Fleetwood Hill. When told it was Chew's battery, Robertson turned to Pleasonton and remarked, "I was all through the Mexican war and in this one from its commencement up to the present time, and I never saw a battery fire so accurately and effectively as that did on that hill today."[150] That accurate and effective fire tore rents in the lines of the attacking bluecoats.

In response, Gregg ordered Kilpatrick to attack with his brigade to the right of Wyndham, and its charge caused the Confederate force to "break…all to pieces…[it] lost all organization and sought safety in flight."[151] As Kilpatrick's troopers struggled up the crest of Fleetwood Hill, things looked bleak for the Rebel cavalry. Kilpatrick rode over and ordered the Tenth New York Cavalry, which was near the railroad tracks coming up to support his attack, to draw sabers and charge into the Confederates atop Fleetwood Hill. "The regiment was well in hand, the formation perfect," recalled a New Yorker. "The enemy in small numbers advanced from the hill to oppose us."[452] Putting spurs to their horses, the New Yorkers surged forward up the right side of Fleetwood Hill, where a large force of Confederate horsemen met them.

"The rebel line that swept down on us came in splendid order, and when the two lines were about to close in, they opened a rapid fire upon us," recalled a member of the Tenth New York Cavalry. "Then followed an indescribable clashing and slashing, banging and yelling…We were now so mixed up with the rebels that every man was fighting desperately to maintain the position until assistance could be brought forward."[453] Lieutenant Colonel William Irvine of the Tenth New York had his horse shot out from under him and was pitched to the ground. Irvine fought alone until the Southerners overpowered and captured him. Major Matthew H. Avery, who succeeded Irvine in command of the regiment, fondly recalled:

> *I never saw so striking an example of devotion to duty. He rode into them slashing with his saber in a measured and determined manner just as he went at everything else, with deliberation and firmness of purpose. I never saw a man so cool under such circumstances.*[454]

Captain Burton B. Porter of the Tenth New York tried to rally enough men to free Irvine, but there were not enough available. "Every man had all he could attend to himself," recalled Porter, who found himself with only two or three troopers available. Just then a big Rebel bore down on him with saber raised. "I parried the blow with my saber," he recounted, "which, however, was delivered with such force as to partially break the parry, and left its mark across my back and nearly unhorsed me." One of Porter's men came to his rescue and dismounted his assailant. "It was plain that I must get out then, if ever," observed the captain while a squadron of enemy cavalry bore down on him. Porter dashed up onto the railroad tracks at the foot of Fleetwood Hill, safely out of their reach. Although the New York captain saw another officer of his regiment shot down in front of him, Porter made good his escape.[455]

Hampton's horsemen were eager to pitch into the fray. "Usually under such circumstances men became demoralized, but it was not so on this occasion," noted one of them. "From our line of battle back over the plain we could get a good view of the situation." The Southerners put spurs to horse and dashed ahead to meet the treat.[456]

As the Confederates were about to give way, Hampton's brigade arrived, along with the balance of Jones's force. With Wade Hampton leading the charge in person, the gray-clad cavalry pitched headlong into the Yankee

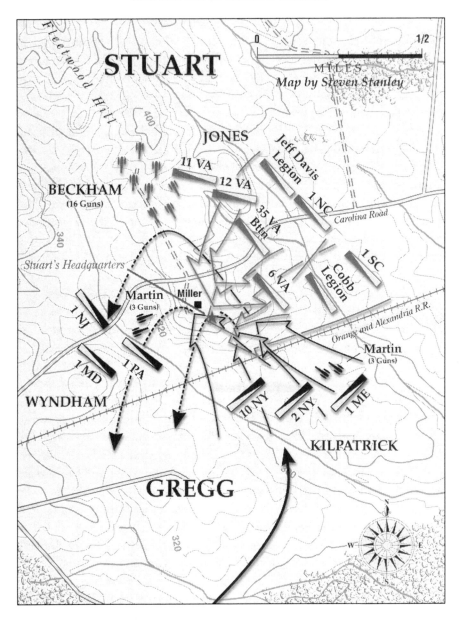

cavalry at the top of Fleetwood Hill, and the mêlée was on. Stuart, following along behind Hampton's column, could be heard to yell, "Give them the sabre, boys!"[157] Saber charge after saber charge occurred, with the whirling mêlée deteriorating into small, isolated fights among pockets of men; all organization disappeared as the horsemen clashed. "What the eye saw as Stuart rapidly fell back from the river and concentrated his cavalry for the

Colonel Pierce M.B. Young, commander of the Cobb Legion Cavalry. Young and his command distinguished themselves in the fight for Fleetwood Hill. *USAHEC.*

defense of Fleetwood Hill, between him and Brandy," recalled a Confederate staff officer, "was a great and imposing spectacle of squadrons charging in every portion of the field—men falling, cut out of the saddle with the sabre, artillery roaring, carbines cracking—a perfect hurly-burly of combat."[458]

"We moved up at a gallop our Regt in the advance and the enemy ran up two guns on our left flank & we were ordered to charge," recounted Lieutenant Colonel Will Delony of the Cobb Legion Cavalry.

> *I was in the head of the Regt and recd the order Col [Pierce M.B.] Young having left us for about 100 yds to communicate with Gen Hampton or rather with one of Stuarts aids—I immediately wheeled the Regt to the left and increased the gait of the horses and the Artillerists did not unlimber their guns Another courier had by this time come to Young saying that Stuarts Hdqtrs were in possession of the Yankees and our guns at that point would soon be captured—Young then ordered us to the right again and off we went in fine style, Young and myself leading.[459]*

With Young leading one column and Delony the other, the brilliant charge of the Georgians swept away everything in their way.

*The day was ours in less time than I can tell it—We killed their Major—
captured their Lt. Col., ten captains and about 40 Lts & privates &
strewn the ground with dead & wounded men and horses—Sabres, pistols
& carbines were lying around loose—We pursued them until called off &
with the Jeff Davis Legion & one Squadron of the 1ˢᵗ S.C. Regt we drove
off the support of their guns which were taken by the 11ᵗʰ Va. which also
did good fighting.*[160]

"As soon as we could recall our dismounted men who were skirmishing in
the woods, we started to the rear, unpursued by the enemy, with whom we
had been engaged all the morning, as they were afraid to venture out in the
open fields; no doubt they thought our falling back was to draw them out,"
recalled a member of the Cobb Legion Cavalry.

*For Stuart's headquarters we made at a sweeping gallop across a beautiful
plain over two miles wide, with scarcely a tree upon its broad expanse; oh,
what a beautiful place for a cavalry fight! And with what a glorious feeling
of emulation did Cobb's Georgia Legion of Cavalry, 1ˢᵗ North Carolina,
1ˢᵗ South Carolina, and the Jeff Davis Legion of cavalry dash across that
plain; and upon that plain we met the Yankee hosts, and in less time than is
required to record it, they were broken, scattered, and dismayed.*[161]

Colonel Pierce M.B. Young proudly noted that his Georgians "swept the
hill clear of the enemy, he being scattered and entirely routed. I do claim
that this was the turning-point of the day in this portion of the field, for in
less than a minute's time the battery would have been upon the hill."[162]

Lieutenant Wiley Howard of Company C of the Cobb Legion recalled that
his unit's charge covered a distance of about two hundred yards from the crest of
the hill, crashing into a line of Yankees there. Making their way through a small
orchard, the Georgians "mixed with them…each man fencing and fighting for
the time with his individual foe." Howard described his fight with his foeman:

*My man, having at the first slash deftly wheeled to the rear, I rushed to the
aid of one of my comrades, who being tangled in the limbs of a peach tree,
was chopped over the head by his adversary, when with a fortunate swing
of the arm my blade touched his neck and the blood flowed, much to the
relief of my friend, who dashed after his man and I was carried* molen
volens *right amid the confused mass of jumbled up retreating Yanks by my
unruly mare, never stopping until she ran up against a piece of artillery they*

were trying to save, drivers and others jumping up and down and running for dear life.[463]

The fierce charge of the Georgians drove the New Yorkers back in disarray.

Jeb Stuart dashed up, doffed his hat—its long, black ostrich plume waving—cried out, "Cobb's Legion, you've covered yourselves with glory, follow me!" and led the charge himself.[464] Stuart's staff officer, Heros von Borcke, turned to Stuart and said, "Young's regiment made the grandest charge I see on either continent."[465] McClellan called this movement "one of the finest which was executed on this day so full of brave deeds."[466]

Black's First South Carolina Cavalry, charging at the same time as Young's Georgians, slammed into the Second New York Cavalry, shattering its ranks and scattering its men across the fields.[467] Lieutenant Colonel Henry E. Davies, the regimental commander, admitted that his regiment became disorganized when "by reason of an order improperly given, as is alleged, the head of the column was turned to the left, and proceeded some distance down the railroad." The regiment had only advanced about one hundred yards when Black spotted it and angled his charge to inflict the most harm possible. "After the first charge, the command was broken up into detachments, which attacked the enemy in different directions," admitted Davies, who had his horse shot out from under him and received a vicious saber cut that nearly severed his saber belt but missed his body.[468] "He rode off the field on a nice horse whose saddle I emptied with extreme satisfaction," reported Davies's adjutant, Lieutenant Edward Whitaker.[469]

"So soon as [we] were under the artillery fire of the enemy, we formed in the field, the whole brigade in line, that is, each regiment on a line, but in column of squadrons, and moved at a gallop toward the enemy positions, over fences, ditches, and the railroad where we met them in repeated charges and for hours, the most desperate and extensive fighting ensued that I ever dreamed of," vividly recounted Whitaker of the Second New York Cavalry.

Charge after charge, retreat and advance, rally and scatter, firing, clubbing, cutting, with pistol, carbine and sabre. Batteries of flying artillery were taken and re-taken on either side, till in amidst the surging masses, the ground was strewn for acres around with dead and wounded, horses and riders, blankets, baggage, broken arms and equipments.

He noted that the fighting continued until nearly every man in the brigade had fought hand to hand and given or received a blow or fired or received a shot.[470]

The Second New York scattered and headed for the protection of the railroad embankment, pursued by Black's screeching South Carolinians, who "were cutting down the fugitives without mercy." When another of Hampton's regiments, probably the Jeff Davis Legion, threatened their flank, the terrified New Yorkers fled, much to the consternation of Kilpatrick.[171] The Second New York was Kilpatrick's old regiment, and "they were repulsed under the very eye of our chief, whose excitement was well-nigh uncontrollable."[172] Kilpatrick later admitted that the two New York regiments—the Second and Tenth—floated away "like feathers on the wind."[173]

Lieutenant Colonel Delony recalled a scene

> *like what we read of in the days of chivalry, acres and acres of horsemen sparkling with sabers, and dotted with brilliant bits of color where their flags danced above them, hurled against each other at full speed and meeting with a shock that made the earth tremble.*[174]

The Sixth Virginia Cavalry of Jones's brigade, which had opened the fighting that morning, charged headlong into five regiments of Yankee cavalry.[175] Rallying his troopers, Kilpatrick shouted to the First Maine Cavalry, "Men of Maine! You must save the day! Follow me!" and personally led a charge by the Maine troopers. "The order was received like an electric shock," remembered a captain of the First Maine. "One idea seemed conveyed to every man throughout those squadrons: This is our opportunity come at last! A spirit of emulation seized them."[176] As the Maine men followed, they saw a magnificent sight. "The whole plain was one vast field of intense, earnest action. It was a scene to be witnessed but once in a lifetime, and one well worth the risks of battle to witness," recalled one. "But the boys could not stop to enjoy this grand, moving panorama of war."[177]

"In one solid mass this splendid regiment circled first to the right, and then moving in a straight line at a run struck the rebel columns in flank. The shock was terrific! Down went the rebels before this wild rush of maddened horses, men, biting sabres, and whistling balls."[178] "A grander sight was seldom ever witnessed," gushed a newspaper correspondent who watched the Maine men attack.[179] Their ferocious charge crashed into the Confederate horsemen. "The two regiments were interwoven," recalled a captain of the First Maine. "It was cut, thrust and fend off; numbers indulged in a personal grapple." The Maine men took about one hundred prisoners, and Corporal Ansel Drew of Company A captured a Virginia battle flag.[180]

The charge of the First Maine saved the Federal guns near Fleetwood Hill from capture. Near Martin's guns, Captain Hampton S. Thomas of Gregg's staff tried to enlist help to protect the abandoned cannons. Thomas spotted Kilpatrick and galloped over to him, begging the colonel to rescue the guns. "To hell with them!" proclaimed Little Kil. "Let Gregg look out for his own guns." Taken aback, Thomas repeated his request. "No! Damned if I will!" came the reply, as Kilpatrick spurred off. Thomas stood his lonely vigil, hoping to salvage Martin's guns.[181]

Some of the Maine men dismounted and opened fire with their carbines. Lieutenant Colonel Charles H. Smith, in command of this contingent, soon found himself alone and almost cut off. "Seconds seemed like minutes," recalled Smith years after the war. A captain of his regiment recalled that Smith "looked and acted as cool as though on dress parade. As soon as he had rallied his scattered men, he remounted the regiment, formed squadrons and moved directly toward those guns which the enemy had by this time succeeded in loading, and were just in the act of training on the regiment." As the gunners were about to fire, he ordered his command, "Fours right, gallop!" turning his command to the right, away from the belching guns. He then called, "Fours left into line!" and dashed for an opening on the opposite side of the Barbour house and into the field beyond, scattering the small force that tried to block their way. "Colonel Smith received a great deal of credit for extricating the regiment from its hazardous situation, by his quick comprehension of the emergency, coolness of decision, and promptness to act under such difficult circumstances," a Maine man recalled.[182] Smith, who was awarded a Medal of Honor and a promotion to brevet brigadier general a year later for his valor at the June 24, 1864 Battle of Samaria Church, slashed his way back through the gauntlet of Southern cavalry to safety.[183]

Kilpatrick himself squared off with a Confederate officer, whom he had known and disliked at West Point. The Southerner spotted Kilpatrick coming, drew his pistol, took aim and fired, missing the hard-charging Little Kil. He drew his saber, and the two officers fenced. "As they met the business commenced. Both men fought like tigers at bay," recalled an observer. The Southerner "gave Kilpatrick a slight cut on the arm," which, instead of disheartening him, only made Kilpatrick "more tigerish." Receiving a vicious slash, the Confederate officer reeled in his saddle. Seeing an opportunity, Kilpatrick killed his injured foe with a slashing cut of his saber. The victorious colonel rejoined his brigade, proclaiming, "That rights a wrong. I have wanted to meet him ever since the war commenced."[184]

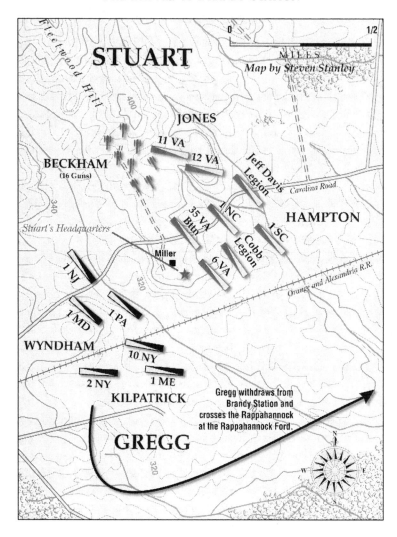

"Here the tide of battle alternated, brilliant charges were being made, routing the enemy and in turn being routed," remembered one of Hampton's troopers.[185] The Jeff Davis Legion of Hampton's command attacked to the east of the railroad tracks, while the balance of Jones's brigade charged to the west. They drove the Federals back,

> *and then, for an hour or more, there was a fierce struggle for the hill, which seemed to have been regarded as the key to the entire situation. This point was taken, and retaken once, and perhaps several times; each side would be in possession for a time, and plant its batteries there, when by a successful charge it would pass into the possession of the other side, and so it continued.[186]*

The defeated Federals melted away, with some of Hampton's troopers in hot pursuit. However, Stuart had ordered two of the South Carolinian's regiments to remain on Fleetwood Hill, supporting the Southern artillery. Deprived of a portion of his command, and frustrated by what he perceived as the cavalry chieftain's meddling, Hampton ordered the recall sounded. "No notice of this disposition of half of my brigade by General Stuart had been given to me by that officer, and I found myself deprived of two of my regiments at the very moment they could have reaped the fruits of the victory they had so brilliantly won," complained Hampton in his after-action report. "This division of my command left me too small a force to operate to advantage, and when the other regiments rejoined me, I received orders to assume a position to protect the hill." He watched, frustrated, as Gregg's battered division withdrew unmolested.[487]

"We saw the circle open up gradually and the clouds of dust move farther and farther into the forest, where the fire of small arms also indicated the direction of the fight," noted Captain Scheibert. "Moreover, we could always tell by the yelling of the Confederates where success had been achieved."[488]

As the blue-clad troopers withdrew, they left Lieutenant Wade Wilson's section of horse artillery exposed to capture about one hundred yards north of the railroad tracks, protected only by dismounted cavalrymen. These artillerists had had a long, hard day, deploying at eight different positions during the savage fighting for Fleetwood Hill. Kilpatrick ordered the gunners to limber up and retreat, but Colonel Lunsford L. Lomax's Eleventh Virginia Cavalry came crashing down on them before they could.[489]

These guns had annoyed Stuart all day, and finally fed up, Stuart had asked Lomax whether he could silence them. "I will do it or lose every man in the attempt," replied Lomax, a West Pointer who came from a distinguished Virginia family. Stuart ordered him to do so, and Lomax, waving his sword, bellowed, "Men, we want those guns; follow me!" He and his Virginians charged down the Carolina Road "like a whirlwind." Bearing down on the battery at an angle, Wilson shifted his guns, "in which the gunners lost their range, so that the volley of grape and canister was not so effective as it might otherwise have been."[490] Seeing the gray wave coming, Captain Thomas tipped his cap to his approaching adversaries and finally abandoned his vigil over Martin's guns, leaving them to the victorious Southerners.[491]

The Virginians then slammed into Wilson's guns, fighting it out with the dismounted Federal troopers supporting the artillery, allowing Wilson's gunners to slash their way to safety, bringing their guns off with them. Wilson stopped from time to time, firing an occasional shell to discourage pursuit. The Virginians were not interested in the guns—they were more interested in the dismounted cavalrymen scurrying for their horses.[192] "Lomax and the men of the bloody Eleventh were among them, slashing left and right." After dispersing Wilson's little band of supports, Lomax veered for the railroad, crashing into three of Wyndham's regiments. "I charged, and drove them from the station," claimed Lomax in his after-action report. Lomax sent a small detachment toward Culpeper, in case Federals were operating near there.

"He advanced his regiment over the captured battery (Martin's 6 N.Y.) covering both sides of the road, driving the enemy pell mell from Brandy Station and for quite a distance on the Stevensburg road. The dust and smoke was so thick that it was impossible at a distance and even nearer to distinguish between friend and foe," recalled an admiring Confederate horse artillerist.[193] Taking the rest of his regiment, Lomax briefly pursued Gregg's retreat along the Stevensburg Road, capturing thirty-four before finally breaking off and returning to Fleetwood Hill.[194]

Gregg had left a company of the Tenth New York Cavalry behind to support a battery. When Gregg's division withdrew, nobody told the Empire Staters that it was time to leave, and they were left behind. Nearly two hours after the rest of Gregg's division had crossed back over the Rappahannock, the New Yorkers realized that they were alone. A body of Confederate cavalry was bearing down on them, sabers waving and Rebel yell keening. The New Yorkers mounted in a hurry and unleashed a volley that slowed the pursuit for a moment. Using the opportunity created by the pause, the New Yorkers turned and skedaddled for the river, nearly three miles away. Even with bullets buzzing around them like bees, the men of the Tenth New York made good their escape without the loss of a man.[195]

Major McClellan noted, "Thus ended the attack of Gregg's division upon the Fleetwood Hill. Modern warfare cannot furnish an instance of a field more closely, more valiantly contested. General Gregg retired from the field defeated, but defiant and unwilling to acknowledge a defeat."[196] After two hours of ferocious hand-to-hand fighting, Gregg re-formed his command in the fields to the south of Brandy Station, where he had staged his initial attacks. "If anyone failed on this day to get all the fighting he wanted his appetite for fighting must haven prodigious," Gregg observed after the war.[197] He noted in his after-action report:

> *The contest was too unequal to be longer continued. The Second Division had not come up; there was no support at hand, and the enemy's numbers were three times my own. I ordered the withdrawal of my brigades. In good order they left the field, the enemy choosing not to follow.*[198]

Chapter 11

THE DUEL ON YEW RIDGE

When Stuart sent Jones and Hampton to counter the threat from Gregg, only Rooney Lee's brigade, still positioned behind the stone wall, remained in Buford's front. Under orders from Pleasonton to hold his position, Buford did not move directly around Lee's flank to Fleetwood Hill but initially remained in a defensive posture along a ridge on the Cunningham farm. "We drove the enemy all along the lines slowly till 5 P.M.," noted a member of the Eighth Illinois Cavalry.[499] Dr. Abner Hard, the surgeon of the Eighth Illinois, watched as a squadron of the Second U.S. Cavalry "were sent to take the wall, and after doing so, were driven back by superior numbers, losing a captain killed, and many of their men wounded." The Eighth Illinois launched the next attack. A sergeant of the Eighth Illinois tried to lead part of a dismounted squadron around the Confederate flank, trying to get into the rear of its position along the wall, but encountered "fire too severe to admit of his turning their flank as easily as had been imagined." Left with no alternative, many of the Illinois horse soldiers went to ground and lobbed potshots at the Confederate troopers holding the stone wall.[500]

The Confederates took a heavy toll on the Union troopers from their stout defensive position. A member of the Ninth Virginia Cavalry left a graphic description of his action that day. "It reminded me more of Bird hunting than any business I was ever engaged in, both parties hiding behind tree stumps & any place suited & firing on each other when ever a head was left uncovered. I am almost certain I killed one & probably more...Whenever a Yank would show himself someone would draw a bead on him and he would fall dead as a wedge."[501] This annoying fire frustrated Buford, who was determined to drive Lee's men off.

Buford then extended his lines in an effort to outflank Lee along the stone wall. Eventually, his dismounted troopers threatened to envelop Lee's lines.[502] The waist-high wall lay in a valley between two ridges, one of which served as Buford's headquarters. The ground on either side of the wall was cleared and provided excellent fields of fire for both sides. At least a part of the low-lying area was swampy and filled with mud and could not be approached while mounted. Confederate artillery firing from the ridge behind Lee's main line covered the formidable defensive position.

A successful attack by Buford would have placed him in the rear of Stuart's position, poised to roll up the Confederate flank from the side and rear. Some of Rooney Lee's sharpshooters took positions behind the stone wall and peppered away at Ames's infantry brigade, which had moved up to support Buford's planned attack. Visibly "annoyed," Buford approached a group of officers of the Third Wisconsin and Second Massachusetts of Ames's brigade and inquired of Captain George W. Stevenson of the Third Wisconsin and Captain Daniel Oakey of the Second Massachusetts, "Do you see those people down there? They've got to be driven out." Stevenson said, "It's about double our force," prompting Oakey to add, "Fully that, if not more." Buford responded, "Well, I didn't order you, mind: but, if you think you can flank them, go in, and drive them off."[503] Buford's "commanding presence and his manly and picturesque simplicity of dress" impressed Stevenson and Oakey.[504]

The two officers thought that they could do so and carefully laid their plans. They really had no choice. "It would hardly do to back out in the presence of so distinguished a cavalry audience, if there was a chance of success," recalled Oakey. Buford's presence drew fire from the concealed Virginians, but he ignored suggestions that he move back to a more protected vantage point.[505]

Stevenson and Oakey ordered several companies of their infantry to advance. They took a circuitous route behind hedges and through cornfields. Screened from Lee's view by woods and the nature of the terrain, the infantrymen sidled around the Virginian's flank until they reached a position from which they could enfilade the Confederate position. Ten carefully chosen marksmen crawled forward into a wheat field while the rest of the infantrymen deployed in a long skirmish line. When in position, the marksmen unleashed a killing fire on Lee's exposed flank, surprising Lee's troopers. "Some crawled off on their hands and knees; others fell dead

Major Henry C. Whelan assumed command of the Sixth Pennsylvania Cavalry after Major Robert Morris Jr. was captured. Whelan's horse was killed under him during the charge on the stone wall on the Cunningham farm. *USAHEC.*

or writhed in wounds; and a number surrendered," recalled the regimental historian of the Third Wisconsin. "The killed, wounded, and captured outnumbered the force that executed this movement." After losing one of the marksmen of the Second Massachusetts, who was mortally wounded, the foot soldiers then retreated to Buford's original position.[506]

Emboldened by the success of the infantry, Buford ordered Major Henry C. Whelan, now commanding the Sixth Pennsylvania, to launch a mounted charge against the Confederate position. Supported by Captain Wesley Merritt's Second U.S., the Pennsylvanians thundered toward the Tenth Virginia through a storm of small arms and artillery fire. Major Whelan, whose horse was shot out from under him, later described the charge as "decidedly the hottest place I was ever in. A man could not show his head or a finger without a hundred rifle shots whistling about…The air [was] almost solid with lead."[507] Spearheaded by the Pennsylvanians, the Federals dashed forward until a vicious countercharge by the Ninth Virginia slammed into them.

Captain Charles B. Davis of the Sixth Pennsylvania Cavalry was killed in action in the charge on the stone wall. *Eric J. Wittenberg.*

With sabers drawn, the Ninth Virginia crashed into the charging Pennsylvanians, sending the Lancers

> *into confusion and forcing them back, not along the line of their retreat, but directly on the stone fence through which there was but a narrow opening; and dealing them some heavy blows during the necessary delay in forcing their way through it. They were followed by men of the Ninth at a gallop through the field beyond the fence to the edge of the woods, where a Federal battery was in position. A good many of the prisoners which the Federals had taken were released by this charge.*[508]

Captain Charles B. Davis of the Sixth Pennsylvania Cavalry was mortally wounded during this charge.

Additional elements of the Sixth U.S. had now arrived on the battlefield and were ready for action. "My regiment lay stretched out, dismounted, behind a fence near a farm house," noted Lieutenant Henry McQuiston, who commanded a company of the Sixth U.S. His company and Captain James Brisbin's company were ordered to extend the line of the Sixth U.S. to the right, to a position about four hundred yards from the fence held by the Confederates.[509]

Elements of the Sixth U.S. Cavalry, which were supporting the attacking Lancers, saw an opportunity. The Regulars spotted a large battle flag atop

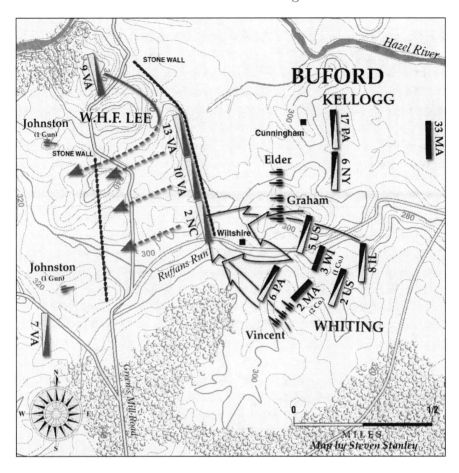

Yew Ridge and headed for it. Lieutenants Isaac M. Ward and Christian Balder led their squadrons forward, "twice charging the enemy and each time driving him with severe loss from his position to a hill beyond and holding him in check against heavy odds till withdrawn, with serious loss, by the brigade commander," wrote Major Charles J. Whiting of the Fifth U.S. Cavalry.[510]

Balder left a vivid description of this action. "When I got half ways through the woods. I heard cheering & shouting as if the infernals had broke loose from the lower regions," he recounted. "Now, thinks I, my bravy Mackerals are giving it to the rebs." Instead, he found a regiment of Confederate cavalry in his front, giving his "Mackerals" hell. Balder looked for the Sixth Pennsylvania and the Second U.S., searching for reinforcements. "The 6th Pa. had indeed made a charge, so I heard but a great many jumped into a ditch, got stuck and were taken prisoners," he reported. "Why the 2d & 6th

Regulars run is impossible for me to say, and I think it is a great shame. On my retreating in the woods I seen cavalries without hats, scratched noses, and the axes of our pioneers bumping against their backs like forty."[511]

"With many cheers our men left their position, rushed forward across the open field, fireing [*sic*] as they moved on. To our left our forces were much stronger than in my immediate vicinity," recounted Lieutenant McQuiston, who mistakenly believed that his men faced Confederate infantry and not dismounted cavalry.

All were repulsed, or failed to reach the rebels, and returned to the position they had left. In my Company we moved forward. I was in advance of all creeping in a shallow ditch toward the enemy. There was an officer of volunteers with and just behind me. When our people on our left fell back we where I was checked our advance, and returned to our old position. The officer of volunteers mentioned was shot in the leg and had to be helped back. The bullets came very plentifully. It is a wonder we were not all killed or disabled. The rebels could have shot directly down the ditch. This they did not do. I suppose none were just at the head of the ditch.[512]

"When we finally crossed this field we found a number of rebel soldiers concealed in the grass on the ridge in front of us. These men did not fire at all, nor did they retreat with their comrades a little way from them. I suppose they were really afraid to let their presence be known for fear we would open on them," he continued. Finally, the Confederates fell back behind Yew Ridge. "We followed on foot a few hundred rods, and then sought our horses." Within about two hundred feet of the fence held by the Confederates lay a ditch that was partially filled with water. As McQuiston's Regulars crossed the ditch, a number of Federal horse soldiers, probably of the Sixth Pennsylvania Cavalry, arose from it, soggy and covered with mud.

In one of the earlier charges of the morning these men had reached this ditch, and unable to go farther, and afraid to return under fire of rebel bullets had sought safety by dropping into the ditch. Here they had lain since morning in the mud and under the broiling sun. The poor fellows must have been greatly relieved when we passed over them. We were in total ignorance of this ditch, and of the fact that it was shielding so many of our men in great peril to themselves. I was greatly surprised when we almost reached the summit of the hill to see several rebel soldiers rise out of the grass to surrender.

After reaching the top of Yew Ridge, McQuiston got orders to mount up to follow the enemy. "Our progress was slow, and never very fast because the enemy stubbornly resisted our progress."[513]

McQuiston and Brisbin finally got orders to attack. Their squadron emerged from a stand of woods, rode up a gentle slope, passing other cavalrymen along the way, and emerged on the summit of Yew Ridge. "At the moment of our appearance from the wood, a troop of cavalry with gray horses was rushing rapidly up the steep slope, while the rebels were disappearing down the slope on the opposite side," recounted McQuiston. "This troop of ours disappeared from view following the rebels, but it did not remain away long, being driven in turn by greater numbers. Meanwhile my troop and that of Capt. Brisbin followed the retreating enemy that had been in our front, down the hill to the fences bounding the fields."[514]

Trooper Sidney M. Davis of the Sixth U.S. watched as Ward positioned his squadron almost at the rear of the Ninth Virginia Cavalry. As the Virginians swept past his position, Ward charged the Southern flank, his men cheering wildly as they went. "It was a curious scene," remembered Davis, "this small body so boldly attacking a large force that was at this moment driving from their front quite a strong regiment [the Sixth Pennsylvania Cavalry], but the movement was successful. The Confederates halted a moment, gave a startled look backward, and then their regiment broke up and fled by a detour westward to the rear." Although Lieutenant Ward was mortally wounded in the breast while reaching to seize a Confederate battle flag, his impetuous charge rescued the beleaguered Pennsylvanians. Later, a Virginian said, "From the noise you men made, we thought it was a whole brigade coming out of those woods."[515]

Lieutenant Christian Balder of the Sixth U.S. Cavalry saw this action unfold. "My blood got up. I wanted my squadron to charge with me. Ward & Tupper done the same, but could not get those cowboys to come on," he recounted.

> *I was in front of the squadron, waving my sabre, and entreating and cursing them alternately, trying to get them on, when all of a sudden, a rebel officer came dashing at me, at full speed, making a tremendous right cut at me, but fortunately, I just perceived him in the nick of time. I parried his cut successfully and striking his sabre clean out of his hand. He fled by me, and one of my men shot him through the heart.*

Balder, a German immigrant who had less than a month left to live, noted that his men and the Confederates stood opposite one another for fully fifteen minutes, staring one another down. "I then seen about a regiment of rebs coming through a field on our right and I thought it time to retire," he wisely thought. "But poor Ward had been killed. He worked like a Trojan to get his men to go in with the sabre, but could not succeed."[516]

Lieutenants Stoll and Carpenter had been ordered to hold the woods to the Sixth U.S.'s right. As Ward's men and the Lancers began withdrawing, the Rebels pursued. The two squadrons of Regulars remained mounted, while the charging Confederates were dismounted. "If I had had command of the squadron, I would have dismounted the men, and fought the enemy equally," reported Carpenter, "but Stoll thought otherwise." Instead, the mounted Regulars waited in the scorching sun. Stoll was badly wounded, and Carpenter took responsibility for withdrawing his beleaguered saddle soldiers.

"I managed in this way, by stopping every minute and fighting the rebels, in getting my men safely out of the wood. The ground sloped downward for 30 or 40 yards and then raised again, just beyond to a little knoll," he continued. "I saw at once that the rebels would have every chance of murdering us, as we crossed this low ground, exposed completely to their fire from behind trees." Carpenter ordered his men to pour in a rapid fire for a few minutes, and then he had them wheel to the right and gallop at full speed. "The minute we commenced to retreat, the rebels arose in multitudes, as if by magic, and poured in a dreadful fire. The next minute however I had gained the knoll with my squadron, and just behind it, I ordered them to stop, and give it to the rebels. We were completely protected by the ground." The Regulars raked the Confederates from the protection of the woods, and Carpenter saw a number of the enemy drop while the remainder retreated "in great haste." Carpenter's horse was wounded on the inside of the foreleg, and the lieutenant lost his hat in the chaos and had to borrow new headgear from an unfortunate Confederate.[517] Captain George C. Cram, who commanded the Sixth U.S. that day, commended Carpenter for the skillful way he brought Stoll's beleaguered squadron to safety.[518]

Lieutenants McQuiston and Wade of the Sixth U.S. had led their men to the Cunningham farmhouse and then into the open ground beyond. "The soldiers had stopped and most of them were returning to the point of departure on the ridge near the wood. The rebels were returning and we knew not their numbers for they were concealed in woods and high brush." McQuiston could see bodies of Federal troops and also could see Buford and his staff in the distance. He rode a gauntlet of heavy fire to cross the field, and his horse was shot in the right flank as they dashed across the field. "I

Brigadier General W.H.F. "Rooney" Lee, second son of General Robert E. Lee, commanded a brigade of veteran Virginia cavalry. Rooney Lee was badly wounded at Brandy Station. *USAHEC.*

then went to my company where I should have been all the time instead of stopping to look about," he wryly observed.[519]

"A rebel bullet struck the second soldier from me just where the visor joins the cap. The noise of course of the contact was heard. The soldier gradually dropped his head, and I could see the blood trickling down his forehead. He was led out of the ranks, and taken to the rear," recalled McQuiston.

> *The next day I learned that the bullet had penetrated the scalp just at the summit of the forehead and had passed between the scalp and skull to the back of his head from which position it had been dislodged. He was doing duty in camp next day. Along the course of the bullet there was a raised, tender welt about two finger widths wide.*[520]

The Confederate success was short-lived. No sooner had they driven the Sixth Pennsylvania from the hill than the Second U.S. counterattacked. The Second U.S. had spent much of the day supporting one of the Federal batteries and eagerly joined the fray. "At last an order—which we all had hoped and all but asked for, and which General Buford told me he was anxious to give, but had not the authority, but which no doubt he carried—finally came," recalled Merritt. "We were ordered to advance and deal on *their* ground with the batteries and sharpshooters which had

Captain Wesley Merritt of the Second U.S. Cavalry engaged in a fencing match with Rooney Lee on Yew Ridge. *Library of Congress.*

wrought such havoc among our men and horses."[521] In addition, Buford ordered Lieutenant Albert O. Vincent's battery of horse artillery to unlimber within four hundred yards of the enemy and to open fire in conjunction with the Regulars' attack.[522]

Following the route of the Sixth Pennsylvania's attack, and supported by the fire of Vincent's battery, the Second U.S. pitched into the flank of the Ninth Virginia, driving it back across Yew Ridge and onto the northern extension of Fleetwood Hill. "Out flew the sabres, and most handsomely they were used," observed Buford.[523] "We rode pell-mell, with sabers in hand at the astonished enemy," recalled Merritt.

> *The next moment* [the Rebel line] *had broken and was flying, while horsemen of the 2nd mingling with the enemy, dealt saber blows and pistol shots on every side. There was little halting to make prisoners, as friend and foe, mixed inextricably together, rode on in this terrible carnage, each apparently for the same destination.*[524]

With Merritt leading the way, the determined charge of the Second U.S. carried up the slope of Yew Ridge, over the plateau and across the crest.

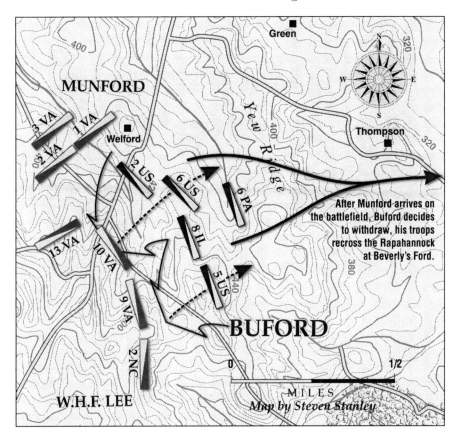

After Munford arrives on the battlefield, Buford decides to withdraw, his troops recross the Rapahannock at Beverly's Ford.

Map by Steven Stanley

Captain Theophilus F. Rodenbough, who commanded a squadron of the Second U.S. Cavalry, pitched into the hand-to-hand fighting and received a slight wound in the process. Lieutenant Charles McK. Loeser, who commanded another squadron of the same regiment, received a serious wound, one of several that he received in combat during the course of the Civil War.[525]

Captain Joseph O'Keeffe, one of Buford's staff officers, rashly joined the charge, riding "boot to boot" with Merritt. Merritt and O'Keeffe became separated when the Confederates broke and the sabers began to fly. Sometime during the mêlée, O'Keeffe was unhorsed, badly wounded in the leg and captured.[526] Major Whiting, the commander of the Reserve Brigade, later noted:

> *I have to regret the loss of Captain O'Keeffe, who requested to act with me during the day, and after affording most valuable service could not resist the temptation of charging with the Second United States Cavalry and was wounded and taken prisoner.*[527]

A depiction of the duel between Captain Wesley Merritt of the Second U.S. Cavalry and Brigadier General Rooney Lee on Yew Ridge. *Library of Congress.*

At that moment, Buford had no time to mourn the loss of his aide—there was more work to do.

Merritt's charge, "in its impetuosity, carried everything before it. It bore up the hill, across the plateau, and to the crest on the other side." The savage attack of the Regulars drove back more than twice their number.[528] "There were discovered in the valley below, fresh regiments of horse moving quietly towards the scene of our combat anxious to strike us while we were in confusion," noted Merritt.[529] Colonel Richard L.T. Beale, the commander of the Ninth Virginia Cavalry, feared a rout until a courier from Stuart reined in, saying, "The General sends his thanks to Colonel Beale and the men of the Ninth for their gallantry in holding the hill, and if you will hold it five minutes longer he will send reinforcements." Stuart delivered on his promise moments later.[530]

Rooney Lee realized that the moment of truth had arrived. He had three uncommitted regiments left, and he quickly decided to commit them to the fight. He ordered the three regiments to attack up the slope of Yew Ridge in a northwesterly direction. The three regiments—the Second North Carolina, the Tenth Virginia and the Thirteenth Virginia—drew sabers and began advancing up Yew Ridge to meet the Union charge. Rooney Lee pushed forward his own skirmishers in an attempt to flank Buford's position and to sever his lines of communication and retreat across Beverly Ford.[531]

"About 4 o'clock in the afternoon Lee put himself at the head of my regiment which was at the foot of a hill out in the open field, standing in column of fours, and gave the order to charge up the hill, he riding at the head of the regiment," recalled William L. Royall of the Ninth Virginia.

The Duel on Yew Ridge

I was very near to the head of the column and could see all that took place. When we got to the summit of the hill, there, some two hundred yards away, stood a long line of blue-coated cavalry. Lee did not hesitate an instant but dashed at the center of this line with his column of fours. The Yankees were of course cut in two at once, but each of their flanks closed in on our column, and then a most terrible affray with sabers and pistols took place. We got the best of it, and we had soon killed, wounded, or captured almost all of them. They had a good many more men over beyond the hill, but the thing was over before the others could come to their assistance.[532]

A charge by the Second North Carolina and the Tenth Virginia reached the hill and shoved the Regulars back toward the Union starting point, prompting an officer of the Ninth Virginia Cavalry to note that their charge drove the Yankee troopers "almost to the mouth of the cannon."[533] An unidentified member of Company F of the Tenth Virginia, in a letter to the *Richmond Daily Dispatch* written the day after the battle, noted, "The 2nd U.S. Cavalry, supported by other cavalry, came up when the 10th Va. Cav…were about to charge them. This regiment charged them gallantly, driving them back precipitately, killing many, chopping many over the head, and taking some prisoners…I think it was the hardest cavalry fight of the war."[534]

Twenty-seven-year-old Colonel Solomon Williams, commander of the Second North Carolina, a member of the West Point class of 1858, got permission from Rooney Lee to commit his troopers, who had spent most of the day supporting a battery, to the fray. Although Williams had been in command of his regiment for a year, this was the first time that he led it in combat.[535] Williams dashed over to his command and ordered it formed by squadron and to advance at a gallop. As they crested Yew Ridge, they could see Buford's troopers driving the Ninth and Thirteenth Virginia back toward them. The Tenth Virginia, which advanced with the Tar Heels, halted and opened fire, while Williams and his Carolinians drew sabers and charged. "The regiment raised the yell as it went by our stationary and retiring companions and the scene was immediately changed," recalled Captain William Graham of the Second North Carolina. "The Federals were the fleers and the Confederates the pursuers. Our regiment drove the enemy about half a mile back upon their reserves of cavalry and infantry, who were posted on a hill, while our advance had reached an angle where two stone walls came together on an opposite hill, about two hundred yards distant."[536]

Colonel Williams, described by Stuart as being "as fearless as he was efficient," led the impetuous charge himself.[537] A volley rang out, desperately wounding the man at Williams's side. As his horse leaped the wall, he cried out, "Second North Carolina, follow me." Captain Graham called out, "Colonel, we had better get a line, they are too strong to take this way." Williams replied, "That will be best: where is the flag?" He turned, began riding back to meet it and was shouting at his men to fall in when he was shot through the head and killed instantly. Williams, who had just been married two weeks earlier, fell alongside his brother-in-law, who drew the sad duty of carrying the colonel's body home to his sister for burial. Seeing their commander fall, the starch went out of the charge of the North Carolinians.[538]

Major Joseph T. Rosser, a lawyer from Petersburg, led the charge of the Tenth Virginia Cavalry. As his men closed on the Second U.S., Rosser spurred his horse toward an officer in an exposed position in advance of the Union line. Rosser drew his saber and fenced with the officer, prompting Private John Smith of Company F of the Tenth Virginia to call out, "Hurray for Hell, Wade in!" The cheering Virginians drove into the Regulars, mixing with them and emptying their revolvers into their ranks.[539]

James Scott, the right guide of the Tenth Virginia, drew his saber back to slash at a Yankee in his front when Lieutenant Thomas Dewees of the Second U.S. Cavalry slashed at his blade from the rear. Scott's right arm went numb from the impact, but he was still able to stab at a Regular in his front. Another trooper of the Tenth Virginia came to Scott's aid, wounding Dewees in the mêlée and permitting Scott to escape.[540]

As the Regulars retreated, Captain Merritt and his aide, Lieutenant James Quirk, found themselves alone among the Confederates. Merritt, who believed that his entire regiment was still alongside him, carried only his saber and his courage. A nearby group of Confederate officers spotted him, and one yelled, "Kill the damned Yankee!" Riding over to the group of officers, Merritt boldly approached the apparent leader of the group, brought his saber to a point and demanded, "Colonel, you are my prisoner!" The officer was not a colonel, but rather Rooney Lee. Lee proclaimed, "The hell I am!" and swung his saber at Merritt's head. Merritt parried the blow, but the thrust of Lee's saber pierced Merritt's hat and a kerchief that he had tied around his head as a sweatband, nicking Merritt's scalp.

Recognizing the danger facing them, Merritt and his aide hastily retreated when other Confederate officers opened fire with their revolvers. With pistol shots and demands for his surrender still ringing in his ears, Merritt safely reached his own lines, where "a kindly Hibernian gave me the hat off his own head."[541] In the course of the fight on Yew Ridge, Rooney Lee suffered a severe leg wound. Deprived of their senior officers,

Colonel Thomas T. Munford
of the Second Virginia Cavalry
commanded Fitz Lee's brigade at
Brandy Station due to Lee's illness.
Virginia Military Institute.

the Confederates did not press their hard-won advantage and retired to their lines along Fleetwood Hill.[542]

When Buford prepared his report of the battle, he wrote that his men "gained the crest overlooking Brandy Station" but could not hold it. He further noted, "The enemy, although vastly superior in numbers was fought hand to hand and was not allowed to gain an inch of ground once occupied. During this fighting, Lt. [Albert O.] Vincent poured his shot into them with terrible execution."[543] Vincent later reported that he maintained his fire for half an hour and that his battery expended four hundred rounds over the course of the day's fighting. Obviously, such heavy fire from a range of only four hundred yards took a toll on the Confederates.[544] Left with no alternative, Buford retreated to the line along the Cunningham farm held by his command for most of the day.

Rooney Lee, "seeing the enemy in retreat, commanded 'Forward,' and was at the same instant wounded," recalled the colonel of the Ninth Virginia Cavalry.[545] Lieutenant George Beale of the Ninth Virginia Cavalry described

161

The Welford house on the northern end of Fleetwood Hill, also known as Farley. *Library of Congress.*

the scene: "General Lee directed in person the countercharge, and as his mounted men swept over the hill…a bullet passed through his leg, in the moment of victory. Directing a soldier to notify the next officer in command that he was wounded, after passing his sword over to an orderly, he was assisted from the field."[516]

Fitz Lee's brigade, commanded in Fitz's absence by Colonel Thomas T. Munford, arrived on Yew Ridge as the fighting was winding down. As the day began, Munford's men were picketing along the Hazel River, a tributary of the Rappahannock. Stuart's orders to Munford were vague, meaning that the colonel and his troops advanced slowly and cautiously.[517] Three of his regiments, the First, Second and Third Virginia, crossed the Hazel River at Starke's Ford and advanced to Welford's Ford on the Rappahannock about 11:00 a.m. Finding the enemy there, they turned to the south and headed toward Beverly Ford. Again finding the enemy there in force, Munford marched his troopers back in the direction of Welford's Ford.[518] They spent a quiet afternoon there with little to do but write letters home.[519]

Munford finally arrived at Welford's Ford about 4:00 p.m. and shook out a skirmish line, advancing sharpshooters. He could see the mêlée raging on Yew Ridge and realized that a very large Federal force lay in front of him. While Captain James Breathed's battery opened on the Union flank, Munford realized that "the enemy's right flank being protected by infantry, artillery, and twice our number of sharpshooters, made it impracticable at any time to engage them in a hand-to-hand fight."[550] As one of Breathed's officers noted of the battery's effective firing, "We had it all our own way the Yankee artillery firing on us almost literally not at all."[551] Munford held his position on the flank, engaging in desultory skirmishing until Buford finally broke off the engagement and began withdrawing. Munford claimed that when he arrived at Farley, he could see "a division of cavalry, a brigade of infantry, and two or three detachments of dismounted cavalry." He slowly followed Buford's withdrawing horsemen but felt "it was impracticable at any time to engage them in a hand-to-hand fight." Munford just let Buford's command go.[552] An officer of the Second Virginia described the brigade's engagement as "quite a close little battle," but that probably overstated the case.[553]

Captain Brisbin and Lieutenant McQuiston of the Sixth U.S. had received orders for their companies to support a battery of horse artillery posted on a nearby hill to defend the withdrawal of the cavalry. Breathed's gunners opened on them, and the Federals returned fire. "The sun was, or had just sunk behind the trees, but the sky was still brilliant above the trees with his light," remembered McQuiston.

> *I remember that the rebel battery with the green of the trees and yellow sky for a background the shallow valley and gently sloping greenly clad hill for a foreground with the smoke curling about the guns, made a pretty sight. The shot could be seen coming like large black balls from the guns.*

One shot in particular stuck in the lieutenant's mind:

> *One shot plainer than the rest seemed to be coming almost directly toward the eye. This shot struck the foremost artillery horse on the upper part of the "nigh" fore leg, disabled the hind leg on same side and the corresponding legs of the two horses immediately in rear of the first.*

That single shot took out an entire gun team.[554]

An order finally arrived for the artillery and for Brisbin and McQuiston to pull back across the Rappahannock. "Fortunately we had but a little distance to go, and were not molested in our withdrawal," observed McQuiston. "The regiment went into camp in a piece of woods, not a great distance from our camp of the morning."[555] With their withdrawal, the guns fell silent on the northern end of the battlefield.

Munford's veteran troopers might have made a difference if they had arrived sooner. Rosser, who despised Munford, could not resist sniping at his old rival in a postwar speech. "On the other flank the unfortunate absence of our gallant and wide-awake Fitz Lee from his brigade (he being absent sick), left his splendid regiments and Breathed's battery in less able hands, which, in consequence of a confusion of orders, did not reach the battlefield until very late in the day."[556]

Had Buford and Gregg coordinated their efforts and linked forces, they may very well have driven the Confederates from Fleetwood Hill and Yew Ridge. Also, the addition of Duffié's command to the fray probably would have tipped the balance. However, the Frenchman and his division had their own adventures that day and did not arrive on the field until the end of the day's fighting.

Chapter 12

DUFFIÉ AT STEVENSBURG

Colonel Alfred N. Duffié received the order to move his command to Kelly's Ford at 12:15 a.m. on June 9. Gregg instructed the Frenchman to march his division "directly upon Stevensburg, following the road leading to Raccoon Ford. Arrived at Stevensburg, you will halt and communicate with our forces at Brandy Station, and from this point communication will be had with you." Gregg's division would follow along behind on the same road. While the Pennsylvanian moved on Culpeper from Brandy Station, Duffié would advance on Culpeper from the south, after leaving a regiment and a section of artillery at Stevensburg to guard the river crossings. "It is intended that when the right of our line at Brandy Station advances toward Culpeper, your division at Stevensburg will also move upon Culpeper," instructed Gregg.[557]

Reveille sounded in his camps at 1:00 a.m. "It was well past twelve before we got down to sleep and I for one was just dozing off—had not lost consciousness—when reveille was somewhere sounded," recalled Captain Charles Francis Adams of the First Massachusetts. "'That's too horrid,' I thought, 'it must be some other division.' But at once other bugles caught it up in the woods around." Soon the blue-clad horsemen were stirring and getting ready to march. They had only five miles to cover to reach the rendezvous point with Gregg's division. They had no idea what lay ahead of them as they set off on the five-hour march to Kelly's Ford.[558]

Upon arriving, the Frenchman was to report to Gregg for further orders, cross the river and advance to Stevensburg, where he was to protect Gregg's flank on the march toward Culpeper.[559] If Duffié controlled the road from

Colonel Luigi Palma di Cesnola of the Fourth New York Cavalry commanded a brigade in Duffié's Second Cavalry Division, Army of the Potomac's Cavalry Corps. *Brown University.*

Stevensburg to Culpeper, the Frenchman and his troopers would be in a perfect position to cut off Stuart and either force the Virginian to fight his way out of the trap or be captured. Gregg ordered the French sergeant not to use guide fires that might give away his position. His division had to traverse an unfamiliar road network through a dark night, and the march took longer than expected. A local guide insisted that a fork in the road led toward Kelly's Ford, so the column proceeded. After continuing on, Duffié realized that the guide was wrong and ordered his men to turn around and backtrack. This misstep delayed their arrival even longer as they pressed on through the dense fog. Once Duffié's troopers reached the rendezvous point, they could hear Buford's fight raging at Beverly Ford, six miles upriver. After meeting Gregg, Duffié crossed the river and deployed in line of battle on the Stevensburg Road.[360] "We crossed the Rappahannock without molestation, the Rebs having been driven back early in the morning, about 4 AM," noted an officer of the Third Pennsylvania Cavalry.[361]

Colonel Luigi Palma di Cesnola's brigade led Duffié's advance. However, the delay meant that instead of crossing at 3:30 a.m., as Gregg had ordered, Cesnola's command began crossing at 6:00 a.m., well behind schedule. The Italian count deployed the First Rhode Island and the Sixth Ohio on the right and the First Massachusetts on the left and kept the Third Pennsylvania in reserve. The sound of the guns booming at St. James Church "buoyed us up—tho some got pale—yet every man looked ready for the fray," a member of the Sixteenth Pennsylvania Cavalry noted.[562] They waded across the fast-moving Mountain Run, a tributary of the Rappahannock that was prone to flooding, near Paoli's Mill and pressed on.

In this array, Duffié advanced slowly toward Stevensburg, sending a battalion of the Sixth Ohio under command of Major Benhamin C. Stanhope forward to scout. "The first squadron found the enemy in some force in the town, but drove them out at a run," reported an officer of the Sixth Ohio. "Soon they were compelled to retire in turn before two regiments of the enemy, who advanced upon them. Slowly retiring, disputing every inch of the ground, they held the enemy in check until the main body came up."[563]

At about 8:30 a.m., Major Stanhope sent back word that he had reached Stevensburg, that the enemy was in sight and that he had sent skirmishers forward to meet it.[564] "From a hill I caught a beautiful glimpse of the advance," reported Lieutenant William Brooke-Rawle of the Third Pennsylvania Cavalry. "The skirmishers deployed in front, supported by their reserves, one column, with the artillery, advancing on our left along the road, & our regiment advancing in echelons of squadrons supporting both the battery & skirmishers. All the guidons flying, & the effect was beautiful."[565] Stanhope's men captured seven pickets, including the lieutenant commanding the vedettes.[566]

Wade Hampton's foresight that morning ensured that Confederate forces guarded Stuart's flank and ultimately helped Stuart win the battle. When he learned that Gregg's command had crossed at Kelly's Ford, Hampton rode to the camp of Colonel Matthew C. Butler's Second South Carolina Cavalry and ordered Butler to mount his regiment and move it to Brandy Station to await further orders. Butler sent a squadron under command of Captain Leonard Williams to picket Stevensburg and moved the rest of his regiment to Brandy Station as ordered. No sooner had these pickets arrived than they spotted Duffié's advance guard approaching. "When a regiment and then a brigade of Yankees came in sight and drew up in battle line, I attracted their attention," recounted Williams. "They threw out their skirmishers the length of a mile in front of me. They advanced briskly. I kept out my vedettes and placed my squadron back across the stream, dismounted the men to hold them in check as long as possible." Williams sent a galloper to Butler bearing this unwelcome news.[567] Knowing there were no other Confederate forces in the area, and without waiting for orders, Butler ordered his entire regiment to move to Stevensburg.[568]

Colonel Matthew C. Butler, commander of the Second South Carolina Cavalry. Butler lost his foot to a Federal artillery shot at Stevensburg. *Library of Congress.*

Matthew Butler was a fine soldier. Born on March 8, 1836, in Greenville, South Carolina, Butler practiced law before the Civil War. He graduated from South Carolina College (now the University of South Carolina) and had no military training before the Civil War. However, he could boast a fine military pedigree as the nephew of War of 1812 naval hero Commodore Oliver Hazard Perry (and his father was a naval surgeon). He married the daughter of South Carolina governor Francis W. Pickens, ensuring him a bright future in state politics. When the war broke out, he received a commission as a captain in the Hampton Legion and was promoted to major after First Bull Run. In August 1862, he became colonel of the Second South Carolina Cavalry. Young, aggressive, fearless and handsome, Butler was one of the Confederate cavalry's better regimental commanders, and he was very much known as Wade Hampton's protégé.[569] This day, he proved to be the right man in the right place.

Protecting the road between Stevensburg and Culpeper was critical—the infantry corps of Lieutenant General James Longstreet was camped around Pony Mountain about midway between Stevensburg and Culpeper, and Lieutenant General Richard S. Ewell's Second Corps was farther north of Culpeper; Brigadier General Junius Daniel's infantry brigade could see some of the action on the main battlefield at Brandy Station from its camps.

Lieutenant Colonel Frank Hampton of the Second South Carolina Cavalry, the younger brother of Brigadier General Wade Hampton, was mortally wounded at Stevensburg. *University of South Carolina.*

The cavalry sought to screen the presence of the Confederate infantry at all costs.[570] Knowing the urgency of the situation, Butler ordered his second in command, Lieutenant Colonel Frank Hampton, younger brother of Wade Hampton, to gallop on to Stevensburg with twenty men to do what they could to delay the Yankee advance. He also sent Major Thomas J. Lipscomb and forty troopers to swing east, cross Mountain Run at Cole's Hill and approach Stevensburg from the north in the hope of cutting off Stanhope's column.[571]

Frank Hampton was eleven years younger than his famous brother. Tall and powerfully built like his brother but considered to be more handsome, Frank Hampton had only recently entered military service after his young wife died unexpectedly in the fall of 1862. General Hampton arranged for his grieving brother to be commissioned as lieutenant colonel of the newly formed Second South Carolina Cavalry, and Frank Hampton had earned Butler's respect; Butler spoke of his second in command's "promptness and gallantry" on the battlefield.[572]

BUTLER'S STAND AT STEVENSBURG

Butler wanted Hampton to buy sufficient time for him to deploy his little force on commanding high ground known as Hansborough's Ridge, just

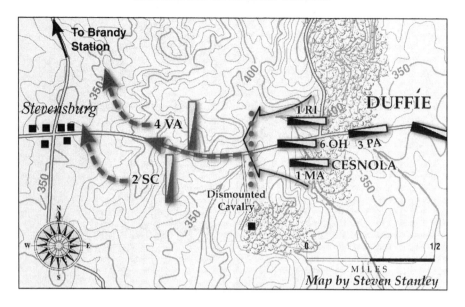

Map by Steven Stanley

outside of Stevensburg. "The position in which Butler awaited attack was well chosen. The woods concealed the smallness of his numbers, and even on the road the sloping ground prevented the enemy from discovering any but the leading files of Hampton's detachment."[573] Butler's lone regiment of two hundred men had to defend a line along Hansborough's Ridge that was nearly a mile long, a difficult task at best. It meant that his deployment would resemble a vedette line, with men positioned thirty to forty feet apart along the front slope of the ridge below the military crest.

When Frank Hampton and his small contingent arrived at Stevensburg, they learned that although the Yankees had already passed through the town, they had withdrawn after Confederate vedettes fired upon them. Hampton dismounted part of his little force in front of a stately plantation house called Salubria and kept part of his command mounted to react.

With a scratch force of thirty-six men, Lieutenant Colonel Hampton ordered his men to charge the Yankee column, which withdrew instead of engaging. "The fight [was] opened by the rebels, who charged the First Massachusetts Cavalry down a hollow road," recounted Captain Walter S. Newhall of the Third Pennsylvania Cavalry. "They came to the conclusion that they 'had the wrong chicken by the tail feathers,' and very shortly changed base, with a loss of twenty-five killed and wounded and a loss of sixty-four prisoners."[574] Thus, Hampton's delaying action bought time for the rest of Butler's regiment to march to Stevensburg and deploy into line of battle.

Colonel Williams Wickham of the Fourth Virginia Cavalry, whose regiment broke and ran at Stevensburg. Wickham was Rooney Lee's father-in-law. *Library of Congress.*

Captain Williams of the Second South Carolina found his little command completely surrounded by bluecoats when the sheer weight of numbers of Yankees finally forced his squadron back. "I discovered that a Yankee regiment was in front of me, the rear vedette, I suppose, captured. I was thus completely cut off, a brigade in my rear, a regiment on the road in my front and neither more than 500 yards from me," he reported. Williams and his thirty men turned into the woods and tried to make their way across country to rejoin Stuart's main body at Brandy Station. "On nearing the place, I halted the column and went towards the road to reconnoiter and found they had passed upon and heard 2 or 3 consecutive charges. On hearing it again, halted to examine."

Williams found no Northerners on the road between Stevensburg and Brandy Station, so he ordered the column forward again. "I discovered that I was encompassed on all sides and then carried my squadron back into the densest wood I could find with the intention of remaining til night and then running the gauntlet through their lines." However, about three o'clock that afternoon, Williams's vedettes reported that the Yankees had been repulsed and that the road between Brandy Station and Stevensburg was clear. "It was universally supposed that we had been captured. I attribute our safety to a divine providence," reported the relieved South Carolinian.[575]

While Butler deployed his troops, the famous Confederate scout, Captain Will Farley, galloped up with a message from Stuart, informing Butler that a single piece of artillery, along with the Fourth Virginia Cavalry, under command of Colonel Williams C. Wickham, was on its way to reinforce Butler.[576] The forty-two-year-old Wickham was a member of one of the first families of Virginia and was a wealthy gentleman planter, lawyer and politician who owned a large plantation on the Pamunkey River near Hanover Courthouse, north and east of Richmond. He was also the father-in-law of Rooney Lee. Although a Union man, Wickham led his militia company, the Hanover Dragoons, into the Confederate service after Virginia seceded. Wounded twice in battle at Williamsburg in May 1862 and again during the 1862 Maryland Campaign, he was commissioned lieutenant colonel of the Fourth Virginia Cavalry in September 1861 and colonel in August 1862.[577]

As the Virginians arrived, Wickham sent Lieutenant Colonel William H. Payne forward to alert Butler that the reinforcements had come. Butler "requested Colonel Payne to inform Colonel Wickham of the disposition I had made of the few men at my disposal and to say to him, as he reached me, I would cheerfully take orders from him."[578] Wickham, who was senior to Butler, declined to assume command, so Butler requested that Wickham bring two mounted squadrons of his command forward to support Hampton's squadron. The rest of the Fourth Virginia would come into line dismounted alongside the balance of Butler's regiment. By this time, it was approximately 11:00 a.m., and the desperate battle raged at Brandy Station as the first elements of Gregg's command reached Fleetwood Hill.

Duffié approached tentatively. He sent mounted skirmishers forward, but they withdrew after a couple of volleys from Butler's dismounted troopers. "As the first brigade of Duffié advanced, the dismounted men, well protected, fired upon our men, who were mounted, and made the advance uncomfortable," recounted an officer of the First Massachusetts. "One carbine in the hands of a dismounted man under cover is certainly worth half a dozen in the hands of men on horseback; and these men of Hampton, on our left of the road, were in the ruins of a large, burned building, a seminary, and delivered a hot fire upon the advance of the 1st Massachusetts, which was opposed to them."[579]

"I sat on my horse skirmishing within 2 rods of the same place for 15 minutes firing as fast as I could get a sight at one they being concealed behind some farm houses and stone walls when they would step out to fire we would pull," recounted a horse soldier from Massachusetts. "We were in an open field. They had got a good range of us and our men and horses began to fall when our supporters came up in line of battle out of some woods." Taking heavy enemy fire that rattled the rails, the Bay Staters pulled down a split rail fence so that their horses could pass through. Even though Duffié had not ordered an attack, the Massachusetts horsemen drew sabers and advanced. "We charged. They mounted their horses in a hurry and skedaddled toward Culpeper. We followed them about 5 miles and met their batteries coming up and had to retreat."[580]

The gray-clad horsemen repulsed a second probing attack, and the Federals shifted the focus of their attack to Hampton's small mounted contingent, waiting in the road.[581] "I immediately threw forward the skirmishers of the First Massachusetts, First Rhode Island and Sixth Ohio Cavalry, who immediately became engaged with the enemy, who were strongly posted and partly concealed in the woods," reported the Frenchman.

> *Pushing steadily forward, the enemy were quickly dislodged from those dense woods into open fields, where the First Rhode Island Cavalry was ordered to charge on the right, the First Massachusetts on the left, and one squadron of the Sixth Ohio Cavalry on the road, in order to cut off the retreat of the enemy on his flank and check him in his front.[582]*

"We drew sabers and started on the charge," recalled Sergeant Albert A. Sherman of the First Massachusetts.

> *The rebels stood until we got within a few yards of them. I thought we had got into a bad fix; but before we got to them, they broke and ran like a flock of sheep toward the village, and we in among them using the sabre. I followed one man and called to him to surrender, but he took no notice of it. I soon reach[ed] him and struck him between the shoulders with the staff of the guidon. It knocked the breath out of him and he surrendered.*

The South Carolinians attempted to make a stand, but the overwhelming force of blue-clad horse soldiers scattered them.[583]

"Imagine my surprise when I learned from the right that a regiment of the enemy's cavalry had charged Colonel Hampton's handful of men and swept him out of the road," recounted Butler. "In the melee, Colonel Hampton received a pistol ball in the pit of his stomach and died that afternoon from the effects of it."[584] Frank Hampton was exchanging saber slashes with a

Yankee trooper when he was shot, and he also received a vicious saber cut to his head and face, disfiguring his handsome features. Unfortunately, Wade Hampton was unable to disengage from Gregg's Federals in time to see his younger brother before he passed away. He felt that he had to stay in order to make certain that his troopers were all placed properly and because he felt he should remain in personal command.[585] Years later, General Hampton wrote to one of his former soldiers that but for "the fact that the Fourth Virginia Cavalry, under the command of Colonel Wickham, broke and ran...my brother, Lieutenant Colonel Frank Hampton, would not have been killed that day."[586]

Duffié's attack crashed into Butler's line. In the process, the force of the Federal charge cut the Fourth Virginia in two and sent it flying from the field in disorder. "No sooner did our sabers appear gleaming in front than a panic seemed to seize the whole mass," recorded an officer of the Sixth Ohio Cavalry. "They broke and fled in the wildest confusion, chased, captured, and cut down, on the road to Culpeper."[587] "We met the Yankees, and they chased us," succinctly reported one of Wickham's troopers.[588] Another said that the Fourth Virginia "ran like sheep and had all the fight taken out of them that day."[589] The Virginians "broke in utter confusion without firing a gun, in spite of every effort of the colonel to rally the men to the charge."[590] "It was a regular steeple chase," recalled a Federal, "through ditches, over fences, through underbrush."[591] The "Yankees cut them in the back as they ran," observed a disgusted Confederate.[592] A.D. Payne, a member of the Fourth Virginia, lamented, "Oh memorable day...A disgraceful rout of the Regiment."[593] Duffié captured more than forty of the Virginians in this charge.[594]

Wickham himself had to flee for his life. About halfway back to Stevensburg, the colonel rallied a handful of men for a countercharge, but only half a dozen followed him. Chased by troopers of the First Massachusetts, Wickham fled through the town with blue-clad horsemen in hot pursuit. He finally halted a mile west of Stevensburg with only three or four officers and five or six men at his side. Most of his regiment fled all the way to the protection of a battery deployed on the slopes of Pony Mountain by Lieutenant General James Longstreet. The Fourth Virginia was out of the fight, leaving Butler to hold off an entire division with a single regiment.[595]

Many years after the battle Butler wrote, "Colonel Wickham not only did not move up his mounted and dismounted squadrons to Colonel Hampton's support, but when the enemy charged they took to their heels toward Culpeper Court House."[596] To his credit, Wickham made no excuses for the conduct of his regiment. "I regard the conduct of my regiment, in which I have heretofore had perfect confidence, as so disgraceful in this instance that…the major general commanding, to whom I request that this be forwarded, may have the facts before him on which to base any inquiry that he may see fit to institute."[597]

Duffié re-formed his command on a hill just to the west of Hansborough's Ridge and pressed forward once again as Butler struggled to rally his small force. Seeing this, Duffié brought up Lieutenant Alexander C.M. Pennington's Battery M, Second U.S. Artillery, and unlimbered a section of two guns on a small rise overlooking the Mountain Run valley below. There, the guns opened on Butler's line, wreaking havoc. Butler and Will Farley were the only Confederates still mounted at that time, and they provided a convenient target for the Federal guns. Supported by the artillery, Duffié ordered another charge.

William Downs Farley was born in Laurensville, South Carolina, on December 19, 1835. He was fond of reading and writing poetry and also showed great athletic prowess. Will Farley studied at the University of Virginia and then returned home to South Carolina to assist his father in the family business. With the coming of the Civil War, he enlisted in the First South Carolina Infantry before earning a reputation as a bold and daring scout. Farley soon became Jeb Stuart's favorite and most dependable scout, and the cavalry chieftain relied on his skills.[598] When the fighting broke out on the morning of June 9, Farley, who had only recently rejoined Stuart's staff after returning home to South Carolina for a time, threw his hat in the air and shouted, "Hurrah, we're going to have a fight!" He would not have long to savor the excitement.[599]

Seeing the approaching Federals, Farley, described by one Confederate officer as "a valuable outpost officer and a skillful marksman," drew his revolver, spurred his horse forward and opened fire.[600] Butler ordered the officer in command of Company G, positioned next to Farley, not to fire too soon in order to protect men of Butler's regiment who might have gone forward to escape the artillery. "When, however, we discovered the enemy making their way through the bushes and opened fire, I gave the command, 'Commence firing' all along the line. I noticed a mounted cavalryman in blue slide off his horse…very easily, and the horse trot back to his rear, and assumed he had dismounted not more than fifty yards down the hill for the purpose of getting the protection of a tree in his future efforts," recalled Butler.

Captain Alexander C.M. Pennington, commander of Battery M, Second U.S. Artillery. Pennington fired the shot that mortally wounded Will Farley and took off Matthew Butler's foot. *Library of Congress*.

Captain Will Farley was Stuart's favorite scout. Farley was mortally wounded at Stevensburg. *Virginia Historical Society*.

About that time a man wearing a striped hat turned to me and said, "Colonel, I got that fellow." I replied by saying, "Got him, the devil; he has dismounted to get you; load your gun." It turned out…he was right. He had killed this man, who proved to be an officer.[601]

Horrified, Butler realized that the rout of the Fourth Virginia had turned his flank, so he redeployed his command in a valley near Norman's Mill on Mountain Run just north of Stevensburg. The narrow (two horses wide) Norman's Mill ford was the only place where horses could cross Mountain Run, which John Buford accurately described just a few months later as "that nasty stream."[602] The creek's banks were steep at Norman's Mill ford, and heavy traffic to and from the mill had eroded them down. A contested crossing there would have been nearly impossible.

Butler sent his adjutant galloping back to Fleetwood Hill to alert Jeb Stuart that he had been forced to abandon Stevensburg by a superior force of the enemy. Butler's men alertly cobbled together a second line of battle on the other side of the creek, using Mountain Run as a natural barrier, and

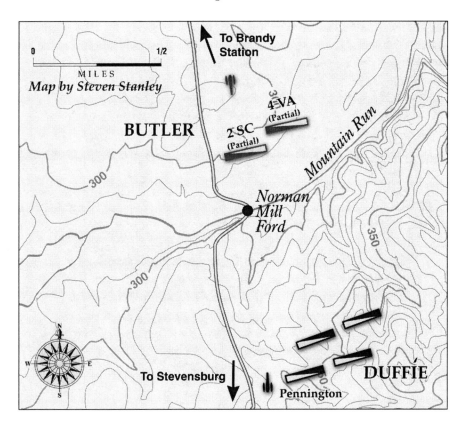

Colonel Butler deployed his single gun there. The gun guarding the ford made it impossible for Duffié to attack, allowing Butler's tired troopers to get their first rest of the morning. His lone gun opened counter-battery fire with Pennington's guns atop the hill. Duffié had to contend with Butler's determined little force. "It being a part of the Federal operations to keep their line of communication by Kelly's open," observed a Tar Heel of Hampton's command, "Col. Butler was to them with his small force, a veritable thorn in the flesh."[603]

As the artillery duel continued, and as Duffié redeployed his forces, a short lull occurred in the fighting. Farley and Butler sat on their horses, facing opposite directions, laughing as Butler recounted to Farley the anecdote about the Federal officer killed by his men. Butler was known for his courage under fire. One observer noted that "so fine was his courage, so unshaken was his nerve, that, if he realized the danger, he scorned it and his chiseled face never so handsome as when cold-set for battle, never showed if or not his soul was in tumult."[604]

Butler had his back to the Federal position, not paying much attention to the artillery fire. "Suddenly, [a] twelve pound shell from the enemy's gun on the hill (we had evidently been located by a field glass), struck the ground about thirty steps from our position in an open field ricocheted and passed through my right leg above the ankle, through Farley's horse, and took off his right leg at the knee," wrote Butler.

> *My horse bounded in the air, threw me, saddle and all, flat on my back in the road, when the poor fellow moved off with his entrails hanging out towards the clover field where he had been grazing in the early morning and died there, as I was afterwards informed.*

Farley's mortally wounded horse dropped in the road, and Farley fell with his head on the horse's side.

> *As soon as we discovered what the trouble was my first apprehension was we would bleed to death before assistance could reach us. I therefore directed Farley to get out his handkerchief and make a tourniquet by binding around his leg above the wound. I got out my handkerchief, and we were doing our best in the tourniquet business when Capt. John Chestnut and Lieutenant John Rhett of my regiment came to our relief, soon followed by…[the] surgeon and assistant surgeon of the regiment.*[605]

The surgeon amputated Butler's shattered leg. Farley was carried from the field on a trough. He asked that his leg be brought to him, remarking, "It is an old friend, gentlemen, and I do not wish to part from it." He clutched it close as the South Carolinians carried him to safety. He died from blood loss later that day. "What a pity, after having gone through so many dangers, for him to be taken off at this late day," lamented a Georgian of Hampton's brigade.[606] Farley had found that fight he was so excited about when he first learned of the Federal advance that morning, and he had paid with his life. That single artillery shot took quite a toll.[607]

With Frank Hampton dead and Butler badly wounded, Major Thomas J. Lipscomb assumed command of the Second South Carolina. Thirty-year-old Lipscomb was trained as a physician before the war but did not get to practice medicine. Shortly after graduation, he was called home to manage his father's plantation in the Laurens, South Carolina area. Before the war, Lipscomb and Butler had clashed, and Butler challenged Lipscomb to a duel when the two got into an argument over precedence on the floor at a dance. Luckily, they settled their differences before resorting to violence.[608]

He was commissioned as a lieutenant in Company B, Third South Carolina Infantry, and served as a staff officer for his uncle, who was a Confederate general, for about a year. He resigned his commission in May 1862 to raise a company for the newly formed Second South Carolina and then became its captain in June. Colonel John Logan Black, who commanded the First South Carolina Cavalry, observed that Lipscomb "would never learn Red Tape." Despite his antipathy for army bureaucracy, Lipscomb was a solid soldier who commanded the Second South Carolina Cavalry for the rest of the war. This day, though, he had his hands full with a full-blown crisis. It was a severe test for an officer new to command.[609]

Although badly wounded, Butler remained calm and collected. "Major Lipscomb, you will continue to fight and fall back slowly toward Culpeper," he instructed, "and if you can save us from capture do it."[610] As Lipscomb attempted to rally his forces, deployed in a thin line in the valley below, Duffié saw that he could carry the position and ordered the First Massachusetts to charge. As the Bay Staters formed, orders reached Duffié from Gregg that he should "return and join the Third Division, on the road to Brandy Station."[611] The Frenchman, standing on the hilltop overlooking the thin line of the South Carolinians along Mountain Run in the valley below, could look straight ahead and see the fight raging on Fleetwood Hill, six miles away.

Instead of ordering his men to overrun Lipscomb's little force and take the direct route to Fleetwood Hill, Duffié obeyed the order explicitly, breaking off and taking a longer, more roundabout route to reach Fleetwood Hill, almost guaranteeing that he would arrive too late to be of any assistance to Gregg. Duffié drew off most of his division, leaving the Third Pennsylvania Cavalry and one section of artillery to watch Lipscomb's men and to keep them from returning to the main Confederate line of battle at Fleetwood Hill. A Rhode Islander claimed that Duffié had obeyed the orders to march to join Gregg promptly, "skirmish all the way. Though at arm's length, the blows were often sharp and telling."[612] However, any skirmishing was desultory at best, but the cautious Frenchman still did not press ahead at anything but a very deliberate pace.

In the meantime, the Palmetto horsemen had to take their commander, the badly wounded Butler, to safety. "I was placed on a blanket," recalled Butler later, "and with a man at each corner…they walked with every possible care. The grating of the bones was anything but pleasant."[613] They carried Butler into a nearby stand of woods, where they placed him on a makeshift stretcher that they quickly assembled. They then moved on, headed in the direction of Culpeper. "Almost at the moment we started, a force of the enemy were reported to be crossing…between us and Brandy Station," recalled one of the stretcher-bearers. "All was excitement and anxiety…our chances of getting safely off with our burden seemed to be very slim." Afraid that he would be left behind to be captured by the Federal cavalry, Butler cried out, "Don't let them take me, boys!"[614] Each step was agony, but each step carried him closer to safety.[615]

Lipscomb withdrew about two miles to the north and west, toward Culpeper, and linked up with Wickham, who had rallied a significant portion of his scattered command. Wickham learned that Duffié was withdrawing and ordered Lipscomb to return to Stevensburg and then find and follow Duffié. Lipscomb backtracked to Stevensburg, passed through the town and shook out vedettes to the right and left. He then cautiously followed Duffié's retreat.[616]

This small force remained at Stevensburg for about an hour, but seeing no enemy and hearing the heavy firing booming at Fleetwood Hill, the Third Pennsylvania Cavalry marched to the sound of the guns. "We were ordered to fall back to the support of General Gregg, who was being badly beaten," claimed an officer of the Third Pennsylvania. "We came up just in time to save the Third Division."[617] The Pennsylvanians arrived at about 4:00 p.m., just as the fighting ended on Fleetwood Hill, and the Federals began withdrawing.[618] "After remaining for about an hour…we withdrew to Rappahannock Station," noted a Pennsylvanian, "and crossed the Ford, having moved along the road which our troops had gained."[619] The Third Pennsylvania then covered the retreat of Duffié's division, squeezing off a few long-range carbine shots at Lipscomb's pursuing Confederates, who slowly followed the long Northern column toward Rappahannock Station as it withdrew.[620]

As he advanced toward the sound of the guns, Duffié encountered a squadron of the Tenth New York Cavalry, fleeing back toward Stevensburg. Learning that a Rebel charge had routed these men, Duffié spent half an hour deploying into line of battle to protect against any Confederate threats. Finally persuaded that the gray-clad horsemen were not about to attack, Duffié resumed his march, connected with Gregg and deployed his guns to cover the retreat of the Cavalry Corps.[621] A member of the First Massachusetts offered an alibi for the Frenchman's lack of aggression. "Their horses were fresh and ours had been marching hard so we did not catch many of them," he claimed.[622] These claims rang hollow.

Thus, the Frenchman and his veteran division played no role at all in the great cavalry fight at Fleetwood Hill, much to the frustration of his command. "We were driven about in a circle all day seeking Pleasonton and finding Rebel batteries," grumbled Colonel William E. Doster of the Fourth Pennsylvania Cavalry. Doster's men, who had been awake and in the saddle for nearly forty-eight hours, finally reached the limits of their endurance about four o'clock that afternoon. Doster gave them permission to lie down and rest for a few minutes.[623] "Our division being on the left, and rather in reserve during the height of the contest," noted one of Doster's company commanders, "was not brought into action until the close of the day, when we had our turn at the enemy."[624]

"Duffié went home satisfied to be left alone," claimed Major John S. Mosby years after the war.[625] The Frenchman had obeyed Pleasonton's orders about guarding the Federal flank, but the flawed premise of the plan meant that an entire division was held out of the great mêlée for Fleetwood Hill. "This country is under obligation to Hampton and his brigade," proudly announced one of Butler's officers.[626] Had he not lost an entire day to the stubborn resistance put up by Butler's small but intrepid band, Duffié's nineteen hundred troopers may very well have tipped the scales in favor of Gregg's men in the fight for Fleetwood Hill. "It so happened that Colonel Duffié's second division went to the left after crossing Kelly's Ford, and only a very insignificant part of one of the brigades was engaged," observed a member of the First Massachusetts

Cavalry. "The rest of the division, two brigades, was not engaged at all; and the loss was comparatively insignificant."[627]

"We were not very actively engaged or under heavy fire and our loss did not exceed ten or a dozen," reported Captain Adams of the First Massachusetts. "The day was clear, hot and intensely dusty; the cannonading lively and the movements, I thought, slow." One thing struck Adams:

> *I saw but one striking object—the body of a dead rebel by the road-side the attitude of which was wonderful. Tall, slim and athletic, with regular sharply chiseled features, he had fallen flat on his back, with one hand upraised as if striking, and with his long light hair flung back in heavy waves from his forehead.*

The vision of that dead Southern horse soldier remained with Adams for years.[628]

That they did not play more of a role at Brandy Station bothered Duffié's men. Sergeant Samuel Cormany of the Sixteenth Pennsylvania, who spent the day watching the battle from a nearby hillside, complained, "Am just too sorry that I and our squad could not perform our part in this day's fighting."[629] An officer of the First Massachusetts observed, "Nothing could have improved our attack, but it was a small affair."[630] That statement by the Bay Stater was not necessarily true. Duffié only committed three regiments—half of his available force—to the fight at Stevensburg. Had he committed his entire force to the fight, he might have broken Butler's line before the South Carolinians took up their strong position on the north bank of Mountain Run. In turn, that might have permitted Duffié's veterans to reach the main battlefield at Fleetwood Hill in time to have made a difference in the outcome of the fighting there.

Chapter 13

THE GREAT BATTLE ENDS

As the fight for Yew Ridge raged, a trooper of the Sixth Virginia Cavalry spotted Robert E. Lee "riding across the fields on his gray horse, 'Traveller,' accompanied by his staff. He seemed as calm and unconcerned as if he were inspecting the land with the view of a purchase."[631] After receiving a dispatch from Stuart describing Pleasonton's furious assault, Lee had decided to ride to the battlefield to see what all of the commotion was about. Lee informed Stuart that two divisions of Confederate infantry were nearby and that Stuart was "not to expose his men too much, but to do the enemy damage when possible. As the whole thing seems to be a reconnaissance to determine our force and position, he wishes these concealed as much as possible, and the infantry not to be seen, if it is possible to avoid it."[632] Lee wanted to avoid tipping his hand regarding the proximity of his infantry if possible. However, as the day dragged on and the fighting grew more desperate, the Confederate commander finally dispatched Confederate infantry to come to Stuart's support. Major General Robert Rodes's Second Corps division advanced as far as John Minor Botts's house, Auburn, which was several miles to the south of Fleetwood Hill. "Got here in a roundabout way and formed in line of battle with two lines of skirmishers in front," a Tar Heel infantryman recorded in his diary.[633] However, Lee had ordered Brigadier General Junius Daniel and Colonel Edward A. O'Neal, Rodes's brigade commanders, to keep their infantrymen concealed from Union observation and only bring them forward in an emergency.[634] Orders to bring them forward never materialized.

Earlier in the afternoon, Hooker had given Pleasonton discretionary orders allowing him to withdraw if he felt it was necessary to do so. By 5:00 p.m., Gregg's command had already withdrawn from the battlefield at Fleetwood Hill, leaving Buford to slug it out alone, just as he had done all morning. Further, Pleasonton's command was fought out, and upon learning that Confederate infantry was filtering onto the battlefield, Pleasonton exercised that discretion. Concluding that his men had done enough for one day, Pleasonton sent one of his staff officers, Captain Frederic C. Newhall of the Sixth Pennsylvania, to go to Buford with orders to withdraw from the field. Newhall found Buford "entirely isolated from the rest of the command under Pleasonton...but paying no attention and fighting straight on."[635] Buford later wrote that once the firing ceased on Gregg's front along Fleetwood Hill,

> *I was ordered to withdraw. Abundance of means was sent to aid me, and we came off the field in fine shape and at our convenience. Capt.* [Richard S.C.] *Lord with the 1st U.S. came up fresh comparatively with plenty of ammunition and entirely relieved my much exhausted but undaunted command in a most commendable style. The engagement lasted near 14 hours.*[636]

One of Ames's infantrymen claimed, "The object of the reconnaissance being accomplished, and the enemy being in motion in great force, our whole force began to retire about three P.M., and recrossed the river about six o'clock."[637]

Although Grimes Davis fell in the first minutes of the battle, his brigade had been fighting nonstop since crossing the Rappahannock. Believing that the Confederates had been reinforced in the afternoon, Davis's men fell back and recrossed the river. Kimber L. John, a member of the Eighth Illinois, noted, "Was struck with a spent ball in the Arm & left the field at 5 P.M." He recorded his regiment's heavy losses that day: "Capt. [Alpheus] Clark, Capt. [George A. "Sandy"] Forsyth and Capt. [J.G.] Smith were wounded. Had 5 Men wounded in our Co, and 50 killed & 4 wounded in the Regt and 150 in the Brigade & some missing."[638] Even with those heavy losses, Davis's men remained full of fight.

Covered by the fresh men of the First U.S., which supported the artillery most of the day, and the men of Ames's infantry brigade, Buford withdrew across Beverly Ford at a leisurely pace. Newhall, who communicated the order to retreat to Buford while the Kentuckian watched the charge of the Second U.S., recalled that Buford himself "came along serenely at a moderate walk."[639] The Thirty-third Massachusetts Infantry of the Eleventh Corps, which advanced nearly three miles beyond the Rappahannock in support of Buford's wing, had the distinction of serving as the rear guard for the entire wing. With the rest of the command across the river, the Bay State foot soldiers then crossed without much harassment from the Confederate cavalry.[640]

Buford then climbed the knoll above the river and joined Pleasonton and a large group of officers to observe the final act of the day's drama as the sun dropped.[641] Pleasonton later noted, "General Buford withdrew his command in beautiful style to this side, the enemy not daring to follow, but showing his chagrin and mortification by an angry and sharp cannonading."[642] A newspaper correspondent traveling with Cavalry Corps headquarters observed, "The fact that the rebels did not take a step toward following the command, though vastly superior in numbers, indicates very clearly that they had had quite enough of the Yankees for one day."[643]

Victorious, Stuart ordered that his headquarters be replanted on Fleetwood as a symbol of his tenacious defense of the hill. However, dead and wounded horses and men littered the hill, with flies "swarming so thick over the blood stains on the ground" that there were no clear spots available for the Southern horsemen to pitch their tents.[644] "Look where you will and see the dead, wounded, and no chance to relieve a great man," noted one of Chew's horse artillerists. "The ground is strewn with blankets, arms, and dead horses...As we move back to camp the boys were too tired to joke and we were very quiet."[645] Many of the tired and hungry men simply collapsed where they were, happy to have an opportunity to eat something and get some rest after the day's tribulations.

About 9:30 p.m., Pleasonton scrawled a note to Hooker. "I did what you wanted, crippled Stuart so that he can not go on a raid," claimed Pleasonton, even though the declaration was untrue. "My own losses were very heavy, particularly in officers. I never saw greater gallantry... exhibited than on the occasion of the fierce 14 hours of fighting from 5 in the morning until 7 at night."[646]

Their withdrawal perplexed Buford's tired but unbowed troopers. "Our cavalry fell back across the river that night. It was a mystery to the boys why they fell back," wrote a New Yorker.[647] Pleasonton reported to Hooker:

Buford's cavalry had a long and desperate encounter, hand to hand, with the enemy, in which he drove handsomely before him very superior forces.

Over two hundred prisoners were captured, and one battle flag. The troops are in splendid spirits, and are entitled to the highest praise for their distinguished conduct.

The corps commander later reported Buford's loss at 36 officers and 435 enlisted men killed, wounded and missing, for total casualties in Buford's division of 471, more than 50 percent of the total Union casualties of 866. The Sixth Pennsylvania suffered the largest loss, 108, including 8 officers.[648] The Second U.S. Cavalry suffered 66 killed or wounded out of 225 present for duty during the day's fight.[649] In addition, many horses were killed or wounded in the fierce fighting, leaving many troopers dismounted. "The proportion of horses killed on both sides in this almost unexampled hand to hand cavalry battle was very large," reported a newspaperman.[650]

John Buford had every reason to be extremely proud of the performance of his Regulars that day. "The men and officers of the entire command without exception behaved with great gallantry," wrote Buford. His men acquitted themselves well, matching their foe charge for charge. "No regiment engaged that day on the Union side had more of it than ours," proudly proclaimed a member of Grimes Davis's Eighth New York Cavalry. "It was first in and last out in our division. It was not later than 4:30 a.m. in going in, and was rear-guard at the Ford."[651] Buford singled out a few officers for commendation, including his protégé, Captain Wesley Merritt. Finally, he praised two captains of Pleasonton's staff, Ulric Dahlgren, of the First U.S., and Elon Farnsworth, of the Eighth Illinois, for their work during the great fight.[652]

When Duffié's division finally arrived, Gregg withdrew about a mile and realigned his position to connect with Buford's northern attack raging on Yew Ridge. Most of the Confederate artillery was concentrated on Fleetwood Hill, and Hampton's and Jones's brigades shifted to meet the Union threat.[653] As Gregg prepared to pitch into the fight once again, Pleasonton ordered the Pennsylvanian to disengage and withdraw. Russell's infantry covered Gregg's retreat. The infantrymen had spent the day pinning down Robertson's brigade, preventing the North Carolinians from reaching the battlefield before the fighting ended. "While Pleasonton was defeated at Brandy Station, he made a masterly withdrawal of his forces," remembered an admiring Virginian.[654] Stuart noted that Buford's attack on the northern end of Fleetwood Hill "made it absolutely necessary to desist from our pursuit of the force retreating toward Kelly's particularly as the infantry known to be on that road would very soon have terminated the pursuit."[655] Thus ended the largest cavalry fight ever seen in the Western Hemisphere.

The day's fighting represented a will-o'-the-wisp of lost opportunities for David Gregg, a veritable litany of "what ifs." His command suffered severe casualties. A brigade commander and 2 regimental commanders were wounded or missing; a third field-grade officer was wounded; 2 line officers were killed and 15 wounded; and 18 enlisted men were killed, 65 wounded and 272 missing. His men captured 8 commissioned officers and two sets of colors. Gregg noted, "The field on which we fought bore evidence of the severe loss of the enemy." He singled out Wyndham and Kilpatrick for particular praise and commended Captain Martin's artillerists for their valiant stand.

At the same time, he squarely and unambiguously placed the blame for his failure to carry Fleetwood Hill on Duffié, both for delaying his crossing and for the Frenchman's tardiness in arriving on the battlefield.[656] When he realized that the whole Confederate cavalry force lay in front of him, Gregg should have called for Duffié's division immediately. He should have used the Frenchman's division as the hammer to drive Stuart's surrounded troopers against the anvil of Gregg's division, holding the high ground on Fleetwood Hill. He failed to do so, and the opportunity to destroy Stuart's command slipped away. The same opportunity would not present itself again.

For his part, Stuart described the fight for Fleetwood Hill as "long and spirited." He generally praised all of his brigade commanders, singling out Jones and Hampton for particular praise. At the same time, he damned Robertson for failing to delay Gregg's advance. Finally, he heaped particular praise on Henry McClellan, for without the enterprising major's help, Fleetwood certainly would have fallen and the outcome of the battle would have been very different indeed.[657]

In return, Robert E. Lee praised Stuart. On June 16, after reading Stuart's report, Lee wrote:

The dispositions made by you to meet the strong attack of the enemy appear to have been judicious and well planned. The troops were well and skillfully managed, and, with few exceptions, conducted themselves with marked gallantry. The result of the action calls for our grateful thanks to Almighty God, and is honorable alike to the officers and men engaged.[658]

Lee evidently did not realize just how close his cavalry corps had come to being completely destroyed that day; if he did, he did a good job of salving Stuart's bruised pride.

Chapter 14

An Analysis of the Battle of Brandy Station

Afcer a day of savage fighting, Stuart won a narrow victory by repulsing Pleasonton's foray. The opposing forces ended up precisely where they had begun, and the Confederate invasion of the North was only delayed by a single day. Seemingly, little was accomplished by it, other than heavy casualties. Stuart claimed victory by virtue of retaining possession of the battlefield at the end of the day. Brandy Station was "a passage of arms filled with romantic interest and splendor to a degree unequaled to anything our [Civil War] produced."[659] Colonel Thomas L. Rosser of the Fifth Viriginia Cavalry, a keen observer, noted:

> After Stuart had driven Pleasonton from the field, he could not pursue him, for the country was wooded and the retreat was covered by the infantry, against which cavalry could not operate successfully in such a country, and, as night came on, Pleasonton was not pursued beyond the river, where his infantry made a stand till dark.

Rosser concluded, "But had Pleasonton been there without infantry, he could never have got his command safely back to its shelter, for Stuart would certainly have destroyed it."[660] While that probably overstated the case, the infantry undoubtedly provided a substantial hindrance to a pursuit by the Southern horsemen.

For nearly fourteen bitter hours, the Federal troopers battled the Confederates to a standoff. "General Pleasonton is handling his troops well," noted a Southern horse artillerist who survived the mêlée at St. James Church, "and I believe if it were not for such level headed officers as General Jones and General Stuart would today have his match."[661] At the same time, Pleasonton did not demonstrate any real aggressiveness once the momentum of Buford's initial assault fizzled after Davis was killed. Instead, he was content to be passive and held Buford's command back from pressing an all-out assault while Stuart tried to contend with Gregg's division at Fleetwood Hill. An all-out assault by Buford's entire wing would probably have stretched Stuart's force too thin and would have prevented the Southern cavalry chief from shifting forces to meet threats. Thus, Pleasonton did not fulfill Hooker's orders to pitch into Stuart's command aggressively.

As well as the Federals did, they also failed in their stated mission of destroying or dispersing Stuart's large force of saddle soldiers. Brigadier General John Gibbon, Buford's old friend, wrote to his wife, "From all accounts, [the fight] must have been a heavy one. Our men behaved well but were overpowered and obliged to come back to this side of the river again, but were not followed."[662]

Lieutenant Edward Whitaker, the adjutant of the Second New York Cavalry, left an apt description of the consequences of Brandy Station for the Union cavalry. "When so many meet on large fields we fight differently now," he wrote. "Sabres are drawn and whole brigades meet in a terrible clash and such cutting and slashing you could not hardly believe, if I should attempt to describe it to you." Just a few months earlier, the Army of the Potomac's Cavalry Corps would not have been able to sustain such intense, large-scale combat, and Brandy Station represented a quantum leap forward for the Federal horsemen.[663]

It seemed that all involved on the Union side tried to claim that their unit had suffered the worst hardships in the long battle. "Today's battle was the heaviest cavalry fight of the war," claimed one of Wyndham's men, "and the brunt of the engagement was born by our brigade."[664]

The Confederates sustained 51 killed, 250 wounded and 132 missing, while the Yankees suffered 484 killed and wounded and 372 taken prisoner. These casualties speak volumes for the severity of the fighting that day. Perhaps the greatest consequence of Brandy Station was its effect on the morale of the Federal cavalry. As Stuart's aide, Henry McClellan, later wrote, "This battle…made the Federal Cavalry. The fact is that up to June 9, 1863, the Confederate cavalry did have its own way…and the record of their success becomes almost monotonous…But after that time we held our ground only by hard fighting."[665] Wesley Merritt of the Second U.S. Cavalry echoed a similar note. "From that day forth the prestige of the Confederate cavalry was broken," he claimed, "and its pre-eminence was gone forever."[666] Another Confederate, trooper John N. Opie of the Sixth Virginia, noted, "In this battle the Federal cavalry fought with great gallantry, and...they exhibited marked and wonderful improvement in skill, confidence, and tenacity."[667]

"They had five brigades of cavalry, ten pieces of artillery, and Longstreet's infantry there. It was their intention to make raids into Maryland and Pennsylvania. We spoiled their fun anyway," recounted a member of the Eighth Illinois two days after the great battle.

> *We had about 10,000 cavalry and two 6 gun batteries, and had 6,000 infantry...Our object was accomplished. We had found out their strength and their intentions. They would have commenced crossing the river in an hour if we had not got the start of them.*[668]

Captain Willard C. Glazier of the Second New York observed that Brandy Station "was a glorious fight, in which the men of the North had proved themselves more than a match for the boasted Southern Chivalry."[669]

The historian of the Tenth New York claimed that the performance of the blue troopers that day "forever settled the question of superiority as between the gray and the blue cavalry in favor of the latter."[670] Edward P. Tobie of the First Maine observed:

> *A higher value attaches to Brandy Station as affecting the regiment...It was...the first time it had ever tasted...the fruit of victory. The battle aroused its latent powers, and awoke it...to a new career. It became self-reliant, and began to comprehend its own possibilities. It became inspired with an invincible spirit that never again forsook it.*[671]

Another member of the First Maine was more succinct in his assessment. "For the first time since we were organized we had a good fair standup fight with him and whipped him at every point," he claimed.[672]

On June 11, upon returning to Warrenton Junction, Pleasonton reported to Hooker that he had "just reviewed [the] cavalry. They are in fine spirits and good condition for another fight."[673] "The day was beautiful, and the troopers made a splendid appearance," noted Captain Glazier of the Second New York Cavalry.

> *To heighten the interest of the occasion, the colors captured by the* [Second New York] *at Urbanna, and those taken by the First Maine in their*

memorable charge at Brandy Station on the ninth instant, were displayed amid the cheers of the enthusiastic cavalry, who past deeds give encouraging promise for the future.[674]

That was undoubtedly the case, but some men remained displeased with the way that the battle had ended. Pleasonton failed to disperse the concentration of Confederate cavalry in the area around Culpeper. He also failed, ultimately, to delay the departure of the Confederates on their march north—the great invasion started one day later than originally planned.

On June 10, a concerned Hooker wrote to Pleasonton:

I am not so certain as you appear to be that the enemy will abandon his contemplated raid. With this impression I have felt a little hesitation in withdrawing the infantry. Will you be able to keep him from crossing the river with the cavalry and batteries with you? If not, and you consider that the infantry will be of service in preventing a passage, pleas[e] have it retained until further orders.[675]

Major changes lay ahead for the Army of the Potomac's Cavalry Corps in the wake of the Battle of Brandy Station. One brigade commander (Grimes Davis) was dead, and another (Sir Percy Wyndham) was badly wounded. A division commander had performed badly. Significant changes had to be made, and quickly. The Confederate army was moving north, headed toward its date with destiny in Pennsylvania less than a month later.

On June 11, Pleasonton reorganized his Cavalry Corps. He placed Buford in command of the First Division, which now consisted of three brigades. Colonel William Gamble of the Eighth Illinois Cavalry, who had been on extended recuperative leave from a severe wound suffered on the Peninsula in August 1862, assumed command of Davis's brigade, redesignated as the First Brigade. Devin continued to command the Second Brigade. The Reserve Brigade, now led by Major Samuel H. Starr of the Sixth U.S., formally joined the First Division.[676]

The Second and Third Divisions merged, forming the Second Division. David Gregg commanded the reconstituted division, which now had three brigades. Although Colonel John B. McIntosh of the Third Pennsylvania Cavalry had commanded a brigade all winter, he learned that Colonel J. Irvin Gregg of the Sixteenth Pennsylvania was senior to him by a few days and that Gregg should have led the brigade all along. McIntosh briefly reverted to regimental command. By July 1, he commanded a different brigade.[677]

Duffié was more problematic. He had performed quite poorly as a division commander. "Colonel Duffié…might be a good man," accurately observed Captain Charles Francis Adams of the First Massachusetts Cavalry, "but he could not run a Division."[678] Although he no longer commanded a division as a result of the consolidation of the Second and Third Divisions, the Frenchman remained the senior colonel in his brigade and was entitled to brigade command as a consequence.

Pleasonton's rabid xenophobia was well known. "I have no faith in foreigners saving our government," he wrote in a June 23, 1863 letter to Congressman John F. Farnsworth of Illinois, a good friend of Abraham Lincoln's who served as the first commander of the Eighth Illinois Cavalry. Pleasonton had a real gift for toadying, and he realized that a powerful ally like Farnsworth could advance his career, so Pleasonton did all he could to develop the relationship, including finding a spot on his staff for the congressman's nephew, Captain Elon J. Farnsworth. "I conscientiously believe that Americans only should rule in this matter & settle this rebellion—& that in every instance foreigners have injured our cause," concluded the corps commander.[679]

In order to solve the Duffié problem, Pleasonton recommended that Judson Kilpatrick receive a promotion to brigadier general of volunteers. In the heady days following Stoneman's Raid, Kilpatrick's officers wrote to Lincoln, requesting Little Kil's promotion. Pleasonton endorsed the request as a means of resolving the conundrum presented by the Frenchman, who was senior to Kilpatrick. When the promotion came through, Pleasonton placed Kilpatrick in command of the brigade, meaning that both Duffié and Cesnola reverted to regimental command. Duffié returned to the First Rhode Island Cavalry. "I know that there was not the most cordial feeling between him and the controlling officers in the cavalry," recalled a Northern horseman. "I suspected that he was more or less a thorn in the side of the higher officers. He was not companionable with them; did not think as they did; had little in common, and, was perhaps inclined to be boastful."[680] However, Pleasonton was not finished with the Frenchman.

On June 17, 1863, Pleasonton dispatched Duffié and the First Rhode Island on a reconnaissance to Middleburg, in Virginia's lush Loudoun Valley. The vastly outnumbered Rhode Islanders were cut to pieces. They lost 6 killed, 9 wounded and 210 missing and captured, leaving a fine regiment gutted. Pleasonton apparently sacrificed the First Rhode Island to rid himself of a hated foreigner.[681] John Singleton Mosby, the notorious Confederate partisan commander, offered his opinion of the Frenchman's leadership skills. "Duffié's folly is an illustration of the truth of what I have often said—that no man is fit to be an officer who has not the sense and courage to know when to disobey an order."[682]

Several weeks earlier, Hooker had endorsed a promotion for Duffié as a consequence of his good work at Kelly's Ford. A few days after the debacle at Middleburg, President Lincoln forwarded a letter to Secretary of War Stanton recommending that Duffié be promoted as a consequence of the Frenchman's good service at the March 17, 1863 Battle of Kelly's Ford.[683] In spite of the mauling received by the Rhode Islanders, Duffié was promoted to brigadier general and was transferred out of the Army of the Potomac in a classic bump upstairs. He never commanded troops in the Army of the Potomac again. He was assigned to lead a brigade of cavalry in the Department of West Virginia. When the division commander was badly wounded, Duffié assumed command of the division, while Brigadier General William W. Averell, formerly Duffié's commander in the Army of the Potomac, served as chief of cavalry in the Army of the Shenandoah. The two men came into conflict as a result of the clumsy command structure.

In September 1864, just after the important Union victories at Third Winchester and Fisher's Hill, Major General Philip H. Sheridan, the new leader of the Army of the Shenandoah, relieved both Averell and Duffié from command. Sheridan directed Duffié to go to Hagerstown, Maryland, to await further orders.[684] On October 21, 1864, Duffié boarded an army ambulance to go see Sheridan about getting another command. Sheridan wanted Duffié to equip and retrain another cavalry force, duty for which the Gallic general was abundantly qualified.[685] After receiving his instructions from Sheridan, on October 24, as Duffié was headed back to Hagerstown to prepare for his new assignment, Mosby's guerrillas fell upon the Frenchman's wagon train. Mosby captured Duffié and quickly sent him back to Richmond as a prisoner of war. Duffié sat out the rest of the war in a prisoner of war camp in Danville and was not exchanged until March 1865. After Duffié's capture, Sheridan put an exclamation point on the Frenchman's career in the United States Army. "I respectfully request his dismissal from the service," sniffed Sheridan in a letter to Major General Henry W. Halleck. "I think him a trifling man and a poor soldier. He was captured by his own stupidity."[686] Duffié never served in the United States Army again, although he remained in public service for the rest of his life.[687]

The new aggressiveness of the Federal cavalry was alarming. Its probing and searching threatened to disclose Lee's plans for the invasion of the North. Major General Lafayette McLaws, who commanded a division in

Lieutenant General James Longstreet's First Corps, summed things up nicely in a letter to his wife on June 10: "They felt our lines to make us show our forces; our infantry was not however displayed to any extent—but I am afraid enough was shown to give notice of our general movement."[688]

After Gettysburg, Pleasonton claimed he had discovered the Confederate plan to invade the North at Brandy Station, but this argument has little merit.[689] Pleasonton's subsequent actions and communications with army headquarters simply do not support this contention. Captain Charles Francis Adams, of the First Massachusetts—never an admirer of Alfred Pleasonton's—grumbled, "I am sure a good cavalry officer would have whipped Stuart out of his boots, but Pleasonton is not and never will be that."[690]

The Federal troopers had performed admirably in exceedingly difficult circumstances, especially Buford's command, which carried the brunt of the fighting, going it largely alone for a good portion of the day. One trooper of the Eighth New York wrote, "The Rebels were going to have a review of their cavalry that day, but our boys reviewed them."[691]

To be sure, much—if not most—of the credit for the Confederate victory at Brandy Station must go to Major Robert F. Beckham and his stalwart horse artillerists. "At every important point of the field, we have found Beckham's guns playing a leading role," observed the historian of the Army of Northern Virginia's artillery.[692] Their massed fire at St. James Church brought Buford's initial assault to a standstill. Their accurate and effective fire at Fleetwood Hill not only bought Stuart time to bring his cavalry forces to bear but also enabled the Southern cavalry chief to shift his forces to meet threats. The Southern gunners fired thousands of rounds that day; Sergeant George Neese of Chew's Battery recorded in his diary that his piece alone fired 160 rounds that day, burning out its breech and rendering it useless.[693]

Stuart recognized the critical role played by his gunners that day, writing in his after-action report:

> *The conduct of the Horse Artillery, under that daring and efficient officer, Maj. R.F. Beckham, deserves the highest praise. Not one piece was ever in the hands of the enemy, though at times the cannoneers had to fight pistol and sword in hand in its defense.*[694]

But for the performance of Beckham's artillerists, Stuart probably would have lost the Battle of Brandy Station.

Another of Stuart's horse artillerists put it best of all. "Thus ended the greatest cavalry fight of modern times, in which the Federal cavalry for the first time began to realize their strength," wrote Henry H. Matthews of Breathed's Battery.

> *This engagement made them a foe, worthy of our steel. Prior to this engagement the Federal troopers were in every respect vastly inferior to the Southern horsemen. They gained confidence in themselves and their officers on that day, which enabled them to so fiercely contest subsequent battle fields.*[695]

Captain Theophilus F. Rodenbough, of the Second U.S. Cavalry, who was wounded and had two horses shot out from under him at Brandy Station and who became the leading early Union cavalry historian of the nineteenth century, wrote a few years later, "Stuart had the advantage of position; the ground, intersected by ravines and low stone fences and interspersed with groves of large trees, rose gradually in the direction of Brandy Station." With such advantages, Stuart should have won decisively, but he did not. Rather, it was too close a margin for Southern comfort. In fact, given the extreme circumstances, Stuart handled his troops well, shifting forces as needed to meet threats. Rodenbough observed:

> *The Confederate cavalry, caught napping, endeavored to repair its fault with promptness and gallantry; it had, however, been checked upon the threshold of an aggressive movement, and its leader was taught a lesson, which sooner or later is learned by the general who undervalues his enemy.*[696]

The key to the Confederate victory was the combination of the stout, superb work by Beckham's gunners and the fact that the Federals never wrested control of the high ground from Stuart. At all times, Stuart and his troopers kept control of the high ground, first at St. James Church and then at Yew Ridge and Fleetwood Hill. As Garnett pointed out, Stuart successfully shifted troops to meet threat after threat, successfully parrying each Federal thrust. Finally, Pleasonton's overly cautious approach prevented Buford from pressing his attack simultaneously with Gregg's assaults at Fleetwood Hill, which made it possible for Stuart to shift Jones and Hampton away from the St. James Church line to meet the threat posed by Gregg's arrival at Fleetwood Hill. While Stuart was clearly surprised that morning, he managed his forces well and was very well served by Fitz Lee, Hampton, Jones, Butler and, especially, Beckham. All of these factors made the Confederate victory at Brandy Station possible.

An Analysis of the Battle of Brandy Station

In spite of the Confederate victory, the Southern newspapers excoriated Stuart for being taken by surprise at Brandy Station. The *Richmond Sentinel* concluded its coverage of the battle by stating, "The fight, on the whole, may be said to have begun in a surprise and ended in a victory. The latter is what we are accustomed to hear of Confederate soldiers; the former we trust never to hear again."

The *Richmond Examiner* had a far harsher appraisal: it referred to Stuart's command as "this much puffed cavalry of the Army of Northern Virginia" and pointed out that, along with the Battle at Kelly's Ford three months earlier, it was at least the second time that Stuart had been surprised by the Federals. The article opined, "If the war was a tournament, invented and supported for the pleasure and profit of a few vain and weak-headed officers, these disasters might be dismissed with compassion. But the country pays dearly for the blunders which encourage the enemy to overrun the land with a cavalry which is daily learning to despise the mounted troops of the Confederacy. It is high time that this branch of the service should be reformed," plainly implying that Stuart should be replaced as its commander. The editorial proclaimed:

> *The enemy is evidently determined to employ his cavalry extensively, and has spared no pains or cost to perfect that arm. The only effective means of preventing the mischief…is to reorganize our own forces, enforce a stricter discipline among the men, and insist on more earnestness among the officers in the discharge of their very important duty.*[697]

The harsh criticism stung the proud Stuart. He wrote home to his wife, Flora, "God has spared me through another bloody battle, and blessed with victory our arms." He then vented his frustration with the media. "The papers are in great error, as usual about the whole transaction," he proclaimed. "It was no surprise, the enemys [*sic*] movement was known, and he was defeated. I lost <u>no paper</u>—no <u>nothing</u>—except the casualties of battle." The offended cavalry chief declared the *Examiner*'s account "lies."[698]

In fact, once Stuart realized the enormity of the situation, he was seemingly everywhere, personally commanding the battlefield, even pitching into the fighting himself. "Learning that he had been flanked and strong units were occupying his previous headquarters blocking his retreat, Stuart's strength and military genius rose to their highest," declared Major von Borcke.[699] "No mortal man—living or dead—ever possessed such readiness and resource as J.E.B. Stuart," observed a North Carolinian. "It took desperation to get up the 'do or die,' and now he had to."[700] "Genl Stuart always fought the hardest when things looked the worst," observed one of his horse soldiers. Another remembered that he was "coldly furious" and that he was "here, there, and everywhere... his black plume floating...where the battle was fiercest."[701] At the end of the day, Stuart's command slept in its camps, held the battlefield and had thwarted Pleasonton's attempt to "destroy or disperse" the concentration of Confederate cavalry in Culpeper County. By any measure, Stuart won the battle, even if he was surprised.

At the same time, though, Stuart's handling of the battle had critics. The Virginian did not commit Fitz Lee's brigade to the fight until the end of the day; earlier involvement by this veteran command might have tipped the balance.[702] Captain Charles Minor Blackford, of Stuart's staff, wrote to his family:

> *The cavalry fight at Brandy Station can hardly be called a victory. Stuart was certainly surprised and but for the supreme gallantry of his subordinate officers and the men in his command, it would have been a day of disaster and disgrace.*[703]

Theodore S. Garnett, who served on Stuart's staff in 1864, noted:

> *By all the laws of war and chances of battle, Stuart should have been crushed and utterly destroyed. But by a rapid change of front to rear Stuart hastened to Fleetwood with regiment after regiment of Jones' and Hampton's Brigades, and by a succession of most gallant and desperate charges wrested victory from the jaws of defeat and drove Gregg and Kilpatrick from the vantage ground of Fleetwood Hill.*[704]

One of Moorman's artillerists noted that the Federals "waked Stuart up this morning and kept him wide-awake all day long. His flank movement was well executed and the enemy fought well."[705] Another Confederate soldier wrote, "Genl Stuart was beautifully surprised and whipped the other day. He drove them back, but not until he had received a considerable chastising. It is amusing to hear the cavalry fellows trying to bluff out of it."[706] John B. Jones, a clerk in the Confederate War Department, noted in his diary:

> *The surprise of Stuart on the Rappahannock has chilled every heart, notwithstanding it does not appear that we lost more than the enemy in the encounter. The question is on every tongue—have the generals relaxed in vigilance? If so, sad is the prospect!*[707]

When he wrote his after-action report, Wade Hampton complained that Stuart had sent his First South Carolina Cavalry without informing him that he had done so, and that by Stuart's orders to his troopers on Fleetwood Hill, "I found myself deprived of two of my regiments at the very moment they could have reaped the fruits of the victory they had so brilliantly won."[708] After the war, Hampton wrote to Henry B. McClellan, "Credit was not given to my Brig. on that occasion for in truth it did the only successful fighting & retrieved the blunders & disasters of the day. I do not think that Robertson was responsible for the passage of enemy behind us & his way left when his command would have been sacrificed but for its withdrawl by myself." He concluded, "Stuart managed badly that day, but I would not say so publicly."[709]

The Confederate cavalry fought superbly that day, living up to its vaunted reputation. Even after it was caught by surprise, the Southern horse gathered itself and prevented the Yankee horsemen from fulfilling their mission that day. Jones's and Hampton's brigades fought especially well, having to hold off the Federals at both St. James Church and again at Fleetwood Hill. "My brigade bore the brunt of action both in the morning and evening, and lost severely in killed and wounded, but had the satisfaction of seeing the enemy worsted in every particular more than ourselves," proudly declared Grumble Jones in his after-action report. "We ended the fight with more horses and more and better small-arms than we had in the beginning."[710]

Hampton's men rushed into the breach at just the right moment on two different occasions during the long day of brutal fighting. The Cobb Legion Cavalry, in particular, distinguished itself. "We were fortunate in retaking Gen. Stuart's Hdqtrs, a very important position at a very critical time when all eyes were turned upon us & our men behaved with gallantry and spirit," recounted Lieutenant Colonel Will Delony.

> *I would not be surprised if our charge made Young a Brigadier—It is the first time we have ever met the enemy in an open field in a charge—Heretofore it has been in byways & roads & we succeeded as I have always told you we would succeed—with such a set of men to follow. I never have seen, nor do I ever again expect to see a field swept in such splendid style, as was that battle field by Hampton's Brigade assisted by one or two Virginia Regts.*[711]

The notable exceptions were Munford's and Roberton's brigades. Munford dilly-dallied and did not arrive on the field until it was almost too late. However, once he got there, his men did a fine job of driving Buford's tired troopers from the northern crest of Fleetwood Hill. Robertson's men did almost nothing, firing a single volley and then stepping aside, opening the way for Gregg's unmolested advance on Fleetwood Hill. Surprisingly, Wade Hampton defended Robertson's performance that day. In a postwar letter to Robertson, Hampton wrote:

> *It gives me pleasure to say now that you carried out the orders you received; that these orders placed your command where it ran great risk of being sacrificed; that in the progress of the fight I took the responsibility of changing your position, and that you did make the necessary changes in a soldierly manner. For a time your brigade was under my command and the men and officers behaved well. I willingly bear this testimony, and I hope that full credit will be done to you.*[712]

Hampton was about Roberton's only defender; most have severely criticized his inactivity that day.

Although Stuart had won the hard fight, Robert E. Lee harbored no illusions. On June 10, the day after the battle, he wrote to President Davis. He now realized that the Federal cavalry claimed superior "numbers, resources, and all the numbers, resources, and means and appliances for carrying on the war." He realized that the Confederacy could not hope to avoid "the military consequences of a vigorous use" of those means. He concluded, "We should not, therefore, conceal from ourselves that our resources in men are constantly diminishing, and that the disproportion in this respect between us and our enemies is steadily augmenting." Stuart's cavalry lost hundreds of horses at Brandy Station, and making good those losses stretched the Confederate supply system to its limits at a time when it could ill afford it. In spite of the glory of the passage of arms at Brandy Station, Lee remained more convinced than ever that the Confederacy's best hope for victory lay in a successful invasion of the North, and he continued preparing for that invasion.[713]

On the other hand, the Army of the Potomac's cavalrymen performed well that day, tangling with the very best that the Confederate cavalry had to offer, and they more than held their own. While they were largely fought out by the end of the day, the Yankee troopers withdrew leisurely and without pursuit. Victory lay within their grasp, but they let it slip away because of poor intelligence work and poor planning by Alfred Pleasonton. Not only was Pleasonton's plan based on shoddy intelligence, but also it did not take into account the possibility that his men might find the enemy on ground where it was not expected. In addition, Pleasonton's plan separated his force and prevented the Northern cavalrymen from delivering a knockout blow; had he concentrated his entire force and made a vigorous attack on one front or the other, he probably would have inflicted a decisive defeat on Stuart and his vaunted cavalry. The combination of poor intelligence work and an unduly complex plan doomed his excursion to failure.

Finally, Pleasonton was unduly cautious and failed to press his advantages. Instead of keeping Buford's troops on a leash for much of the day, Pleasonton could have unleashed Buford's command, which would have placed such pressure on Stuart's hard-pressed command that he might not have been able to shift forces successfully to meet threats. Luther Hopkins, a member of the Sixth Virginia Cavalry, summed it up nicely. "Our enemies could have driven us back farther if they had tried to, but they seemed to be afraid of getting into trouble," he said.[714] Pleasonton's failings, however, do not take away from the performance of the individual troopers, who fought long and hard, earning the respect of their gray-clad foes.

In the big scheme of things, Brandy Station meant little to the outcome of the Gettysburg Campaign. Instead of the bulk of the Army of Northern Virginia's infantry moving as scheduled on June 9, it marched the next day, meaning that the beginning of the second invasion of the North was delayed by a single day. Stuart's cavalry spent several days in place at Brandy Station, licking its wounds and regrouping for the coming campaign. "I think we will move forward in a few days tho' I know nothing," observed a Georgian. "Gen Lee may keep us all here for some time yet and certain indications looks that way—He keeps his own counsel."[715]

Epilogue

A TALE OF TWO SOLDIERS

Captain Henry W. Sawyer of the First New Jersey Cavalry was now a prisoner of war. He was treated at a home in Culpeper, and his two combat wounds from Brandy Station were declared "very dangerous, if not mortal." However, he recovered enough to be transported from Culpeper to Richmond's notorious Libby Prison, "only to face the horrible fate which this heroic captain wished he had escaped by death through the bullet he had previously received through his head in battle."[716]

On April 9, 1863, Federal soldiers arrested Confederate captains William F. Corbin and T.G. McGraw near Rouse's Mills, Kentucky. They were tried before a military commission convened by Major General Ambrose E. Burnside, commander of the Department of the Ohio, and were convicted of being spies and recruiting within Federal lines. On May 15, Corbin and McGraw were executed at the prisoner of war camp at Johnson's Island, near Sandusky, Ohio.[717]

When Colonel Robert Ould, the Confederate agent for the exchange of prisoners of war, learned of these executions through the press, he informed his Union counterpart, Lieutenant Colonel William H. Ludlow, that the Confederate authorities had ordered two Union captains in their custody to be selected for execution in retaliation for this perceived barbarity. On May 25, 1863, Lieutenant Colonel Ludlow informed Ould that Captains Corbin and McGraw were being executed for being spies and

that if he proposed to select brave and honorable officers who had been captured in fair open fight on the battlefield and barbarously put to death in just retribution for the punishment of spies, he gave him formal notice that the United States Government would exercise their discretion in selecting such persons as they thought best for the purpose of count retaliation.[718]

Ludlow had already received notice that the Confederates had condemned Captain Samuel McKee of the Fourteenth Kentucky Cavalry and a Lieutenant Shepherd as the two officers to be executed. However, some influential politicians intervened with Confederate president Jefferson Davis, and the two men were spared.[719]

Brigadier General John H. Winder, who commanded the Department of Henrico, Virginia, issued Special Orders No. 160 on July 6, 1863, ordering Captain Thomas P. Turner, the commandant of Libby Prison, to select by lot two captains from among the prisoners to be shot in retaliation for the deaths of Corbin and McGraw. Turner summoned all of the seventy-five Union captains being held in Libby Prison and announced, "Gentlemen, it is my painful duty to communicate to you an order I have received from General Winder, which I will read."[720]

After reading the order, Turner had the men form into a hollow square, in the center of which was placed a table. The names of all of the Union captains were written on slips of paper, carefully folded up and placed in a box. The first two names drawn would be the two men shot. He gave the officers the choice of who would draw the names, but nobody came forward. Instead, Sawyer suggested a chaplain of the U.S. Army. Three chaplains were called down, and Reverend Joseph T. Brown of the Sixth Maryland Infantry drew the first name, which was Sawyer's. The second name drawn was that of Captain John M. Flinn of the Fifty-first Indiana Infantry.[721] "When the names were read out," reported the *Richmond Dispatch*, "Sawyer heard it with no apparent emotion, remarking that some one had to be drawn, and he could stand it as well as any one else. Flynn [*sic*] was very white and depressed." The two men were placed in solitary confinement to await their execution. No date for the execution was set.[722]

Sawyer realized that if he could bring his plight to the attention of the Federal government, something might be done to save his life. He asked for, and received, permission to write to his wife. Sawyer penned a lengthy letter to his wife explaining the fate that awaited him and declared, "I have no trial, no jury, nor am I charged with any crime, but it fell to my lot." Upon completing his letter, Sawyer burst into tears at the thought of leaving his wife and children behind to fend for themselves.[723]

A Tale of Two Soldiers

Captain Henry W. Sawyer of the First New Jersey Cavalry was wounded and captured at Brandy Station. *USAHEC.*

Sawyer and Flinn were placed in close confinement in an underground dungeon and fed only corn bread and water, their clothing molding in the dank, damp dungeon. The vault was only about six feet wide and had no place for light or air, except a hole about six inches square cut in the door. A sentry constantly stood duty in front of this door to challenge the inmates once in each half hour and receive a reply. This, of course, rendered it impossible for both the inmates to sleep at one time. Sleep would have been impossible anyway. One of the two had to remain awake to keep the rats, which swarmed in the cell, off his comrade.[724] The two men understandably grew deeply depressed as they awaited their cold fate, unaware of the efforts being undertaken to save their lives.[725]

On July 11, they penned a letter to Winder, pleading for their lives. "You are aware in obedience to your order we were by lot selected from among the Federal captains for execution," they wrote.

> *No crime is charged against us, nor have we been guilty of any. It seems our lives are demanded as a measure of retaliation on our Government for the execution of two persons in Burnside's department of our army. Of these persons we know nothing, nor of the circumstances attending them. We never had any connection with that part of the army.*

They suggested that they should only be held for events that occurred in their theater of the war and suggested that Winder instead consider several officers from the Western Theater. They concluded by pleading, "Innocent as we are of any offense against the rules of war, in the name of humanity we ask you if our lives are to be exacted for the alleged offense of other men in other departments of the army than that in which we served?"[726]

In the interim, Colonel Ludlum, who was an astute observer, wrote to recommend a course of action to save the lives of Sawyer and Flinn.

> *I respectfully and earnestly recommend that two Confederate officers in our hands be immediately selected for execution in retaliation for the threatened one of Sawyer and Flinn, and that I be authorized to communicate their names to the Confederate authorities, with the proper notice.*[727]

This wise suggestion provided the basis for a strategy that saved the lives of the two unfortunate captains.

Upon learning her husband's fate, a horrified Mrs. Sawyer hastened to Washington, D.C., to present the case to President Abraham Lincoln. She traveled with a friend, Captain W. Whelden, and Representative J.T. Nixons of New Jersey and met with the president on July 14. Lincoln immediately ordered Major General Henry W. Halleck, the commanding general of the U.S. Army, to send the following communication to Lieutenant Colonel Ludlow at Fortress Monroe, Virginia:

> *Washington, July 15, 1863*
> *Colonel Ludlow, Agent for Exchange of Prisoners of War:*
>
> *The President directs that you immediately place General W.H.F. Lee and another officer selected by you not below the rank of captain, prisoners of war, in close confinement and under strong guard, and that you notify Mr. R. Ould, Confederate agent for exchange and prisoners of war, that if Capt. H.W. Sawyer, First New Jersey Volunteer Cavalry, and Capt. John M. Flinn, Fifty-first Indiana Volunteers, or any other officers or men in the service of the United States not guilty of crimes punishable with death by the laws of war, shall be executed by the enemy, the aforementioned prisoners will be immediately hung in retaliation. It is also directed that immediately on receiving official or other authentic information of the execution of Captain Sawyer and Captain Flinn, you will proceed to hang General Lee and the other rebel officer designated as hereinabove directed, and that you notify Robert Ould, Esq., of said proceeding, and assure him that the Government of the United States*

will proceed to retaliate for every similar barbarous violation of the laws of civilized war.

H.W. Halleck,
General-in-Chief[728]

Like Henry Sawyer, Rooney Lee had received two serious combat wounds at Brandy Station. One was a saber cut, and the other, more serious, was a gunshot wound to the leg that narrowly missed the tibia and the main artery. He was taken to Hickory Hill, the Wickham family home, in Hanover County, Virginia, to recuperate.[729] A task force of more than one thousand Federal cavalrymen, stationed near Yorktown, Virginia, raided deep into Hanover County and seized Rooney Lee from his father-in-law's house on June 26, 1863. Colonel Samuel P. Spear of the Eleventh Pennsylvania Cavalry, commander of the task force, whom Lee knew from the prewar Regular Army, refused Lee's request to be paroled, and the Confederate general became a prisoner of war. He was taken to Fortress Monroe and held there and soon became a pawn in the great game of human chess that also involved Henry Sawyer.[730]

Immediately after receiving this telegram, Ludlow had Rooney Lee placed in close confinement in a dungeon at Fortress Monroe, where Captain Robert H. Tyler of the Eighth Virginia Infantry, a prisoner of war being held in Old Capitol Prison in Washington, D.C., drawn by lot, joined him the next day. This action saved the lives of Sawyer and Flinn. Ludlow then informed Ould of what had occurred and what the new policy of the United States government would be.[731] As one Union officer commented, the Union high command had rightly surmised "that the influential connection of these two officers in the Confederacy would prevent the threatened execution of the Union captains who had drawn their death warrants in the dreadful lottery in which they had been compelled to take tickets."[732]

After remaining in the dungeon until August 16, 1863, Sawyer and Flinn were relieved and placed back in with the general prisoner population on the same footing as the other prisoners, even though the Richmond newspapers continued to claim that the two Yankee captains would be executed.[733] "About the 10th of August the prisoners were removed from this vault to the upper rooms among the other prisoners, where 1100 men were confined in six rooms, averaging about 37 by 100 feet each," later reported the *Philadelphia Inquirer*.[734]

On November 13, Lee was transferred to Fort Lafayette in New York Harbor. Captain Tyler joined him there a month later.[735] Finally, in February 1864, the Confederate authorities proposed an exchange that was acceptable.

Lee and Tyler were to be exchanged for Brigadier General Neal Dow of Maine, who was the highest-ranking Union officer in captivity, Sawyer and Flinn.[736] Lee and Tyler were transferred back to Fortress Monroe in anticipation of their exchange. Finally, on March 14, the exchange was completed, and the prisoners returned to their respective commands.[737]

Although he did not know it, Rooney Lee had been promoted to major general while in captivity and assumed command of a division of cavalry created specifically for him. He ended the war with the rank of major general. After the end of the Civil War, Rooney Lee became a gentleman farmer and became involved in veterans' affairs and in politics. He was elected to the Virginia State Senate in 1875 and served as its presiding officer. Lee served in the state senate until 1878, when he was appointed to serve as the president of the state agricultural society. In 1887, he ran as a Democrat and was elected to serve three terms in Congress. He served from 1888 until his death of congestive heart failure on October 15, 1891. Rooney Lee was interred in a family burial ground in Ravensworth, Virginia, and was later reinterred in the Lee family crypt at the Lee Memorial Chapel, Washington and Lee University, in Lexington, Virginia, in September 1922.[738]

The unfortunate Captain Flinn, who never got over his long confinement in Libby Prison, seven weeks of which were spent in a dungeon, died six months after his release. His jet-black hair had turned completely white, and he died at age thirty-nine of alcoholism and tuberculosis contracted in prison.[739]

Henry Sawyer was promoted to major of the First New Jersey Cavalry on March 22, 1864, to date to October 12, 1863. He rejoined his regiment and served out the duration of the war, receiving his honorable discharge on July 24, 1865. He received two more combat wounds at the Second Battle of Kernstown in July 1864. After the close of the war, he was brevetted lieutenant colonel by United States Commission. At the close of the Civil War, the ranks of the Regular Army being recruited up, Secretary of War Edwin M. Stanton offered him a lieutenancy in the Regular Army, having been recommended by a division officer. Sawyer declined the offer. During the time that he was in the field he had received four wounds, two of which were of a serious character. One ball he carried in his body until he died. Sawyer settled in the pretty beach town of Cape May, New Jersey, where he was active in local politics. He died on October 16, 1893, at the age of sixty-four.[740]

This cautionary tale of two warriors demonstrates that in wartime, even good people do brutal things, for which there is almost always a heavy human toll. At least Henry Sawyer and Rooney Lee received reprieves and were able to live out their lives as good citizens. Their journey, which began in the beautiful hills and dales surrounding Brandy Station, had a happy ending.

Appendix A

ORDER OF BATTLE

THE BATTLE OF BRANDY STATION

JUNE 9, 1863

***

ARMY OF THE POTOMAC
CAVALRY CORPS
BRIGADIER GENERAL ALFRED PLEASONTON

Right Wing
Brigadier General John Buford

FIRST CAVALRY DIVISION
BRIGADIER GENERAL JOHN BUFORD
COLONEL THOMAS C. DEVIN

Appendix A

First Brigade
Colonel Benjamin F. Davis (mortally wounded in action); Major William S. McClure

Eighth New York Cavalry (Major Edmund M. Pope)
Eighth Illinois Cavalry (Captain Alpheus Clark, MWIA; Captain George
 A. Forsyth, WIA; Captain Elon J. Farnsworth)
Third Indiana Cavalry (Major William S. McClure; Major Charles Lemmon)
Ninth New York Cavalry (five companies; Major William B. Martin, WIA)
Third (West) Virginia Cavalry (two companies; Captain Seymour B. Conger)

Second Brigade
Colonel Thomas C. Devin
Colonel Josiah H. Kellogg

Sixth New York Cavalry (Major William E. Beardsley)
Seventeenth Pennsylvania Cavalry (Colonel Josiah H. Kellogg; Lieutenant
 Colonel J.Q.A. Anderson)

Reserve Brigade
Major Charles J. Whiting

First U.S. Cavalry (Captain Richard S.C. Lord)
Second U.S. Cavalry (Captain Wesley Merritt)
Fifth U.S. Cavalry (Captain James E. Harrison)
Sixth U.S. Cavalry (Captain George C. Cram)
Sixth Pennsylvania Cavalry (Major Robert Morris Jr., taken prisoner; died
 in Libby Prison; Major Henry C. Whelan)
U.S. Horse Artillery (Captain James M. Robertson)
First U.S. Artillery, Battery K (Captain William M. Graham)
Second U.S. Artillery, Batteries B and L (consolidated; Lieutenant Albert
 O. Vincent)
Fourth U.S. Artillery, Battery E (Lieutenant Samuel S. Elder)

SELECT BRIGADE OF INFANTRY (FIFTEEN HUNDRED OFFICERS AND MEN)
BRIGADIER GENERAL ADELBERT AMES

86ᵗʰ New York Infantry (3ʳᵈ Corps; Major Jacob H. Lansing; East of
 Beverly Ford Road)

124th New York Infantry (3rd Corps; Lieutenant Colonel Francis M. Cummins)
33rd Massachusetts Infantry (11th Corps; Colonel Adin B. Underwood)
2nd Massachusetts Infantry (12th Corps; Lieutenant Colonel Charles R. Mudge)
3rd Wisconsin Infantry (12th Corps; Lieutenant Colonel Martin Flood)

Left Wing
Brigadier General David McM. Gregg

SECOND CAVALRY DIVISION
COLONEL ALFRED N. DUFFIÉ

First Brigade
Colonel Luigi P. di Cesnola

First Massachusetts Cavalry (Lieutenant Colonel Greely S. Curtis)
Sixth Ohio Cavalry (Major William Steadman)
First Rhode Island Cavalry (Lieutenant Colonel John L. Thompson)

Second Brigade
Colonel John Irvin Gregg

Third Pennsylvania Cavalry (Lieutenant Colonel Edward S. Jones)
Fourth Pennsylvania Cavalry (Lieutenant Colonel William E. Doster)
Sixteenth Pennsylvania Cavalry (Major William H. Fry, in reserve and
    dismounted)
Second U.S. Artillery, Battery M (Lieutenant Alexander C.M. Pennington)

THIRD CAVALRY DIVISION
BRIGADIER GENERAL DAVID McM. GREGG

First Brigade
Colonel Hugh Judson Kilpatrick

Second New York Cavalry (Lieutenant Colonel Henry E. Davies)
Tenth New York Cavalry (Lieutenant Colonel William Irvine, captured;
    Major M. Henry Avery)

Appendix A

First Maine Cavalry (Colonel Calvin S. Douty)
Orton's Independent Company D.C. Vols. (Captain William H. Orton;
attached for the battle)

Second Brigade
Colonel Sir Percy Wyndham—WIA; Colonel John P. Taylor

First New Jersey Cavalry (Lieutenant Colonel Virgil Brodrick, KIA; Major
John H. Shelmire, KIA; Major Myron H. Beaumont)
First Pennsylvania Cavalry (Colonel John P. Taylor; Lieutenant Colonel
David Gardner)
First Maryland Cavalry (Lieutenant Colonel James M. Deems)
New York Light Artillery, Sixth Independent Battery (Captain Joseph W. Martin)
Third U.S. Artillery, Battery C (Lieutenant William D. Fuller)

SELECT BRIGADE OF INFANTRY (FIFTEEN HUNDRED OFFICERS AND MEN)
BRIGADIER GENERAL DAVID A. RUSSELL

56th Pennsylvania Infantry (1st Corps; Colonel J. William Hoffman)
7th Wisconsin Infantry and two companies from 2nd Wisconsin Infantry (1st
Corps; Colonel William Robinson commanding both)
6th Maine Infantry (6th Corps; Colonel Hiram Burnham)
119th Pennsylvania Infantry (6th Corps; Major Henry P. Truefitt Jr.)
5th New Hampshire Infantry and 81st Pennsylvania Infantry (2nd Corps;
Colonel Edward E. Cross commanding both)

Order of Battle

✱✱✱

ARMY OF NORTHERN VIRGINIA
CAVALRY DIVISION
MAJOR GENERAL J.E.B. STUART

Jones's Brigade
Brigadier General William E. "Grumble" Jones

Sixth Virginia Cavalry (Major Cabell E. Flournoy)
Seventh Virginia Cavalry (Lieutenant Colonel Thomas C. Marshall)
Eleventh Virginia Cavalry (Colonel Lunsford L. Lomax)
Twelfth Virginia Cavalry (Colonel Asher W. Harman, WIA; remained in command)
Thirty-fifth Battalion Virginia Cavalry (Lieutenant Colonel Elijah V. White, WIA; remained in command)

W.H.F. Lee's Brigade
Brigadier General William H.F. "Rooney" Lee, WIA; Colonel James Lucius Davis; Colonel John R. Chambliss Jr.

Second North Carolina Cavalry (Colonel Solomon Williams, KIA: Lieutenant Colonel William H.F. Payne)
Ninth Virginia Cavalry (Colonel Richard L.T. Beale)
Tenth Virginia Cavalry (Colonel James Lucius Davis, WIA; Major Joseph Rosser)
Thirteenth Virginia Cavalry (Colonel John R. Chambliss Jr.)

Hampton's Brigade
Brigadier General Wade Hampton

Cobb's Legion Cavalry (Colonel Pierce M.B. Young, WIA; remained in command)

First South Carolina Cavalry (Colonel John L. Black)
First North Carolina Cavalry (Colonel Laurence S. Baker)
Jeff Davis Legion Cavalry (Lieutenant Colonel Joseph F. Waring)
Second South Carolina Cavalry (Colonel Matthew C. Butler, WIA; Major
   Thomas J. Lipscomb; regiment detached at Stevensburg)

Fitzhugh Lee's Brigade
Colonel Thomas T. Munford

First Virginia Cavalry (Colonel James H. Drake)
Second Virginia Cavalry (Lieutenant Colonel James W. Watts)
Third Virginia Cavalry (Colonel Thomas H. Owen)
Fourth Virginia Cavalry (Colonel Williams C. Wickham; regiment
   detached at Stevensburg)

Robertson's Brigade
Brigadier General Beverly H. Robertson

Fourth North Carolina Cavalry (Colonel Dennis C. Ferebee)
Fifth North Carolina Cavalry (Colonel Peter G. Evans)

Stuart's Horse Artillery
Major Robert F. Beckham

Hart's Battery (Captain James F. Hart)
Breathed's Battery (Captain James Breathed)
Chew's Battery (Captain Roger Preston Chew)
Moorman's Battery (Captain Marcellus Moorman)
McGregor's Battery (Captain William M. McGregor)

Note: Fifteenth Virginia Cavalry (Rooney Lee's brigade), Phillips Legion
Cavalry (Hampton's brigade) and Fifth Virginia Cavalry (Fitz Lee's brigade)
were detached and serving picket duty at the time of battle and are not
included in this order of battle.

A WALKING AND DRIVING TOUR OF THE BATTLE OF BRANDY STATION

What follows is a walking/driving tour of the Battle of Brandy Station. This tour includes detailed driving directions, as well as global positioning satellite (GPS) coordinates for thirty-five positions throughout the tour route. It is important to note that a significant portion of the battlefield remains entirely in private hands and is not accessible to the general public. Consequently, there are no directions or GPS coordinates for the Yew Ridge and northern Fleetwood Hill battlefield from the late afternoon phase of the battle. Please do not trespass there, and please respect the private property rights of the landowners who own that sector of the battlefield.

The GPS coordinates appear at the end of this driving tour. Simply program these coordinates into your GPS unit, and you will be able to follow this driving tour easily.

Begin at the Graffiti House, which is the visitor center for the Brandy Station battlefield and the headquarters of the Brandy Station Foundation. It is located at 19702 Brandy Road, Brandy Station, Virginia (GPS BENCHMARK 1).

Leave the parking lot and travel 0.1 mile to Alanthus Road and turn right (GPS BENCHMARK 2). Go 0.1 mile and turn right onto U.S. 15 North (GPS BENCHMARK 3). After 0.8 mile, you will see Fleetwood Hill on your left. The high ground on your left was the focus of the fighting on the southern end of the battlefield. There is a Virginia historical marker along the road there.

The Graffiti House, which serves as the visitor center for the Brandy Station battlefield. Our tour begins and ends here. *Mike Noirot.*

Proceed another 2.4 miles north and turn right onto the Kelly's Ford Road (**GPS BENCHMARK** 4). Continue along the Kelly's Ford Road for 4.8 miles and then turn left onto County Route 620 (**GPS BENCHMARK** 5).

Go about one hundred yards and then turn right into the gravel parking lot. Proceed to the end of the parking lot and park your car. Although the signage there indicates that this was the location of Kelly's Ford, it was not. It was actually the site of John Kelly's mill and millrace. If you proceed to the edge of the river, you will see a narrow trail to the right that leads through the woods along the bank of the river. Take that trail, proceed for 0.2 mile and you will reach the actual location of Kelly's Ford, which is marked. This is private property owned by the Inn at Kelly's Ford, which is accommodating to visitors, but you should be considerate of anyone enjoying the equestrian trail there. Also, this path is very narrow and can be badly overgrown with, among other things, poison ivy, so plan and dress accordingly. In spite of the presence of the poison ivy, the actual site of Kelly's Ford is well worth a visit, since it was the subject of so much action during the Civil War and because David Gregg's and Alfred Duffié's cavalry divisions, and Brigadier General David A. Russell's infantry brigade, all crossed there on June 9, 1863 (**GPS BENCHMARK** 6). Reset your odometer when you leave the parking lot.

Above: Kelly's Ford on the Rappahannock River. The Second and Third Cavalry Divisions crossed here, as did Brigadier General David Russell's ad hoc infantry brigade. *Mike Noirot.*

Right: A sign marking the actual location of Kelly's Ford. *Mike Noirot.*

This is the area where Colonel Benjamin F. "Grimes" Davis received his mortal wound along the Beverly Ford Road. It is also the area where Major Robert F. Beckham parked most of his horse artillery. *Mike Noirot.*

Turn left out of the parking lot and proceed one hundred yards. Turn right onto the Kelly's Ford Road. Proceed north for 4.8 miles and then turn left on U.S. 15 South. Continue for 0.3 mile and then turn right onto the Beverly Ford Road (**GPS BENCHMARK 7**).

Proceed along the Beverly Ford Road for two miles and you will reach the approximate location where Colonel Benjamin F. "Grimes" Davis, commander of Brigadier General John Buford's First Cavalry Division, received his mortal wound (**GPS BENCHMARK 8**).

Turn around and proceed for 0.2 mile and turn right into the gravel parking area. Park your car and get out. This is the site where Major Robert F. Beckham's horse artillery was parked and where the artillerists had their camps. Here there are several walking trails and interpretive markers that address the crossing of Buford's right wing, the opening engagements of the battle between the Eighth New York Cavalry and Captain Bruce Gibson's company of the Sixth Virginia Cavalry and the escape of the Confederate horse artillery. Walk 0.75 mile down the driveway (crossing Ruffin's Run along the way) and you will reach Buford's Knoll, the position that was John Buford's headquarters for much of the Battle of Brandy Station. There are two interpretive markers atop Buford's Knoll, and there is a spectacular view of most of the battlefield from there, including the stone wall on the

A Walking and Driving Tour of the Battle of Brandy Station

This picture was taken from the top of Buford's Knoll and faces west. The tree line in the distance is where the stone wall was located on the Cunningham farm, with Yew Ridge rising beyond. *Mike Noirot.*

Cunningham farm, Yew Ridge and the Hazel River. You can walk out to the stone wall on the Cunningham farm, but the ground is very swampy and badly overgrown with chiggers and burrs. You may also encounter snakes there. Caution is encouraged (**GPS BENCHMARK 9**). After your visit to Buford's Knoll, return to your car and reset your odometer.

Proceed out of the gravel parking lot and turn right on the Beverly Ford Road. After you proceed for 0.3 mile, you will see some heavy woods on your right. That position marks the spot held by the 124th New York Infantry for much of the morning of June 9, 1863 (**GPS BENCHMARK 10**).

Proceed another 0.5 mile and turn right onto the St. James Church Road. Continue to the gravel parking lot and park your car. The location of the Emily Gee house was on the small knoll on the property of the Culpeper County Airport just across the Beverly Ford Road. The location of St. James Church was 250 yards down the St. James Church Road to the right. There are two plaques marking the approximate location of where the church stood. There is also a mile-long walking trail with several interpretive markers that discuss the charge of the Sixth Pennsylvania Cavalry and the Sixth U.S. Cavalry at St. James Church. The ditch where Major Robert Morris Jr., commander of the Sixth Pennsylvania Cavalry, went down and was captured is part of that

A modern-day view of the woods from where the Sixth Pennsylvania Cavalry and Sixth U.S. Cavalry charged the Confederate guns at St. James Church. *Mike Noirot.*

This view looks west from the position held by Grumble Jones's cavalry brigade at St. James Church. Yew Ridge rises in the distance. *Mike Noirot.*

walking trail and is found at the low ground where the small wooden footbridge is located. The Confederate artillery was deployed along the St. James Church Road, with Brigadier General Wade Hampton's cavalry on the right and Brigadier General William E. "Grumble" Jones's cavalry on the left (GPS BENCHMARK 11). Reset your odometer when you leave the parking lot.

Turn right onto the Beverly Ford Road. Proceed for 0.35 mile until you come to a fork in the road. Take the right fork, which is Cobb's Legion Lane (GPS BENCHMARK 12). Proceed along Cobb's Legion Lane for 0.2 mile and then turn right onto the Fleetwood Heights Road (the old Carolina Road) at the dead end (GPS BENCHMARK 13).

Proceed south on the Fleetwood Heights Road for 0.8 mile and stop at the United Daughters of the Confederacy marker, which will be on your left under a large tree on Fleetwood Hill. This marker commemorates the site of Jeb Stuart's headquarters tent during the Battle of Brandy Station. The Miller home, also called Fleetwood House, was between the UDC marker and the large modern house that stands on the crest of Fleetwood Hill. Everything around the UDC marker is private property, so please respect the property rights of the landowner. Cross the street and stand on the knoll at Stuart Lane. You will be able to see Beauregard, the large house in the distance to the right, from where Robert E. Lee watched a portion of the Battle of Brandy Station. The valley is where Lieutenant Colonel Elijah V. White's Thirty-fifth Battalion of Virginia Cavalry captured Captain Joseph Martin's guns of the Sixth New York Independent Battery. This valley saw the heaviest fighting in the contest for Fleetwood Hill. The railroad is on your left, on the other side of U.S. 15 (GPS BENCHMARK 14).

Continue south along the Fleetwood Heights Road for 0.4 mile. You will pass through the valley, and you will get the closest view of Beauregard that you will have during this driving tour. You will come to a pullover with two interpretive markers. Stop here, read the markers and take in the Union perspective of Gregg's approach to Fleetwood Hill. From this perspective, you will come to have a real appreciation of how dominating a piece of high ground Fleetwood Hill is and why it controls the entire position (GPS BENCHMARK 15).

Continue 0.5 mile south along Fleetwood Heights Road to the traffic light. Turn left onto Alanthus Road (GPS BENCHMARK 16). Go one hundred yards and turn right onto U.S. 15 South (GPS BENCHMARK 17). Proceed south on U.S. 15. After 1.9 miles, you will see a white farmhouse on your left. This is Auburn, the home of John Minor Botts, a prominent Union sympathizer. Stuart held his three grand reviews on Botts's property.

A view of Fleetwood Hill from the south. Stuart's headquarters was where the large tree to the left appears. *Mike Noirot.*

Proceed south for another 0.6 mile. Take the exit for Culpeper (GPS BENCHMARK 18). Proceed 0.25 mile and then turn left onto Brandy Road, 15/29 Business (GPS BENCHMARK 19).

Proceed north on Brandy Road for 0.2 mile. The field where the grand reviews of May 22, June 5 and June 8, 1863, occurred is immediately on your left. It is presently municipal property. The area where you have stopped is the location of the reviewing stand where Robert E. Lee and other notable dignitaries watched the grand reviews. The lines of Confederate troopers extended north from here for 1.5 miles (GPS BENCHMARK 20).

Travel north along Brandy Road for 1.5 miles until you come to Jonas Run. This marks the northern end of the grand review field (GPS BENCHMARK 21). Proceed north for 0.9 mile and then turn right onto the Carrico Mill Road, Route 669 (GPS BENCHMARK 22).

Proceed along the Carrico Mill Road for 3.1 miles to Mountain Run, which was the site of Carrico's Mill. The mill was on the right of the road (GPS BENCHMARK 23). Proceed another 2.5 miles to the intersection of the Carrico Mill Road and Virginia Route 3. Virginia Route 3 follows the path of what was called Kirtley's Rolling Road at the time of the Battle of Brandy Station. Turn right onto Route 3. You are now following the route

of march taken by Colonel Alfred N. Duffié's Second Cavalry Division as it headed toward Stevensburg (**GPS BENCHMARK** 24).

Proceed 1.4 miles to the intersection of Route 3 and Clay Hill Road. Pull over here and take in the view of Hansborough's Ridge, which is the commanding high ground in front of you. Colonel Matthew C. Butler's Second South Carolina Cavalry was deployed along Hansborough's Ridge (**GPS BENCHMARK** 25).

Proceed 0.6 mile along Route 3 until you see the Virginia historical marker for Salubria. Carefully pull over and park your car here. Route 3 is a very busy road, and there is usually a lot of traffic. The logging road taken by Colonel Williams C. Wickham's Fourth Virginia Cavalry intersected with Kirtley's Rolling Road about one hundred yards to the east. The Fourth Virginia Cavalry was routed here. Salubria, a handsome wartime plantation house just on the other side of the line of trees that borders the road, is the approximate location where Lieutenant Colonel Frank Hampton of the Second South Carolina made his charge with his small command and received the mortal wound that took his life. Hampton was then taken to Salubria, where he died (**GPS BENCHMARK** 26).

Proceed west on Route 3 for 0.2 mile and then turn right onto York Road, which is the historic road trace of Kirtley's Rolling Road (**GPS BENCHMARK** 27).

A monument to Captain Will Farley erected near the site of Norman's Mill in Stevensburg. *Mike Noirot.*

Proceed for 0.3 mile and turn right into the parking lot of the Stevensburg Baptist Church. Please keep in mind that this is an active congregation and is also private property. Please be respectful of that fact. Proceed around the church to the parking area behind it for a view of the field where Butler's troopers took position after being driven off Hansborough's Ridge. The knoll to your right is the position where Lieutenant Alexander C.M. Pennington deployed his Battery M, Second U.S. Artillery, and the spot from which Pennington fired the shot that took off Butler's leg and inflicted the mortal wound on Will Farley. The tree line in the distance marks Mountain Run (GPS BENCHMARK 28). Reset your odometer when you leave the parking lot.

Turn right onto York Road. Proceed 0.3 mile to Stevensburg Road (Route 663). This was the historic intersection of Kirtley's Rolling Road and the Carolina Road. This was a major intersection and a major commerce center in 1863. Turn right onto the Stevensburg Road (GPS BENCHMARK 29).

Go 0.8 mile north on the Stevensburg Road, cross Mountain Run at the site of Norman's Mill and then turn right into the small parking area where the commemorative kiosk and small monument are located. The small monument there is to Will Farley, who was mortally wounded at Stevensburg. A local man who had a deep and abiding interest in the fight at Stevensburg placed the interpretive kiosk and monument there. There is also a trail along the road back to the site of Norman's Mill if you want to take it. If you stand on the north bank of Mountain Run, you will have a good view of the commanding high ground held by Duffié and by Pennington's artillery (GPS BENCHMARK 30).

A Walking and Driving Tour of the Battle of Brandy Station

Carefully leave the parking area. Stevensburg Road can be busy, so watch for approaching traffic as you exit. Turn right onto Stevensburg Road and proceed north for 0.4 mile. On your right, you will see a cleared area at the northern end of Hansborough's Ridge called Cole's Hill. Cole's Hill has no particular significance to the Battle of Brandy Station, but it marks the spot where Lieutenant General Ulysses S. Grant first reviewed troops of the Army of the Potomac once he arrived at the army's winter encampment site in March 1863 (GPS BENCHMARK 31).

Proceed north on Stevensburg Road for 0.4 mile. You will see two houses located back-to-back, separated by only a few feet. The small yellow house in the back is where Matthew C. Butler was taken after he was wounded. This is private property, so please respect the rights of the property owner (GPS BENCHMARK 32). Proceed north on Stevensburg Road for 2.5 miles to a stop sign. Turn left onto the Carrico Mill Road (GPS BENCHMARK 33). Continue 0.1 mile and turn right onto Brandy Road (GPS BENCHMARK 34). Go 0.1 mile and turn right into the parking lot for the Graffiti House, which is the beginning and end point for this tour (GPS BENCHMARK 35).

I hope that you have enjoyed this walking and driving tour of the Battle of Brandy Station and that you have gained an appreciation for the terrain that played such an important role in the battle.

GPS Benchmarks

BENCHMARK 1: N38°30.149'
W077°53.455'

BENCHMARK 2: N38°30.117'
W077°53.604'

BENCHMARK 3: N38°30.205'
W077°53.648'

BENCHMARK 4: N38°30.841'
W077°51.119'

BENCHMARK 5: N38°28.635'
W077°46.965'

BENCHMARK 6: N38°28.613'
W077°46.900'

BENCHMARK 7: N38°30.795'
W077°51.388'

BENCHMARK 8: N38°32.026'
W077°51.245'

BENCHMARK 9: N38°31.889'
W077°51.495'

BENCHMARK 10: N38°31.707'
W077°51.683'

BENCHMARK 11: N38°31.300'
W077°51.923'

BENCHMARK 12: N38°30.981'
W077°51.946'

BENCHMARK 13: N38°30.807'
W077°51.988'

BENCHMARK 14: N38°30.587'
W077°52.757'

BENCHMARK 15: N38°30.385'
W077°53.189'

BENCHMARK 16: N38°30.294'
W077°53.678'

BENCHMARK 17: N38°30.240'
W077°53.673'

BENCHMARK 18: N38°29.504'
W077°56.151'

BENCHMARK 19: N38°29.320'
W077°56.320'

BENCHMARK 20: N38°29.409'
W077°56.012'

BENCHMARK 21: N38°29.683'
W077°54.423'

BENCHMARK 22: N38°30.132'
W077°53.531'

BENCHMARK 23: N38°28.045'
W077°51.568'

BENCHMARK 24: N38°25.858'
W077°51.288'

BENCHMARK 25: N38°26.594'
W077°52.555'

BENCHMARK 26: N38°26.533'
W077°53.199'

BENCHMARK 27: N38°26.507'
W077°53.366'

BENCHMARK 28: N38°26.579'
W077°53.679'

BENCHMARK 29: N38°26.592'
W077°53.987'

BENCHMARK 30: N38°27.329'
W077°54.038'

BENCHMARK 31: N38°27.644'
W077°54.124'

BENCHMARK 32: N38°27.997'
W077°54.113'

BENCHMARK 33: N38°30.081'
W077°53.466'

BENCHMARK 34: N38°30.140'
W077°53.513'

BENCHMARK 35: N38°30.149'
W077°53.455'

NOTES

CHAPTER 1

1. Obviously, it is not possible to chronicle fully a four-day battle the size and scope of the fight at Chancellorsville in a few paragraphs, and doing so strays far beyond the scope of this book. For an excellent and well-balanced study of the campaign, see Earnest B. Furgurson, *Chancellorsville 1863: The Souls of the Brave* (New York: Alfred A. Knopf, 1992). For a study of the campaign that defends Hooker's conduct of the battle, see Stephen W. Sears, *Chancellorsville* (Boston: Houghton-Mifflin, 1996).

2. Quoted in Jeffry D. Wert, *Cavalryman of the Lost Cause: A Biography of J.E.B. Stuart* (New York: Simon & Schuster, 2008), 234.

3. Edwin C. Fishel, *The Secret War for the Union: The Untold Story of Military Intelligence in the Civil War* (Boston: Houghton-Mifflin, 1996), 414; and *The War of the Rebellion: A Compilation of the Official Records of the Union and Confederate Armies*, 128 vols., 3 series (Washington, D.C.: United States Government Printing Office, 1889), series 1, vol. 25, part 1, 1109 (hereafter cited as "O.R." All further references are to series 1, unless otherwise noted).

4 Abner N. Hard, *History of the Eighth Cavalry Regiment Illinois Volunteers* (Aurora, IL: privately published, 1868), 228.

5. Ibid., 239.

6. O.R., vol. 25, part 1, 1112.

7. Hard, *History of the Eighth Cavalry Regiment*, 241.

8. Margeurite Merington, ed., *The Custer Story: The Life and Letters of General George A. Custer and His Wife Elizabeth* (New York: The Devin-Adair Co., 1950), 53–54.

9. O.R., vol. 25, part 1, 1116.

10. Merington, *The Custer Story*, 54.

11. Alfred Pleasonton to Austin Blair, May 30, 1863, George A. Custer Papers, Special Collections, United States Military Academy Library, West Point, New York.

12. Daniel Oakey, *History of the Second Massachusetts Regiment of Infantry. Beverly Ford. A Paper Read at the Officers' Reunion in Boston, May 12, 1884* (Boston: Geo. H. Ellis, Printer, 1884), 2.

13. O.R., vol. 25, part 2, 782–83.

14. Joseph W. McKinney, *Brandy Station, Virginia, June 9, 1863: The Largest Cavalry Battle of the Civil War* (Jefferson, NC: McFarland, 2006), 40.

15. Frank S. Robertson to his sister, May 22, 1863, quoted in Robert J. Trout, *With Pen and Saber: The Letters and Diaries of J.E.B. Stuart's Staff Officers* (Mechanicsburg, PA: Stackpole Books, 1995), 265.

16. Walbrook D. Swank, ed., *Sabres, Saddles and Spurs* (Shippensburg, PA: Burd Street Press, 1998), 66.

17. O.R., vol. 25, part 2, 528. This was just one of a number of extremely accurate intelligence reports that Colonel Sharpe generated over the course of the coming Gettysburg Campaign. Even in the Civil War, good military intelligence was critical to an army's success.

18. Ibid., vol. 27, part 3, 3.

19. Ibid., 32.

20. Ibid., vol. 25, part 2, 536. The Confederate concentration observed by Gregg's scouts was the beginning of the great massing of Confederate cavalry at Brandy Station. The brigades were the commands of Brigadier General Fitzhugh Lee, Brigadier General William H.F. Lee, Brigadier General Wade Hampton and Brigadier General Beverly H. Robertson, although the report claimed that Brigadier General Charles Field commanded it.

21. Ibid., 537.

22. Ibid., 538; and John Buford to Captain A.J. Cohen, May 29, 1863, Letters Received, Telegrams, Reports and Lists Received by Cavalry Corps, 1861–1865, National Archives, Washington, D.C.

23. O.R., vol. 25, part 2, 571–72.

24. Ibid., 595.

25. Buford to Lieutenant Colonel A.J. Alexander, June 2, 1863, Letters Received, Telegrams, Reports and Lists Received by Cavalry Corps, 1861–1865, National Archives, Washington, D.C.

26. O.R., vol. 27, part 3, 5.

27. Buford referred to the brigade of Brigadier General Albert G. Jenkins, a Harvard-trained lawyer who commanded a rough-and-tumble brigade of Confederate mounted infantry. This brigade became part of Stuart's command after the Battle of Brandy Station.

28. O.R., vol. 27, part 3, 8.

29. *New York Times*, June 10, 1863.

30. Kimber L. Johns diary, entry for June 5, 1863, Diaries and Letters, Friends Historical Library, Swarthmore College, Swarthmore, Pennsylvania.

31. O.R., vol. 27, part 3, 10.

32. Ibid., 12.

33. John Singleton Mosby, *Stuart's Cavalry in the Gettysburg Campaign* (New York: Moffatt, Yard & Co., 1908), 10.

34. Fishel, *The Secret War for the Union*, 426–28.

35. O.R., vol. 27, part 3, 13.

36. Ibid., 14.

37. Ibid.

38. Fishel, *The Secret War for the Union*, 429.

Chapter 2

39. Ezra J. Warner, *Generals in Blue: The Lives of the Union Commanders* (Baton Rouge: Louisiana State University Press, 1964), 373.

40. P.J. Staudenraus, ed., *Mr. Lincoln's Washington: Selections from the Writings of Noah Brooks, Civil War Correspondent* (South Brunswick, NJ: Thomas Yoseloff, 1976), 210.

41. Jeffry D. Wert, *Custer: The Controversial Life of George Armstrong Custer* (New York: Simon & Schuster, 1996), 75.

42. Worthington C. Ford, ed., *A Cycle of Adams Letters, 1861–1865*, 2 vols. (Boston: Houghton-Mifflin, 1920), 2:8.

43. Edward W. Emerson, ed., *Life and Letters of Charles Russell Lowell* (Port Washington, NY: Kennikat Press, 1971), 279.

44. John Gibbon, "The John Buford Memoir," John Gibbon Papers, Pennsylvania Historical Society, Philadelphia, Pennsylvania.

45. Ibid.

46. Warner, *Generals in Blue*, 52–53.

47. John Buford to George Stoneman, February 9, 1863, Letters Sent and Received, First Cavalry Division, Army of the Potomac, National Archives, Washington, D.C.

48. Allan L. Tischler, *The History of the Harpers Ferry Cavalry Expedition, September 14 & 15, 1862* (Winchester, VA: Five Cedars Press, 1993), 26. The West Point class of 1854 also included Generals O.O. Howard and John Pegram. *New York Herald*, June 11, 1863.

49. Dan L. Thrapp, *Encyclopedia of Frontier Biography*, 3 vols. (Lincoln: University of Nebraska Press, 1991), 1:379.

50. O.R., vol. 11, part 1, 425–32. Davis was recommended for a brevet to lieutenant colonel in the Regular Army for this action, but the Senate never confirmed the brevet. *New York Herald*, June 11, 1863.

51. *Rochester Daily Union and Advertiser*, June 20, 1863.

52. Wesley Merritt, "Personal Recollections—Beverly's Ford to Mitchell's Station, 1863," in *From Everglade to Canon with the Second Dragoons*, edited by Theophilus F. Rodenbough (New York: D. Van Nostrand, 1875), 285–86.

53. For the only detailed treatment of this adventure, see Tischler, *The History of the Harpers Ferry Cavalry Expedition.*

54. Henry Norton, *Deeds of Daring: or History of the Eighth New York Volunteer Cavalry* (Norwich, NY: Chenango Telegraph Printing House, 1889), 30–33.

55. Wert, *Custer*, 78.

56. Elias W. Beck, MD, "Letters of a Civil War Surgeon," *Indiana Magazine of History* (June 1931), 154.

57. Samuel J.B.V. Gilpin diary, entry for June 9, 1863, Gilpin Papers, Manuscripts Division, Library of Congress, Washington, D.C.

58. Warner, *Generals in Blue*, 124. That promotion did not come until the spring of 1865 and was long overdue when it finally happened.

59. Henry Edwin Tremain, *The Last Hours of Sheridan's Cavalry* (New York: Bonnell, Silver & Bowers, 1904), 37.

60. Edward G. Longacre, *The Cavalry at Gettysburg: A Tactical Study of Mounted Operations During the Civil War's Pivotal Campaign, 9 June–14 July 1863* (Rutherford, NJ: Fairleigh-Dickinson University Press, 1986), 51.

61. Frederic C. Newhall, *With General Sheridan in Lee's Last Campaign* (Philadelphia: J.B. Lippincott, 1866), 228.

62. Warner, *Generals in Blue*, 124.

63. Tremain, *The Last Hours of Sheridan's Cavalry*, 39.

64. George F. Price, *Across the Continent with the Fifth Cavalry* (New York: Noble Offset Printers, 1883), 331–32.

65. Rodenbough, *From Everglade to Canon With the Second Dragoons*, 445; and James R. Arnold, *Jeff Davis's Own: Cavalry, Comanches, and the Battle for the Texas Frontier* (New York: John Wiley & Sons, 2000), 108.

66. George T. Ness Jr., *The Regular Army on the Eve of the Civil War* (Baltimore, MD: The Toomey Press, 1993), 223.

67. Price, *Across the Continent*, 333.

68. Arnold, *Jeff Davis's Own*, 320.

69. Price, *Across the Continent*, 332.

70. His father, Jean August Duffié, served as mayor of the village of La Ferte sous Juarre. At least one contemporary source states that the Duffié family had its roots in Ireland and that the family fled to France to escape Oliver Cromwell's Reign of Terror. See Charles Fitz Simmons, "Hunter's Raid," in *Military Essays and Recollections, Papers Read Before the Commandery of the State of Illinois Military Order of the Loyal Legion of the United States* 4 (Chicago, 1907), 395–96.

71. Napoleon Alexandre Duffié military service records, French Army Archives, Vincennes, France. I am grateful to Jean-Claude Reuflet, a relative of Duffié's, for making these obscure records available and for providing me with a detailed translation of their contents.

72. Ibid.

73. Jeremiah M. Pelton, *Genealogy of the Pelton Family in America* (Albany, NY: Joel Munsell's Sons, Publishers, 1892), 565. The true state of the facts differs dramatically from the conventional telling of Duffié's life, as set forth in Warner's *Generals in Blue*.

74. Warner, *Generals in Blue*, 131–32.

75. A document prepared by Duffié's son indicates that Duffié attended the cadet school at Versailles, that he took and passed the entrance examinations for the Military College of St. Cyr and that he was admitted to St. Cyr in 1851. Daniel A. Duffié claimed that his father dropped out of St. Cyr after a year to enlist in the Sixth Regiment of Dragoons. Procuration executed by Daniel A. Duffié, heir of Jean August Duffié, March 16, 1885, Pelton-Duffié Family Papers, Staten Island Historical Society, New York, New York.

76. For an example of the elaborate ruse spun by Duffié, see George N. Bliss, "Duffié and the Monument to His Memory," *Personal Narratives of Events in the War of the*

Rebellion, Being Papers Read Before the Rhode Island Soldiers and Sailors Historical Society VI (Providence: Published by the Society, 1890), 316–76. Bliss presents a detailed biographical sketch of Duffié that includes all of the falsehoods. Duffié himself apparently provided Bliss with most of his information. See pages 317 to 320 for the recitation of this litany of falsehoods.

77. James E. Taylor, *The James E. Taylor Sketchbook* (Dayton, OH: Morningside, 1989), 134.

78. Gregory J.W. Urwin, *The United States Cavalry: An Illustrated History* (Poole, Dorset, UK: Blandford Press, 1983), 98–99.

79. Benjamin W. Crowninshield, *A History of the First Regiment Massachusetts Cavalry Volunteers* (Boston: Houghton-Mifflin Co., 1891), 113.

80. William H. Beach, *The First New York (Lincoln) Cavalry from April 19, 1861, to July 7, 1865* (New York: Lincoln Cavalry Association, 1902), 399.

81. Albinus Fell to Dear Lydia, March 8, 1863, Albinus Fell Papers, Archives, Western Reserve Historical Society, Cleveland, Ohio.

82. Emmons D. Guild to his parents, March 20, 1863, Fredericksburg National Military Park ("FNMP"), Fredericksburg, Virginia.

83. Jacob B. Cooke, "The Battle of Kelly's Ford, March 17, 1863," *Personal Narratives of Events in the War of the Rebellion, Being Papers Read Before the Rhode Island Soldiers and Sailors Historical Society* IV (Providence: Published by the Society, 1887), 9.

84. Robert F. O'Neill Jr., *The Cavalry Battles of Aldie, Middleburg, and Upperville: Small But Important Riots, June 10–27, 1863* (Lynchburg, VA: H.E. Howard Co., 1993), 36.

85. Crowninshield, *First Regiment of Massachusetts Cavalry*, 307–08. In fact, John Buford despised this regiment. He believed it had failed him at Second Manassas, and he would take away its regimental colors in the fall of 1863 as a result of another perceived failure.

86. An interesting and detailed account of this episode can be found in Elizabeth McFadden, *The Glitter and the Gold: A Spirited Account of the Metropolitan Museum of Art's First Director, the Audacious and High-Handed Luigi Palma di Cesnola* (New York: Dial Press, 1971), 40–44.

87. Samuel P. Bates, *Martial Deeds of Pennsylvania* (Philadelphia: T.H. Davis & Co., 1875), 851.

88. Ibid.

89. Ibid., 851–52.

90. Ibid., 852.

91. For a detailed discussion of the Battle of Kelly's Ford, see Eric J. Wittenberg, *The Union Cavalry Comes of Age: Hartwood Church to Brandy Station* (Dulles, VA: Brassey's, 2003).

92. Bates, *Martial Deeds of Pennsylvania*, 854.

93. Newhall, *With General Sheridan*, 229.

94. Warner, *Generals in Blue*, 187–88.

95. Bates, *Martial Deeds of Pennsylvania*, 772.

96. "David McMurtrie Gregg," Circular No. 6, Series of 1917, Military Order of the Loyal Legion of the United States, Commandery of Pennsylvania, May 3, 1917, 2.

97. Bates, *Martial Deeds of Pennsylvania*, 772. There is no satisfactory biography of David M. Gregg available. The only published biography is Milton V. Burgess, *David Gregg: Pennsylvania Cavalryman* (N.p.: privately published, 1984).

98. Hampton S. Thomas, *Some Personal Reminiscences of Service in the Cavalry of the Army of the Potomac* (Philadelphia: L.R. Hamersly & Co., 1889), 8.

99. Samuel J. Martin, *"Kill-Cavalry": Sherman's Merchant of Terror—The Life of Union General Hugh Judson Kilpatrick* (Madison, NJ: Fairleigh-Dickinson University Press, 1996), 1–63.

100. Edward G. Longacre, "Judson Kilpatrick," *Civil War Times Illustrated* 10 (April 1971): 25.

101. Ford, *A Cycle of Adams Letters*, 2:44–45.

102. Longacre, "Judson Kilpatrick," 25.

103. Percy Wyndham, "The Wyndham Question Settled," *New York Herald*, September 16, 1863. Wyndham referred to himself as a mercenary, writing in the fall of 1863 that people could "call me a soldier of fortune, if you will."

104. James H. Kidd, *Personal Recollections of a Cavalryman in Custer's Michigan Brigade* (Ionia, MI: Sentinel Publishing Co., 1908), 90–91.

105. Edward G. Longacre, "Sir Percy Wyndham," *Civil War Times Illustrated* 8 (December 1968): 12 ,14.

106. Samuel Harris, *The Personal Reminiscences of Samuel Harris* (Detroit: The Robinson Press, 1897), 14.

107. Walter S. Newhall to My Dear George, October 2, 1863, Newhall Family Papers, Historical Society of Pennsylvania, Philadelphia, Pennsylvania.

108. Most artillery was called "mounted artillery." With mounted artillery, the guns were mounted and drawn by mules or horses, and the men who served those guns either walked or rode on the limber chests. With horse artillery, the men who served the guns each had his own horse, and they used those horses to travel from place to place. They moved almost as quickly as the cavalry and were sometimes known as "flying artillery."

109. Eugene C. Tidball, *"No Disgrace to My Country": The Life of John C. Tidball* (Kent, OH: Kent State University Press, 2002), 300.

110. Francis E. Heitman, *Historical Register and Dictionary of the U.S. Army*, 2 vols. (Washington, D.C.: U.S. Government Printing Office, 1903), 1:836.

111. Ibid., 1:961. For an excellent full-length biography of John C. Tidball, see Tidball, *"No Disgrace to My Country,"* which fully documents his long and fascinating career.

CHAPTER 3

112. Emory N. Thomas, *Bold Dragoon: The Life of J.E.B. Stuart* (New York: Harper & Row, 1986), 31.

113. Ezra J. Warner, *Generals in Gray: The Lives of the Confederate Commanders* (Baton Rouge: Louisiana State University Press, 1959), 296–97.

114. Historian Emory N. Thomas is the primary advocate of this theory. See Thomas, *Bold Dragoon*, for his version of these events.

115. William W. Hassler, ed., *The General to His Lady: The Civil War Letters of William Dorsey Pender to Fanny Pender* (Chapel Hill: University of North Carolina Press, 1965), 239.

116. John Esten Cooke, "General Stuart in Camp and Field," in *The Annals of the War, Written by Leading Participants, North and South* (Philadelphia: Times Publishing Co., 1879), 665.

117. G. Moxley Sorrel, *Recollections of a Confederate Staff Officer*, edited by Bell I. Wiley (Jackson, TN: McCowat-Mercer Press, 1958), 243.

118. Robert T. Hubard Jr., *The Civil War Memoirs of a Virginia Cavalryman*, edited by Thomas P. Nanzig (Tuscaloosa: University of Alabama Press, 2007), 146.

119. Quoted in Jeffry D. Wert, *Cavalryman of the Lost Cause: A Biography of Jeb Stuart* (New York: Simon & Schuster, 2008), 372.

120. Two additional brigades of Virginia cavalry, commanded by Brigadier Generals John D. Imboden and Albert G. Jenkins, joined Stuart's division after the Battle of Brandy Station, meaning that the Army of Northern Virginia's mounted arm was the strongest it would ever be as the Gettysburg Campaign started.

121. Arnold, *Jeff Davis's Own*, 243–44.

122. Ibid., 282–84.

123. Warner, *Generals in Gray*, 178.

124. James Longstreet to Thomas T. Munford, September 9, 1894, Munford-Ellis Family Papers, Perkins Library, Duke University, Durham, North Carolina.

125. Edward G. Longacre, *Lee's Cavalrymen: A History of the Mounted Forces of the Army of Northern Virginia, 1861–1865* (Mechanicsburg, PA: Stackpole Books, 2002), 190.

126. Bruce S. Allardice, *More Generals in Gray* (Baton Rouge: Louisiana State University Press, 1995), 171.

127. George W. Beale, *A Lieutenant of Cavalry in Lee's Army* (Boston: Gorham, 1918), 220.

128. Warner, *Generals in Gray*, 184.

129. Longacre, *Lee's Cavalrymen*, 33.

130. Warner, *Generals in Gray*, 122–23. There are five published biographies of Wade Hampton. By far, the best is Rod Andrew Jr., *Wade Hampton: Confederate Warrior to Southern Redeemer* (Chapel Hill: University of North Carolina Press, 2008).

131. Henry B. McClellan, "The Campaign of 1863—A Reply to Kilpatrick," *Philadelphia Weekly Times*, February 7, 1880.

132. Wert, *Cavalryman of the Lost Cause*, 194.

133. James G. Holmes, "The Fighting Qualities of Generals Hampton, Butler, and Others Related by Adjutant-General Holmes of Charleston," *Sunny South*, June 13, 1896.

134. John Esten Cooke, *Wearing of the Gray, Being Personal Portraits, Scenes & Adventures of the War* (New York: E.B. Treat & Co., 1867), 48–49.

135. Wert, *Cavalryman of the Lost Cause*, 116.

136. J.E.B. Stuart to Flora Cooke Stuart, September 12, 1862, Thomas D. Perry Collection, Special Collections, Virginia Polytechnic University, Blacksburg, Virginia.

137. Warner, *Generals in Gray*, 259–60. Robertson was Stuart's principal rival for the hand of Flora Cooke, and many historians speculate that rivalry was the root of Stuart's animosity toward Robertson.

138. John W. Busey and David G. Martin, *Regimental Strengths and Losses at Gettysburg* (Hightstown, NJ: Longstreet House, 1994), 197.

139. J.E. Copeland, "The Fighting at Brandy Station," *Confederate Veteran* 30 (1922): 451.

140. George Dallas Mosgrove, *Kentucky Cavaliers in Dixie: The Reminiscences of a Confederate Cavalryman* (Louisville, KY: Courier-Journal Job Printing Co., 1895), 85.

141. Thomas W. Colley, "Brigadier General William E. Jones," *Confederate Veteran* 6 (1898): 267.

142. John D. Imboden, "Fire, Sword and the Halter," in *The Annals of the War, Written by Leading Participants, North and South* (Philadelphia: Weekly Times Publishing Co., 1879), 173.

143. Adele H. Mitchell, ed., *The Letters of Major General James E.B. Stuart* (Richmond, VA: Stuart-Mosby Historical Society, 1990), 221.

144. J.E.B. Stuart to Samuel Cooper, October 24, 1862, J.E.B. Stuart Papers, Virginia Historical Society, Richmond, Virginia.

145. Quoted in Dobbie Edward Lambert, *Grumble: The W.E. Jones Brigade 1863–64* (Wahiawa, HI: Lambert Enterprises, Inc., 1992), 8.

146. O.R., vol. 25, part 2, 789.

147. William E. Jones to James A. Seddon, May 24, 1863, RG 94, Letters Received by the Confederate Adjutant General and Inspector General, 1861–1865, NARA. The relationship fell apart altogether in September 1863, when Robert E. Lee transferred Jones to avoid his being court-martialed at the behest of Stuart. Jones never served in the Army of Northern Virginia again.

148. O.R., vol. 12, part 2, 727; and Mosby, *Stuart's Cavalry*, 18.

149. Busey and Martin, *Regimental Strengths and Losses*, 198. The Thirty-fifth Battalion Virginia Cavalry normally served with this brigade, but it was with Ewell's Corps on detached duty. Later, when Jones finally received orders to come to Pennsylvania, the Twelfth Virginia Cavalry was left behind to guard river crossings and did not participate in the invasion of Pennsylvania.

150. Robert J. Trout, *"The Hoss": Officer Biographies and Rosters of the Stuart Horse Artillery Battalion* (Myerstown, PA: JebFlo Press, 2003), 4–8.

151. Clark B. Hall, "Robert F. Beckham: The Man Who Commanded Stuart's Horse Artillery After Pelham Fell," *Blue & Gray* 10 (December 1991): 35.

152. Robert J. Trout, *Galloping Thunder: The Stuart Horse Artillery Battalion* (Mechanicsburg, PA: Stackpole Books, 2002), 211.

153. Trout, *"The Hoss,"* 8.

154. William W. Blackford, *War Years with Jeb Stuart* (New York: Charles Scribner's Sons, 1945), 168.

155. For a detailed discussion of cavalry operations during the first half of 1863, see Eric J. Wittenberg, *The Union Cavalry Comes of Age: Hartwood Church to Brandy Station, 1863* (Dulles, VA: Potomac Books, 2002).

CHAPTER 4

156. Thomas Marshall to Dear Bettie, June 4, 1863, Manuscripts Collection Brandy Station Foundation (BSF), Brandy Station, Virginia.

157. Swank, *Sabres, Saddles and Spurs*, 65.

158. Douglas Southall Freeman, *R.E. Lee: A Biography*, 4 vols. (New York: Charles Scribner's Sons, 1951), 3:30.

159. Henry B. McClellan, *The Life and Campaigns of Major General J.E.B. Stuart* (Boston: Houghton-Mifflin, 1895), 261; see also, Blackford, *War Years with Jeb Stuart*, 211–12.

160. Festus P. Summers, ed., *A Borderland Confederate* (Pittsburgh, PA: University of Pittsburgh Press, 1962), 71.

161. Trout, *Galloping Thunder*, 218.

162. William N. McDonald, *A History of the Laurel Brigade* (Baltimore, MD: Sun Job Printing Office, 1907), 131.

163. W.P. Shaw, "Fifty-ninth Regiment (Fourth Cavalry)," in *Histories of the Several Regiments and Battalions from North Carolina in the Great War 1861–65*, 5 vols., edited by Walter Clark (Goldsboro, NC: Nash Brothers, 1901), 3:460.

164. Daniel A. Grimsley, *Battles in Culpeper County, Virginia, 1861–1865* (Culpeper, VA: Raleigh Travers Green, 1900), 7.

165. Blackford, *War Years with Jeb Stuart*, 212.

166. George H. Moffat, "The Battle of Brandy Station," *Confederate Veteran* 14 (February 1906): 74.

167. Heros von Borcke, *Memoirs of the Confederate War for Independence*, 2 vols. (Philadelphia: J.B. Lippincott, 1867), 2:264–67.

168. Trout, *Galloping Thunder*, 217.

169. Ada Bruce D. Bradshaw, ed., *Civil War Diary of Charles William McVicar* (Washington, D.C.: privately published, 1977), 9–10.

170. Borcke, *Memoirs*, 402.

171. Francis H. Wigfall to Louise Wigfall, June 4, 1863, Manuscripts Division, Library of Congress, Washington, D.C.

172. McDonald, *A History of the Laurel Brigade*, 132.

173. John Minor Botts, *The Great Rebellion: The Political Life of the Author Vindicated* (New York: Harper & Bros., 1866), 294.

174. Hall, "Robert F. Beckham," 35; and Clark B. Hall, "Auburn: Culpeper's Architectural and Historical Gem," *Culpeper Star Exponent*, May 1, 2008.

175. *Vermont Chronicle*, November 28, 1863.

176. Botts, *The Great Rebellion*, 301–02.

177. Myrta Lockett Avary, *A Virginia Girl in the Civil War* (New York: D. Appleton & Co., 1903), 238–40.

178. O.R., vol. 27, part 3, 14, 18.

179. Ibid., 24–25.

180. Ibid., 24, 27.

181. Johns diary, entry for June 7, 1863.

182. John Esten Cooke, *Wearing of the Gray, Being Personal Portraits, Scenes & Adventures of the War* (New York: E.B. Treat & Co., 1867), 227.

183. Burke Davis, *Jeb Stuart: The Last Cavalier* (New York: Rinehart, 1957), 304.

184. Henry H. Matthews, "The Great Cavalry Fights of the War, Fleetwood Hill or Brandy Plains, June 9, 1863," *St. Mary's Beacon*, March 9, 1905.

185. George M. Neese, *Three Years in the Confederate Horse Artillery* (New York: Neale Publishing Co., 1911), 169–70.

186. Blackford, *War Years with Jeb Stuart*, 212–13.

187. J.M. Monie, "Cavalry Operations Relating to the Campaign of Gettysburg, Brandy Station or Fleetwood, and Stevensburg," *News and Observer*, August 29, 1894.

188. Blackford, *War Years with Jeb Stuart*, 210.

189. Francis Smith Robertson, "Reminiscences, 1861–1865," Archives, Virginia Historical Society, Richmond, Virginia.

190. Dabney Herndon Maury, *Recollections of a Virginian in the Mexican, Indian, and Civil Wars* (New York: Charles Scribner's Sons, 1894), 239; and Peter Wellington Alexander, *Writing & Fighting the Confederate War: The Letters of Peter Wellington Alexander, Confederate War Correspondent*, edited by William B. Styple (Kearny, NJ: Belle Grove Publishing Co., 2002), 146.

191. Grimsley, *Battles in Culpeper County*, 8.

192. Summers, *A Borderland Confederate*, 71.

193. Robert J. Trout, ed., *Memoirs of the Stuart Horse Artillery: Moorman's and Hart's Batteries* (Knoxville: University of Tennessee Press, 2008), 49.

194. Susan P. Lee, *Memoirs of William Nelson Pendleton, D.D.* (Philadelphia: J.B. Lippincott, 1893), 277–78.

195. Charles T. O'Ferrall, *Forty Years of Active Service* (New York: The Neale Publishing Co., 1904), 65.

196. McClellan, *The Life and Campaigns of Major-General J.E.B. Stuart*, 262.

197. Grimsley, *Battles in Culpeper County*, 8.

198. G. Moxley Sorrel, *Recollections of a Confederate Staff Officer* (New York: Neale Publishing Co., 1905), 129.

199. Blackford, *War Years with Jeb Stuart*, 212–13.

200. O.R., vol. 27, part 3, 872–73.

201. Captain Robert E. Lee, *Recollections and Letters of Robert E. Lee* (Garden City, NY: Garden City, 1924), 96.

202. J.E. Copeland, "The Fighting at Brandy Station," *Confederate Veteran* 30 (1922): 451.

203. John Blue, *Hanging Rock Rebel: Lt. John Blue's War in West Virginia and the Shenandoah Valley*, edited by Dan Oates (Shippensburg, PA: Burd Street Press, 1994), 198.

204. Alonzo West diary, entry for June 8, 1863, Alonzo West papers, Tom K. Savage collection, Atlanta, Georgia.

205. O'Ferrall, *Forty Years of Active Service*, 64–65.

Chapter 5

206. Heros von Borcke and Justus Scheibert, *The Great Cavalry Battle of Brandy Station*, translated by Stuart T. Wright and F.D. Bridgewater (1893; repr., Gaithersburg, MD: Olde Soldier Books, 1976), 35.

207. Edwin E. Bryant, *History of the Third Regiment of Wisconsin Veteran Volunteer Infantry 1861–1865* (Madison, WI: Published by the Veteran Association of the Regiment, 1891), 165.

208. Oakey, *Beverly Ford*, 3.

209. *New York Times*, June 11, 1863.

210. O.R., vol. 27, part 3, 27–28.

211. William F. Moyer, "Brandy Station: A Stirring Account of the Famous Cavalry Engagement," *National Tribune*, March 28, 1884.

212. Ibid.

213. Noble D. Preston, *History of the Tenth Regiment of Cavalry, New York State Volunteers, August, 1861 to August, 1865* (New York: D. Appleton & Co., 1892), 82.

214. Alfred Pleasonton to John Buford, June 8, 1863, Order Book of the Chief of Cavalry for 1863, Civil War Miscellaneous Collection, USAHEC. The only evidence of Pleasonton's intention to turn his raid into a chase of Stuart is a letter by Captain George A. Custer to his sister, written on the eve of battle, wherein he indicated that Pleasonton had instructed the men to pack three days' rations for a pursuit of the enemy. George A. Custer to Anne Reed, June 8, 1863, Lawrence Frost Collection of Custeriana, Monroe County Library System, Monroe, Michigan.

215. James H. Wilson, *The Life and Services of Brevet Brigadier-General Andrew Jonathan Alexander, United States Army* (New York: privately published, 1887), 34.

216. Grimsley, *Battles in Culpeper County*, 3.

217. Chiswell Dabney to Dear Father, June 14, 1863, quoted in Trout, *With Pen and Saber*, 213; and Eric J. Wittenberg, "John Buford and the Gettysburg Campaign," *Gettysburg: Historical Articles of Lasting Interest* 11 (July 1994): 27.

218. James S. Brisbin to Dearest Wife, June 8, 1863, Civil War Times Illustrated Collection, USAHEC.

CHAPTER 6

219. Alonzo H. Quint, *The Potomac and the Rapidan: Army Notes, from the Failure at Winchester to the Reinforcement of Rosecrans, 1861–1863* (Boston: Crosby and Nichols, 1864), 327.

220. Bryant, *History of the Third Regiment*, 165–66.

221. Oakey, *Beverly Ford*, 4.

222. Gilpin diary, entry for June 8, 1863.

223. John diary, entry for June 8, 1863.

224. Hard, *History of the Eighth Cavalry Regiment*, 242.

225. Gracey, *Annals of the Sixth Pennsylvania Cavalry*, 156–57. Evidently, not all of the Union troopers were permitted to sleep as they waited to cross at Beverly Ford. See for example Hillman A. Hall, ed., *History of the Sixth New York Cavalry (Second Ira Harris Guards), Second Brigade-First Division-Cavalry Corps, Army of the Potomac 1861–1865* (Worcester, MA: Blanchard Press, 1908), 127. ("No fires were permitted at night, the men standing 'to horse,' noiseless and alert.")

226. Oakey, *Beverly Ford*, 5.

227. Gracey, *Annals of the Sixth Pennsylvania Cavalry*, 156–57.

228. Custer to Anne Reed, June 8, 1863.

229. Frank Moore, ed., *The Rebellion Record: A Diary of American Events, With Documents, Narratives, Illustrative Incidents, Poetry, Etc.*, 11 vols. (New York: D. Van Nostrand, 1864–68), 7:16.

230. Sidney Morris Davis, *Common Soldier, Uncommon War: Life as a Cavalryman in the Civil War*, edited by Charles F. Cooney (Bethesda, MD: SMD Group, 1994), 391.

231. Frederic C. Newhall, "The Battle of Beverly Ford," in *The Annals of the War as Told by the Leading Participants* (Dayton, OH: Morningside, 1988), 138–39.

232. Hard, *History of the Eighth Cavalry Regiment*, 243.

233. John Buford to Lieutenant Colonel A.J. Alexander, June 13, 1863, Joseph Hooker Papers, Huntington Library, San Marino, California. For some reason, Buford's official report of the Battle of Brandy Station never made it into the *Official Records of the Civil War*.

234. *Rochester Daily Union & Advertiser*, June 18, 1863.

235. Robert N. Shipley to his father, included in R.L. Murray, ed., *Wayne County Troops in the Civil War* (Wolcott, NY: Benedum Books, 2003), 63.

236. Hard, *History of the Eighth Cavalry Regiment*, 243.

237. John W. Peake, "Recollections of a Boy Cavalryman," *Confederate Veteran* 34 (1926): 261.

238. Blue, *Hanging Rock Rebel*, 198.

239. Norton, *Deeds of Daring*, 65; Frederick Phisterer, *New York in the War of the Rebellion, 1861–1865*, 5 vols. (Albany, NY: Weed and Parsons, 1890), 2:895.

240. Blue, *Hanging Rock Rebel*, 198.

241. Luther W. Hopkins, *From Bull Run to Appomattox: A Boy's View* (Baltimore, MD: Press of Fleet-McGinley Co., 1908), 90–91.

242. Matthews, "The Great Cavalry Fights of the War."

243. Hopkins, *From Bull Run to Appomattox*, 89–90.

244. McDonald, *History of the Laurel Brigade*, 134; and T.J. Young, "The Battle of Brandy Station," *Confederate Veteran* 23 (April 1915): 171–72.

245. Norton, *Deeds of Daring*, 65. According to the regimental historian of the Eighth New York, the surprise in the Confederate camps was complete, and mass confusion resulted from the Confederates being caught unaware.

246. *Rochester Daily Union & Advertiser*, June 18, 1863.

247. Marcus A. Reno, "Boots and Saddles: The Cavalry of the Army of the Potomac," *National Tribune*, April 29, 1886.

248. Hopkins, *From Bull Run to Appomattox*, 90.

249. John N. Opie, *A Rebel Cavalryman with Lee, Stuart, and Jackson* (Chicago: Charles B. Conkey, 1899), 147.

250. Major James F. Hart in the *Philadelphia Weekly Times*, June 26, 1880, quoted in McClellan, *The Life and Campaigns of Major-General J.E.B. Stuart*, 266.

251. McDonald, *History of the Laurel Brigade*, 134.

252. Hard, *History of the Eighth Cavalry Regiment*, 243.

253. Hopkins, *From Bull Run to Appomattox*, 91.

254. G.N. Saussy, "Anniversary of Brandy's Battle: Fought 46 Years Ago Today," *Memphis Commercial Appeal*, June 9, 1909.

255. Christian Balder to Tattnall Paulding, June 12, 1863, Paulding Family Papers, Historical Society of Pennsylvania, Philadelphia, Pennsylvania.

256. Norton, *Deeds of Daring*, 65; McClellan, *The Life and Campaigns of Major-General J.E.B. Stuart*, 265; and Longacre, *Cavalry at Gettysburg*, 67.

257. Buford to Alexander, June 13, 1863.

258. Merritt, "Recollections of the Civil War," 286.

259. Robertson, "Reminiscences, 1861–1865."

260. Frank Robertson to My Dear Kate, June 12, 1863, quoted in Trout, *With Pen and Saber*, 208. Captain Robertson was one of Stuart's engineering officers and traveled with Stuart's headquarters. Thus, he was present when the sounds of the firing reached Stuart's ears that morning.

261. Borcke and Scheibert, *The Great Cavalry Battle of Brandy Station*, 88.

262. Quoted in Wert, *Cavalryman of the Lost Cause*, 243.

263. Justus Scheibert, *Seven Months in the Rebel States During the North American War, 1863*, translated by Joseph C. Hayes (Tuscaloosa, AL: Confederate Publishing Co., 1958), 87.

264. Chiswell Dabney, "The Battle of Brandy Station," in *Writings of Maud Carter Clement* (Chatham, VA: Pittsylvania Historical Society, 1982), 59.

265. Murray, *Wayne County Troops*, 66.

266. P.J. Kennedy to Dear Parents, June 11, 1863, *Morrison-Whiteside Journal*, June 25, 1863.

267. John diary, entry for June 9, 1863.

268. Quoted in Daniel E. Sutherland, *Seasons of War: The Ordeal of a Confederate Community, 1861–1865* (New York: Free Press, 1995), 246.

269. Buford to Alexander, June 13, 1863.

270. Gracey, *Annals of the Sixth Pennsylvania Cavalry*, 158.

271. Monie, "Cavalry Operations."

272. Hard, *History of the Eighth Cavalry Regiment*, 244.

273. Ibid., 244–45; and O.R., vol. 27, part 1, 1046–47.

274. O.R., vol. 27, part 1, 1046. The myth of Custer assuming command of Davis's brigade began with an earlier biographer and has been repeated a number of times. See for example Gregory J.W. Urwin, *Custer Victorious: The Civil War Battles of General George Armstrong Custer* (East Rutherford, NJ: Combined University Presses, 1983), 53. ("Custer took command of the [8th New York] and two other [regiments], the 8th Illinois and 3rd Indiana, leading them through the surrounding Confederates in a smart saber charge that brought them out safely.") Historian Jeffry D. Wert, who has written the most balanced biography of Custer to date, specifically refutes that myth. Wert, *Custer*, 78.

275. Frederick Whittaker, *A Complete Life of General George A. Custer* (New York: Sheldon, 1876), 147.

276. C.R. Starnes, "A Few Incidents in My Life," *Recollections and Reminiscences 1861–1865 through World War I* (Columbia: South Carolina Division United Daughters of the Confederacy, 1990), 11.

277. *Weekly Raleigh Register*, June 17, 1863. The next morning, the Confederates retook the two guns that they had lost on the Beverly Ford Road.

278. Trout, *Memoirs of the Stuart Horse Artillery Battalion*, 204–05.

279. O.R., vol. 27, part 2, 748.

280, Ibid., 49.

281. George M. Neese, *Three Years in the Confederate Horse Artillery* (New York: Neale Publishing Co., 1911), 171.

282. John J. Shoemaker, *Shoemaker's Battery, Stuart Horse Artillery, Pelham's Battalion, Army of Northern Virginia* (Memphis, TN: privately published, n.d.), 38.

283. Jennings Cropper Wise, *The Long Arm of Lee, or the History of the Artillery of the Army of Northern Virginia*, 2 vols. (Lynchburg, VA: J.P. Bell Co., Inc., 1915), 2:586.

284. Moffat, "The Battle of Brandy Station," 74. Moffat stated that Jones "gave the enemy such a stiff fight that he held them in check until the remainder of the corps could be mounted and Gen. Stuart form his line of battle." This may be a bit of an overstatement.

285. O.R., vol. 27, part 2, 748.

286. Trout, *Memoirs of the Stuart Horse Artillery Battalion*, 322.

287. O'Ferrall, *Forty Years of Active Service*, 65.

288. O.R., vol. 27, part 2, 772–73.

289. Shoemaker, *Shoemaker's Battery*, 38.

290. Clark B. Hall, "Buford at Brandy Station," *Civil War* (July–August 1990): 16.

291. Henry P. Moyer, *History of the Seventeenth Regiment, Pennsylvania Volunteer Cavalry* (Lebanon, PA: privately published, 1911), 45; and Hall, *History of the Sixth New York Cavalry*, 127.

292. Frank M. Myers, *The Comanches: A History of White's Battalion, Virginia Cavalry* (Baltimore, MD: Kelly, Piet & Co., 1871), 181.

293. O.R., vol. 27, part 2, 749.

294. Dennis E. Frye, *12th Virginia Cavalry*, 2nd ed. (Lynchburg, VA: H.E. Howard, 1988), 36.

295. Myers, *The Comanches*, 182; and Frye, *12th Virginia Cavalry*, 36. Lieutenant Colonel Elijah Veirs White commanded the Thirty-fifth, a veteran raiding unit. The Comanches had not seen much classic cavalry combat, and they were largely untested in a stand-up fight. As Jones had no other available reserve, he threw in the Thirty-fifth, and it performed well.

296. O'Ferrall, *Forty Years of Active Service*, 65–66.

297. "The Georgia Cavalry in the Brandy Station Fight," *Savannah Republican*, June 26, 1863.

298. O.R., vol. 27, part 2, 721.

299. William G. Delony to Dear Rosa, June 10, 1863, William G. Delony Papers, Special Collections, Hargrett Library, University of Georgia, Athens, Georgia.

300. Davis, *Common Soldier, Uncommon War*, 391–92.

301. O.R., vol. 27, part 3, 38.

CHAPTER 7

302. Gracey, *Annals of the Sixth Pennsylvania Cavalry*, 159.

303. Alfred R. Waud, "The Cavalry Fight Near Culpeper," *Harper's Weekly*, July 10, 1863.

304. The cavalry charge was trained in three types: in-line, in-column and as foragers. It was most important to keep the horses straight and toward the objective. The charge consisted of the commands: "Forward, Guides right (or left), March!" After twenty paces, the command was "Trot March!" and after another sixty paces, "Gallop March!" After another eighty paces, the final command was "CHARGE!" The area of ground to be covered by the charge should be as short as possible so as to arrive in good order and without fatiguing the horses. J.R. Poinsett, *Cavalry Tactics, Second Part, School of the Trooper, of the Platoon and of the Squadron Mounted* (Washington, D.C.: J. and G.S. Gideon Printers, 1841), 173.

305. Gracey, *Annals of the Sixth Pennsylvania Cavalry*, 159.

306. Richard L.T. Beale, *History of the Ninth Virginia Cavalry in the War Between the States* (Richmond, VA: B.F. Johnson Publishing Co., 1899), 85.

307. Longacre, *Cavalry at Gettysburg*, 73.

308. Buford to Alexander, June 13, 1863.

309. Quoted in Sutherland, *Seasons of War*, 248.

310. Trout, *Memoirs of the Stuart Horse Artillery Battalion*, 206.

311. Waud, "The Cavalry Fight Near Culpeper."

312. Henry C. Whelan to Charles C. Cadwalader, June 11, 1863, Cadwalader Family Collection, Historical Society of Pennsylvania, Philadelphia.

313. John A. Dahlgren, *Memoir of Ulric Dahlgren* (Philadelphia: J.B. Lippincott, 1872), 148.

314. Ibid., 149.

315. Alfred Pleasonton to Joseph Hooker, June 9, 1863, Hooker Papers.

316. For additional information on the critical role played by Ulric Dahlgren in the Gettysburg Campaign, see Eric J. Wittenberg, "Ulric Dahlgren in the Gettysburg Campaign," *Gettysburg Magazine: Historical Articles of Lasting Interest* 22 (December 1999): 96–111.

317. Fairfax Downey, *Clash of Cavalry: The Battle of Brandy Station* (New York: David McKay Co., 1959), 103.

318. Wise, *The Long Arm of Lee*, 2:587.

319. Bradshaw, *Diary of Charles McVicar*, 11.

320. Gracey, *Annals of the Sixth Pennsylvania Cavalry*, 160. Major Robert Morris Jr., commanding officer of the Sixth Pennsylvania, was captured during the charge. Morris, great-grandson of the financier of the American Revolution, died a prisoner of war in Richmond's notorious Libby Prison, another casualty of this most fratricidal of wars.

321. William H. Carter, *From Yorktown to Santiago with the Sixth U.S. Cavalry* (1900; repr.; Austin, TX: State House Press, 1989), 84. One squadron of the Sixth U.S. remained on the other side of the Rappahannock in support of the Union guns positioned there.

322. Louis H. Carpenter to his father, June 11, 1863, Louis Henry Carpenter Letters from the Field, 1861–1865, Historical Society of Pennsylvania, Philadelphia, Pennsylvania.

323. Neese, *Three Years in the Confederate Horse Artillery*, 172.

324. Charles McVicar memoirs, Manuscripts Division, Library of Congress, Washington, D.C.

325. Hall, "Buford at Brandy Station," 16.

326. George Baylor, *Bull Run to Bull Run; or, Four Years in the Army of Northern Virginia* (Richmond, VA: B.F. Johnson Publishing Company, 1900), 143.

327. Carpenter to his father, June 11, 1863.

328. George C. Cram to Sir, June 10, 1863, Hooker Papers.

329. Thomas C. Devin to Lieutenant Colonel A.J. Alexander, June __, 1863, Hooker Papers.

330. Lieutenant Samuel S. Elder to Captain James M. Robertson, June 20, 1863, Henry Jackson Hunt Papers, Manuscripts Collection, Library of Congress, Washington, D.C.

331. O.R., vol. 27, part 2, 772–73.

332. Abner Hard to Editor Beacon, June 11, 1863, *Aurora Beacon,* June 18, 1863.

333. O.R., vol. 27, part 2, 768.

334. Monie, "Cavalry Operations."

335. "The Georgia Cavalry in the Brandy Station Fight," *Savannah Republican,* June 26, 1863.

336. Jack Welsh, *Medical Histories of the Confederate Generals* (Kent, OH: Kent State University Press, 1995), 14.

337. "The Georgia Cavalry in the Brandy Station Fight."

338. Robertson to My Dear Kate, June 12, 1863, quoted in Trout, *With Pen and Saber,* 209; and Devin to Cohen, June __, 1863.

CHAPTER 8

339. Thomas T. Hoskins to his father, June 10, 1863, BSF.

340. McClellan, *The Life and Campaigns of Major-General J.E.B. Stuart,* 267.

341. Buford to Alexander, June 13, 1863; Captain James E. Harrison to Sir, June 16, 1863, James Harrison Papers, United States Military Academy Special Collections, West Point, New York, Reference No. 173. Those casualties included two officers wounded (one severely), four killed, three mortally wounded, fifteen wounded and another fifteen missing. Price, *Across the Continent,* 654.

342. O.R., vol. 27, part 1, 903.

343. Jasper Cheney diary, entry for June 9, 1863, Civil War Miscellaneous Collection, USAHEC.

344. Buford to Alexander, June 13, 1863.

345. Charles H. Weygant, *History of the One Hundred and Twenty-Fourth Regiment, N.Y.S.V.* (Newburgh, NY: Journal Printing House, 1877), 145.

346. Ibid., 148–51.

347. Ibid.

348. Adin B. Underwood, *The Three Years' Service of the Thirty-Third Mass. Infantry Regiment 1862–1865* (Boston: A. Williams & Co., 1881), 107.

349. Bryant, *History of the Third Regiment,* 169.

350. Julian Wisner Hinkley, *A Narrative of Service with the Third Wisconsin Infantry* (Madison: Wisconsin History Commission, 1912), 80.

351. Oakey, *Beverly Ford,* 8.

352. Bryant, *History of the Third Regiment,* 169–70.

353. Underwood, *The Three Years' Service,* 107–08.

354. Scheibert, *Seven Months in the Rebel States,* 88.

355. Gilpin diary, entry for June 9, 1863.

356. Newhall, "The Battle of Beverly's Ford," 141.

357. Underwood, *The Three Years' Service,* 108.

Chapter 9

358. Charles W. Ford, "Charge of the First Maine Cavalry at Brandy Station," *War Papers Read Before the Commandery of the State of Maine, Military Order of the Loyal Legion of the United States* 2 (Portland, ME: Lefavor-Tower Co., 1902), 276–78.

359. William P. Lloyd, *History of the First Reg't Pennsylvania Reserve Cavalry, from Its Organization, August 1861, to September, 1864, with List of Names of All Officers and Enlisted Men* (Philadelphia: King & Baird, 1864), 53.

360. Ford, "Charge of the First Maine Cavalry," 273–74.

361. William Child, *A History of the Fifth Regiment New Hampshire Volunteers in the American Civil War, 1861–1865* (Bristol, NH: R.W. Musgrove, 1893), 200–01.

362. Ibid., 201–02.

363. *New York Times,* June 16, 1863.

364. Edward G. Longacre, *Jersey Cavaliers: A History of the First New Jersey Volunteer Cavalry, 1861–1865* (Hightstown, NJ: Longstreet House, 1992), 141–42.

365. *New York Times,* June 14, 1863.

366. Edward P. Tobie, *Service of the Cavalry in the Army of the Potomac* (Providence, RI: N.B. Williams, 1882), 18.

367. Samuel H. Merrill, *The Campaigns of the First Maine and First District of Columbia Cavalry* (Portland, ME: Bailey & Noyes, 1866), 106.

368. O.R., vol. 27, part 2, 734–35.

369. Ibid., 734–36.

370. Ibid., 733.

371. Ibid., 734.

372. Ibid., 736.

373. Alonzo West to his parents, June 12, 1863, Alonzo West papers, Tom K. Savage collection, Atlanta, Georgia.

374. O.R., vol. 27, part 2, 680.

375. Ibid., 735. For a detailed examination of Beverly Robertson's role in the Battle of Brandy Station, see Patrick A. Bowmaster, "Beverly H. Robertson and the Battle of Brandy Station," *Blue & Gray* 14 (Fall 1996).

376. Tobie, *Service of the Cavalry,* 18.

377. Joseph W. McKinney, *Brandy Station, Virginia, June 9, 1863: The Largest Cavalry Battle of the Civil War* (Jefferson, NC: McFarland, 2006), 139.

378. O.R., vol. 27, part 1, 950.

379. Lloyd, *History of the First Reg't,* 53.

380. *New York Times,* June 14, 1863.

381. Burton B. Porter, *One of the People: His Own Story* (N.p.: privately published, 1907), 140.

382. Myers, *The Comanches,* 183.

Chapter 10

383. McClellan, *The Life and Campaigns of Major-General J.E.B. Stuart,* 270.

384. Wise, *The Long Arm of Lee,* 2:589.

385. McClellan, *The Life and Campaigns of Major-General J.E.B. Stuart*, 270.

386. Ibid., 271.

387. "The North Carolina Cavalry: Its First Fight—War Records—Curious Reports—A Great Cavalry Battle—Virginia and North Carolina Exultant," *News and Observer*, May 11, 1883.

388. Baylor, *From Bull Run to Bull Run*, 143.

389. O'Ferrall, *Forty Years of Active Service*, 66.

390. Summers, *A Borderland Confederate*, 72.

391. Saussy, "Anniversary of Brandy's Battle."

392. Robert J. Trout, ed., *In the Saddle With Stuart: The Story of Frank Smith Robertson of Jeb Stuart's Staff* (Gettysburg, PA: Thomas Publications, 1998), 67; and Trout, *Memoirs of the Stuart Horse Artillery Battalion*, 324.

393. Harriett Bey Mesic, *Cobb's Legion Cavalry: A History and Roster of the Ninth Georgia Volunteers in the Civil War* (Jefferson, NC: McFarland, 2008), 64.

394. Scheibert, *Seven Months in the Rebel States*, 89.

395. O.R., vol. 27, part 1, 1054.

396. Henry R. Pyne, *The History of the First New Jersey Cavalry* (Trenton, NJ: J.A. Beecher, 1871), 118.

397. Matthews, "The Great Cavalry Battles of the War."

398. O.R., vol. 27, part 1, 1053.

399. Quoted in Rod Andrew Jr., *Wade Hampton: Confederate Warrior to Southern Redeemer* (Chapel Hill: University of North Carolina Press, 2008), 148.

400. McClellan, *The Life and Campaigns of Major-General J.E.B. Stuart*, 271.

401. Theodore S. Garnett, *J.E.B. Stuart (Major General) Commander of the Cavalry Corps, Army of Northern Virginia, C.S.A.: An Address Delivered at the Unveiling of the Equestrian Statue of General Stuart, at Richmond, Virginia, May 30, 1907* (New York: The Neale Publishing Co., 1907), 35.

402. Blackford, *War Years with Jeb Stuart*, 215.

403. James Moore, MD, *Kilpatrick and Our Cavalry* (New York: W.J. Widdleton, 1865), 58.

404. Borcke, *Memoirs*, 406–07.

405. McClellan, *The Life and Campaigns of Major-General J.E.B. Stuart*, 277.

406. Trout, *Memoirs of the Stuart Horse Artillery Battalion*, 207.

407. Quoted in Longacre, *Lee's Cavalrymen*, 194.

408. Frye, *12th Virginia Cavalry*, 38.

409. Quoted in Sutherland, *Seasons of War*, 250.

410. Frye, *12th Virginia Cavalry*, 39.

411. O.R., vol. 27, part 2, 769.

412. Pyne, *The History of the First New Jersey Cavalry*, 149.

413. Frye, *12th Virginia Cavalry*, 39.

414. Longacre, *Jersey Cavaliers*, 144–45.

415. Robert H. Moore, *The 1st and 2nd Stuart Horse Artillery* (Lynchburg, VA: H.E. Howard Co., 1985), 64–65.

416. Wise, *The Long Arm of Lee*, 2:591.

417. Howard, *Sketch of Cobb Legion Cavalry*, 7.

418. James F. Hart, in the *Philadelphia Weekly Times*, June 26, 1880.

419. Thomas L. Cox to John S. Brodrick, June 11, 1863, Virgil Brodrick Papers, Blair Graybill collection, Charlottesville, Virginia. Brodrick was laid to rest in the National Cemetery in Culpeper.

420. Pyne, *The History of the First New Jersey Cavalry*, 121.

421. O.R., vol. 27, part 1, 1055.

422. Pyne, *The History of the First New Jersey Cavalry*, 121.

423. *Philadelphia Inquirer*, March 23, 1864; and Dr. C.E. Godfrey, *Sketch of Major Henry Washington Sawyer, First Regiment, Cavalry, New Jersey Volunteers: A Union Soldier and Prisoner of War in Libby Prison Under Sentence of Death* (Trenton, NJ: MacCrellish & Quigley, 1907), 4.

424. Pyne, *The History of the First New Jersey Cavalry*, 122.

425. Lloyd, *History of the First Reg't*, 55.

426. Ibid., 55–56.

427. Hampton S. Thomas, *Some Personal Reminiscences of Service in the Cavalry of the Army of the Potomac* (Philadelphia: L.R. Hamersly & Co., 1889), 9.

428. Lucas to his wife, June 14, 1863.

429. David M. Gregg, "The Union Cavalry at Gettysburg," in *The Annals of the War, Written by Leading Participants North and South* (Philadelphia: Times Publishing Co., 1879), 7.

430. "The North Carolina Cavalry."

431. Wiley C. Howard, *Sketch of Cobb Legion Cavalry and Some Scenes and Incidents Remembered* (Atlanta: Atlanta Camp 159, SCV, 1901), 6.

432. Dabney, "The Battle of Brandy Station," 60.

433. McKinney, *Brandy Station*, 164.

434. Peake, "Recollections of a Boy Cavalryman," 261.

435. Lloyd, *History of the First Reg't*, 54.

436. West to his parents, June 12, 1863.

437. Matthews, "The Great Cavalry Fights of the War."

438. *Supplement to the Official Records of the Union and Confederate Armies*, 100 vols. (Wilmington, NC: Broadfoot, 1995), vol. 5, 250 (hereafter referred to as "O.R. Supp.").

439. Ibid., 250–51.

440. Scheibert, *Seven Months in the Rebel States*, 90–91.

441. Henry C. Meyer, *Civil War Experiences Under Bayard, Gregg, Kilpatrick, Custer, Raulston, and Newberry, 1862, 1863, 1864* (New York: Knickerbocker Press, 1911), 28.

442. *New York Times*, June 14, 1863.

443. Myers, *The Comanches*, 185.

444. Saussy, "Anniversary of Brandy's Battle."

445. Myers, *The Comanches*, 185.

446. O.R., vol. 27, part 1, 1025.

447. Thomas, *Some Personal Reminiscences of Service in the Cavalry*, 10.

448. *New York Times*, June 14, 1863.

449. Bradshaw, *Diary of Charles McVicar*, 12.

450. George M. Neese to Roger P. Chew, October 22, 1900, Roger Preston Chew Papers, Jefferson County Museum, Charles Town, West Virginia.

451. Opie, *A Rebel Cavalryman*, 153.

452. Burton, *One of the People*, 140.

453. Preston, *History of the 10th Regiment of Cavalry*, 85.

454. Ibid.

455. Ibid., 86–87.

456. Monie, "Cavalry Operations."

457. Grimsley, *Battles in Culpeper County*, 11.

458. Cooke, *Wearing of the Gray*, 219.

459. Delony to Dear Rosa, June 10, 1863.

460. Ibid.

461. "The Georgia Cavalry in the Brandy Station Fight."

462. O.R., vol. 27, part 2, 732.

463. Howard, *Sketch of the Cobb Legion Cavalry*, 8.

464. Ibid.

465. "The Beau Sabreur Of Georgia," *Southern Historical Society Papers* 25 (1897): 149.

466. McClellan, *The Life and Campaigns of Major-General J.E.B. Stuart*, 277.

467. Moyer, "Brandy Station."

468. O.R., vol. 27, part 1, 997; and M.K. Adams, ed., *Salt Horse and Sabers: Whitaker's War—Bull Run to Appomattox, 4 Years—82 Battles* (Privately published, 2003), 76.

469. Adams, *Salt Horse and Sabers*, 76.

470. Ibid.

471. Eleanor D. McSwain, ed., *Crumbling Defenses; Or Memoirs and Reminiscences of John Logan Black, C.S.A.* (Macon, GA: privately published, 1960), 133.

472. Edward P. Tobie, *History of the First Maine Cavalry 1861–1865* (Boston: Press of Emory & Hughes, 1887), 154.

473. Gary W. Gallagher, "Brandy Station: The Civil War's Bloodiest Arena of Mounted Combat," *Blue & Gray* 9 (October 1990): 46.

474. Delony to Dear Rosa, June 10, 1863.

475. O.R., vol. 27, part 2, 755.

476. Ford, "Charge of the First Maine," 278.

477. Tobie, *First Maine Cavalry*, 148–49.

478. Moore, *Kilpatrick and Our Cavalry*, 59; and Willard Glazier, *Three Years in the Federal Cavalry* (New York: R.H. Ferguson & Co., 1873), 220.

479. *New York Times*, June 14, 1863.

480. Ford, "The Charge of the First Maine Cavalry," 279.

481. Thomas, *Some Personal Reminiscences of Service in the Cavalry*, 11.

482. Ford, "The Charge of the First Maine Cavalry," 283.

483. Tobie, *First Maine Cavalry*, 150–52.

484. George H. Chase, "A Scrap of History," *National Tribune*, September 2, 1882.

485. Monie, "Cavalry Operations."

486. Grimsley, *Battles in Culpeper County*, 11.

487. O.R., vol. 27, part 2, 722.

488. Scheibert, *Seven Months in the Rebel States*, 92.

489. O.R., vol. 27, part 1, 1027.

490. Moffatt, "The Battle of Brandy Station," 75.

491. Thomas, *Some Personal Recollections of Service in the Cavalry*, 11.

492. Moffatt, "The Battle of Brandy Station," 75.

493. Matthews, "The Great Cavalry Battles of the War."

494. O.R., vol. 27, part 2, 763.

495. Ron Matteson, ed., *Civil War Campaigns of the 10th New York Cavalry With One Soldier's Personal Correspondence* (Morrisville, NC: Lulu.com, 2007), 120.

496. McClellan, *The Life and Campaigns of Major-General J.E.B. Stuart*, 279.

497. Handwritten note by Gregg, David M. Gregg Papers, Manuscripts Division, Library of Congress, Washington, D.C.

498. O.R., vol. 27, part 1, 951.

CHAPTER 11

499. John diary, entry for June 9, 1863.

500. Hard, *History of the Eighth Cavalry Regiment*, 244.

501. Thomas T. Hoskins to his father, June 10, 1863, Hoskins Family Papers, Virginia Historical Society, Richmond, Virginia.

502. McClellan, *The Life and Campaigns of Major-General J.E.B. Stuart*, 282.

503. Bryant, *History of the Third Regiment*, 171.

504. Oakey, *Beverly Ford*, 10.

505. Ibid., 11.

506. Bryant, *History of the Third Regiment*, 171.

507. Whelan to Cadwalader, June 11, 1863.

508. Beale, *A Lieutenant of Cavalry in Lee's Army*, 96.

509. Henry McQuiston memoirs, McQuiston Papers, Special Collections, U.S. Military Academy, West Point, New York.

510. Cram to Sir, June 10, 1863.

511. Balder to Paulding, June 12, 1863.

512. McQuiston memoir.

513. Ibid.

514. Ibid.

515. Davis, *Common Soldier, Uncommon War*, 395. Ward was originally listed as being a prisoner of war and not as dead or mortally wounded. The next day, Stuart gave notice that an officer of the Sixth U.S. Cavalry had been killed in action at Brandy Station, and word came from Libby Prison that Ward had never been held there as a prisoner of war. During the winter encampment of the Army of the Potomac in January 1864, a local farmer recognized the insignia of the Sixth U.S. and informed the men that he had helped to bury an officer after the Battle of Brandy Station near Pleasonton's winter headquarters on the Greene farm. The farmer led officers of the regiment to the spot, and the body was disinterred and sent home to Ward's family for burial. William Harding Carter, *The Life of Lieutenant General Chaffee* (Chicago: University of Chicago Press, 1917), 28–29.

516. Balder to Paulding, June 12, 1863.

517. Carpenter to his father, June 11, 1863.

518. George C. Cram to Carpenter, June 11, 1863, Carpenter letters.

519. McQuiston memoir.

520. Ibid.

521. Merritt, "Recollections of the Civil War," 287.

522. Lieutenant Albert O. Vincent to Lieutenant J. Hamilton Bell, June 16, 1863, Hunt Papers.

523. Buford to Alexander, June 13, 1863.

524. Merritt, "Recollections of the Civil War," 287–88.

525. Ibid., 288, 328.

526. Ibid., 288.

527. Major Charles J. Whiting to Captain Theodore C. Bacon, June 12, 1863, Hooker Papers.

528. Merritt, "Recollections of the Civil War," 289.

529. Ibid.

530. Beale, *History of the Ninth Virginia Cavalry*, 69.

531. McKinney, *Brandy Station*, 189.

532. William L. Royall, *Some Reminiscences* (New York: The Neale Publishing Company, 1909), 13–14.

533. Beale, *A Lieutenant of Cavalry in Lee's Army*, 96.

534. *Richmond Daily Dispatch*, June 15, 1863.

535. Robert K. Krick, *Lee's Colonels*, 2nd ed. (Dayton, OH: Morningside House, 1992), 400.

536. W.A. Graham, "From Brandy Station to The Heights of Gettysburg," *News & Observer*, February 7, 1904.

537. O.R., vol. 27, part 2, 684.

538. Graham, "From Brandy Station to The Heights of Gettysburg."

539. James McClure Scott, "War Record," edited by Sarah Travers Lewis Scott Anderson, Archives, Virginia Historical Society, Richmond, Virginia.

540. Ibid.; and Merritt, "Recollections of the Civil War," 288.

541. Merritt, "Recollections of the Civil War," 289.

542. Robert Driver Jr., *10th Virginia Cavalry* (Lynchburg, VA: H.E. Howard, 1992), 37. Two days after the great battle, Robert E. Lee reported on his son's condition in a letter to his wife, Mary. "I saw him the night after the battle. Indeed met him on the field as they were bringing him from the front," recounted General Lee. "At night he appeared comfortable & cheerful. Neither the bone or artery of the leg I am informed is injured. He is young & healthy & I trust will soon be up again. He seemed to be more concerned about his brave men & officers who had fallen in battle than himself." Robert E. Lee, *The Wartime Papers of R.E. Lee*, edited by Clifford Dowdey and Louis H. Manarin, 2 vols. (Boston: Little, Brown, & Co., 1961), 2:511. Rooney Lee was taken to Williams Wickham's home in Hanover County to recuperate. Northern cavalrymen found out that he was there and captured him. Lee spent the next six months as a prisoner of war before he was exchanged.

543. Buford to Alexander, June 13, 1863.

544. Vincent to Bell, June 16, 1863.

545. Beale, *History of the Ninth Virginia Cavalry*, 68.

546. Beale, *A Lieutenant of Cavalry in Lee's Army*, 223.

547. The first orders, written at seven o'clock that morning by one of Fitz Lee's staff officers, were that Munford should "pack up your train, and keep everything ready to move; **_to bring your command a little farther in this direction_**, and keep up communication with him, and to look out for your picket line" (emphasis added). A second order, received a few minutes later, indicated, "General Stuart wishes all of Colonel Munford's regiments but one brought this way, leaving a guard for the baggage, which can be sent toward Culpeper." O.R., vol. 27, part 2, 737. Given the conflicting and unclear orders, Munford's confusion is no surprise.

548. Swank, *Sabres, Saddles and Spurs,* 66.

549. Catherine M. Wright, ed., *Lee's Last Casualty: The Life and Letters of Sgt. Robert W. Parker, Second Virginia Cavalry* (Knoxville: University of Tennessee Press, 2008), 106.

550. O.R., vol. 27, part 2, 737–38.

551. Wigfall to his sister, June 14, 1863, Wigfall Papers.

552. Quoted in Mary Bandy Daughtry, *Gray Cavalier: The Life and Wars of General W.H.F. "Rooney" Lee* (New York: DaCapo Press, 2002), 136.

553. Wright, *Lee's Last Casualty,* 106.

554. McQuiston memoir.

555. Ibid.

556. Thomas L. Rosser, *Addresses of Gen'l T.L. Rosser at the Seventh Annual Reunion of the Association of the Maryland Line* (New York: L.A. Williams Printing Co., 1889), 37.

CHAPTER 12

557. O.R., vol. 27, part 3, 41–42.

558. Worthington C. Ford, ed., *A Cycle of Adams Letters, 1861–1865,* 2 vols. (Boston: Houghton-Mifflin, 1920), 2:31.

559. O.R., vol. 27, part 1, 961.

560. Ibid.

561. William Brooke-Rawle to his mother, June 12, 1863, William Brooke-Rawle Papers, Special Collections, Spahr Library, Dickinson College, Carlisle, Pennsylvania.

562. James C. Mohr and Richard E. Winslow III, eds., *The Cormany Diaries: A Northern Family in the Civil War* (Pittsburgh: University of Pittsburgh Press, 1982), 316.

563. *Western Reserve Chronicle,* June 15, 1863.

564. Mohr and Winslow, *The Cormany Diaries,* 316.

565. Brooke-Rawle to his mother, June 12, 1863.

566. *New York Times,* June 16, 1863.

567. Williams to My Dear Anna, June 11, 1863.

568. McClellan, *The Life and Campaigns of Major-General J.E.B. Stuart,* 284.

569. Warner, *Generals in Gray,* 40–41. For a good treatment of Butler's life and career that places him in his proper historic context, see Samuel J. Martin, *Southern Hero: Matthew Calbraith Butler—Confederate General, Hampton Red Shirt, and U.S. Senator* (Mechanicsburg, PA: Stackpole Books, 2001).

570. McClellan, *The Life and Campaigns of Major-General J.E.B. Stuart,* 285.

571. McKinney, *Brandy Station,* 141.

572. U.R. Brooks, ed., *Butler and His Cavalry in the War of Secession, 1861–1865* (Columbia, SC: The State Co., 1909), 152.

573. McClellan, *The Life and Campaigns of Major General J.E.B. Stuart*, 286.

574. Sarah Butler Wister, *Walter S. Newhall: A Memoir* (Philadelphia: The Sanitary Commission, 1864), 104.

575. Williams to My Dear Anna, June 11, 1863.

576. Matthew C. Butler to O.G. Thompson, August 17, 1907, in *Butler and His Cavalry in the War of Secession, 1861–1865*, edited by U.R. Brooks (Columbia, SC: The State Co., 1909), 152.

577. Warner, *Generals in Gray*, 335.

578. Butler to Thompson, *Butler and His Cavalry*, 152–53.

579. Crowninshield, *History of the First Regiment*, 129.

580. Robert W. Frost and Nancy D. Frost, eds., *Picket Pins and Sabers* (Privately published, 1971), 48–49.

581. McClellan, *The Life and Campaigns of Major-General J.E.B. Stuart*, 287.

582. O.R., vol. 27, part 1, 961.

583. Crowninshield, *History of the First Regiment*, 133.

584. Butler to Thompson, *Butler and His Cavalry*, 153.

585. Rod Andrew Jr., *Wade Hampton: Confederate Warrior to Southern Redeemer* (Chapel Hill: University of North Carolina Press, 2008), 151.

586. Brooks, *Butler and His Cavalry*, 169.

587. *Western Reserve Chronicle*, June 15, 1863.

588. Lewis Marshall Helm, *Black Horse Cavalry: Defend Our Beloved Country* (Falls Church, VA: Higher Education Publications, 2004), 163.

589. Alexander Hunter, *Johnny Reb and Billy Yank* (New York: Neale Publishing Co., 1905), 357.

590. Kenneth L. Stiles, *4th Virginia Cavalry* (Lynchburg, VA: H.E. Howard, Co., 1985), 28.

591. Brooke-Rawle to his mother, June 12, 1863.

592. Brooks, *Butler and His Cavalry*, 153.

593. Stiles, *Fourth Virginia Cavalry*, 29.

594. O.R., vol. 27, part 1, 961.

595. McKinney, *Brandy Station*, 145.

596. Butler to Thompson, *Butler and His Cavalry*, 153.

597. O.R., vol. 27, part 2, 744–45.

598. Robert J. Trout, *They Followed the Plume: The Story of J.E.B. Stuart and His Staff* (Mechanicsburg, PA: Stackpole Books, 1993), 106–12.

599. Frank S. Robertson, *Reminiscences of the Years 1861–1865* (Abingdon: Historical Society of Washington County, Virginia, 1986), 20.

600. G.N. Saussy, "Anniversary of Brandy's Battle: Fought 46 Years Ago Today," *Memphis Commercial Appeal*, June 9, 1909; and Brooks, *Butler and His Cavalry*, 154.

601. Brooks, *Butler and His Cavalry*, 154.

602. O.R., vol. 28, part 1, 348.

603. J.M. Monie, "War Recollection: Cavalry Operations Relating to the Campaign of Gettysburg, Brand Station or Fleetwood, and Stevensburg," *News and Observer*, August 29, 1894.

604. James G. Holmes, "The Fighting Qualities of Generals Hampton, Butler, and Others Related by Adjutant-General Holmes of Charleston," *Sunny South*, June 13, 1896.

605. Brooks, *Butler and His Cavalry*, 154.

606. "A Savannah Boy in the Cavalry Fight at Brandy Station—A Perilous Scout," *Savannah Daily News*, June 20, 1863.

607. Trout, *They Followed the Plume*, 112–13. Farley became delirious just before he died. His final words were "To your post, men! To your post!" He died a few moments later. Stuart lamented the scout's passing almost as much as he mourned the loss of Major John Pelham at the Battle of Kelly's Ford three months earlier. Farley was buried in Fairview Cemetery in Culpeper, where his body remained until 2005. In 2005, he was disinterred and taken home for burial in the family plot in Laurens, South Carolina.

608. Martin, *Southern Hero*, 9–10.

609. Bruce S. Allardice, *Confederate Colonels: A Biographical Register* (Columbia: University of Missouri Press, 2008): 241–42. In fact, Lipscomb was promoted to lieutenant colonel to replace the fallen Frank Hampton the next day, June 10, 1863. Then, when Butler was promoted to brigadier general in September 1863, Lipscomb was promoted to colonel of the Second South Carolina, a rank he held for the rest of the war. After the war, he was a cotton merchant in Newberry, South Carolina, for a time. He moved to Columbia in 1878 to become head of the state penitentiary for South Carolina and was later elected mayor of Columbia. He died on November 4, 1908, and was buried in Rosemont Cemetery in Newberry.

610. Brooks, *Butler and His Cavalry*, 160.

611. O.R., vol. 27, part 1, 962.

612. Reverend Fredric Denison, *Sabres and Spurs: The First Rhode Island Cavalry in the Civil War, 1861–1865* (Providence: The First Rhode Island Cavalry Veteran Assoc., 1876), 230.

613. Brooks, *Butler and His Cavalry*, 156.

614. Dr. T.M. Braskillien, "Chapters of Unwritten History: A Sharp Cavalry Clash: The Personal Recollections of a South Carolina Trooper at Brandy Station: Butler at Stevensburg," *Philadelphia Weekly Times*, March 24, 1883.

615. Butler was taken to the home of a woman named Fitzhugh, where the shattered leg was amputated below the knee. He then began the long road to recovery, returning to duty in the fall of 1863. When Wade Hampton was promoted to major general and command of a division in the fall of 1863, Butler was promoted to brigadier general and given the task of organizing and training a brigade of South Carolina mounted infantry that performed admirably during the campaigns of 1864.

616. Brooks, *Butler and His Cavalry*, 171.

617. Wister, *Walter S. Newhall*, 104.

618. O.R., vol. 27, part 1, 975.

619. Brooke-Rawle to his mother, June 12, 1863.

620. William Brooke-Rawle, *History of the Third Pennsylvania Cavalry, Sixtieth Regiment Pennsylvania Volunteers, in the American Civil War 1861–1865* (Philadelphia: Franklin Printing Co., 1905), 247.

621. O.R., vol. 27, part 1, 962.

622. Frost and Frost, *Picket Pins and Sabers*, 49.

623. William E. Doster, *Lincoln and Episodes of the Civil War* (New York: G.P. Putnam's Sons, 1915), 208.

624. William Hyndman, *History of a Cavalry Company: A Complete Record of Company "A," 4th Pennsylvania Cavalry* (repr.; Hightstown, NJ: Longstreet House, 1997), 59.

625. Mosby, *Stuart's Cavalry*, 12.

626. Williams to My Dear Anna, June 11, 1863.

627. Crowninshield, *History of the First Regiment*, 128.

628. Ford, *A Cycle of Adams Letters*, 32.

629. Mohr and Winslow, *The Cormany Diaries*, 316.

630. Crowninshield, *History of the First Regiment*, 142.

CHAPTER 13

631. Hopkins, *From Bull Run to Appomattox*, 92.

632. O.R., vol. 27, part 3, 876.

633. Louis Leon, *Diary of a Tar Heel Confederate Soldier* (Charlotte, NC: Stone Publishing Co., 1913), 29–30.

634. Borcke and Scheibert, *The Great Cavalry Battle at Brandy Station*, 98.

635. Newhall, "The Battle of Beverly Ford," 143.

636. Buford to Alexander, June 13, 1863.

637. Quint, *The Potomac and the Rapidan*, 328.

638. John diary, entry for June 9, 1863. The wounds to Smith and Clark were mortal; Forsyth recovered from his leg wound and returned to duty. He served in the Regular Army until 1890 and attained fame as an Indian fighter.

639. Newhall, "The Battle of Beverly Ford," 144.

640. Underwood, *The Three Years' Service*, 109.

641. Newhall, "The Battle of Beverly Ford," 144.

642. O.R., vol. 27, part 1, 1045.

643. *New York Times*, June 14, 1863.

644. Blackford, *War Years with Jeb Stuart*, 217; and John R. Porter diary, entry for June 9, 1863, Perkins Library, Duke University, Durham, North Carolina.

645. Bradshaw, *Diary of Charles McVicar*, 13.

646. Pleasonton to Hooker, June 9, 1863, Hooker Papers.

647. Norton, *Deeds of Daring*, 67.

648. O.R., vol. 27, part 1, 903–04.

649. Joseph I. Lambert, *One Hundred Years with the Second Cavalry* (Topeka, KS: Press of the Caper Print Co., 1939), 70.

650. *New York Herald*, June 11, 1863.

651. H.A. Bull, "Brandy Station: Where the 8th N.Y. Cav. Had Its Full Share of Fighting," *National Tribune*, January 20, 1887.

652. Buford to Alexander, June 13, 1863.

653. Grimsley, *Battles in Culpeper County*, 12.

654. Moffatt, "The Battle of Brandy Station," 75.

655. O.R., vol. 27, part 2, 682.

656. Ibid., part 1, 951.

657. Ibid., part 2, 683–84.

658. Ibid., 687.

CHAPTER 14

659. Blackford, *War Years with Jeb Stuart*, 215.

660. Rosser, *Addresses*, 38.

661. Bradshaw, *Diary of Charles McVicar*, 12.

662. John Gibbon to My Dearest Mama, June 11, 1863, Gibbon Papers.

663. Adams, *Salt Horse and Sabers*, 78.

664. William Penn Lloyd, Memoranda from May 13, 1863, to May 31, 1863, entry for June 9, 1863, William Penn Lloyd Papers, Southern Historical Collection, Wilson Library, University of North Carolina, Chapel Hill.

665. McClellan, *The Life and Campaigns of Major-General J.E.B. Stuart*, 234.

666. Merritt, "Recollections of the Civil War," 291.

667. Opie, *A Rebel Cavalryman*, 157.

668. *Morrison-Whiteside Journal*, June 25, 1863.

669. Glazier, *Three Years in the Federal Cavalry*, 223.

670. Preston, *History of the 10ᵗʰ Regiment of Cavalry*, 85.

671. Tobie, *History of the First Maine Cavalry*, 155.

672. Charles Gardner, *Three Years in the Cavalry: The Civil War Remembrances of Charles Gardner* (Tucson, AZ: A Plus Printing, 1998), 45.

673. O.R., vol. 27, part 3, 58.

674. Glazier, *Three Years in the Federal Cavalry*, 223–24.

675. O.R., vol. 27, part 3, 45–46.

676. Ibid., 64.

677. Ibid.; John B. McIntosh to his wife, May 13, 1863, John B. McIntosh letters, Special Collections, Brown University, Providence, Rhode Island.

678. Ford, *A Cycle of Adams Letters*, 2:22.

679. Alfred Pleasonton to John F. Farnsworth, June 23, 1863, Alfred Pleasonton Papers, Manuscripts Division, Library of Congress, Washington, D.C.

680. George Bliss, *The First Rhode Island Cavalry at Middleburg* (Providence, RI: privately published, 1889), 48.

681. For a detailed examination, see Robert F. O'Neill Jr., *The Cavalry Battles of Aldie, Middleburg and Upperville, Small but Important Riots, June 10–27, 1863* (Lynchburg, VA: H.E. Howard Co., 1993), 66–76.

682. John S. Mosby, *Stuart's Cavalry in the Gettysburg Campaign* (New York: Moffatt, Yard & Co., 1908), 71.

683. Abraham Lincoln to Edwin M. Stanton, June 22, 1863, Pearce Civil War Collection, Archives, Navarro College, Corsicana, Texas.

684. O.R., vol. 37, part 2, 896–97.

685. *New York Times*, October 7, 1864.

686. O.R., vol. 43, part 2, 475.

687. In 1869, President Ulysses S. Grant appointed Duffié U.S. consul to Spain and sent him to Cadiz, on the Iberian Peninsula's southwest seacoast. While he served in Spain, the Frenchman contracted tuberculosis, which claimed his life in 1880. Because of his conviction for desertion, Duffié never was able to return to his native France. His body was brought home and buried in his wife's family plot in Fountain Cemetery in Staten Island, New York. Unfortunately, the cemetery was abandoned long ago, and the grave is badly overgrown with vegetation. It is nearly impossible to find and is as forgotten to history as the proud soldier who rests there. The veterans of the First Rhode Island Cavalry, who remained loyal to their former commander, raised money to erect a handsome monument to Duffié in the North Burying Ground in Providence. Captain George Bliss, who commanded a squadron in the First Rhode Island, wrote a lengthy and eloquent tribute to Duffié that was published and distributed to the veterans of the regiment. See Bliss, "Duffié and the Monument to His Memory."

688. John C. Oeffinger, ed., *A Soldier's General: The Civil War Letters of Major General Lafayette McLaws* (Chapel Hill: University of North Carolina Press, 2002), 189.

689. In fact, an infantryman of the Eighty-sixth New York Infantry of the Third Corps, part of Ames's select brigade of infantry, claimed, "I found General Lee's General Orders to his army. From them we learned that Hooker had been outwitted, that he was hopelessly in the rear, while Lee, unopposed, was marching northward. In the orders Lee enjoined perfect discipline, declaring that depredators would be severely punished." However, this account was written forty-one years after Brandy Station and cannot be corroborated. It supports Pleasonton's fictions and may have been based on his unsupported claims. Samuel G. Inram, "Beverly Ford: The Third Corps Helps the Cavalry Surprise Jeb Stuart and Give Him a Rough House," *National Tribune*, April 28, 1904.

690. Ford, *A Cycle of Adams Letters*, 2:32.

691. Norton, *Deeds of Daring*, 66. Interestingly, another member of the same regiment said something similar. "It was talked by our boys that the Union cavalry would do the reviewing instead of Gen. Stuart." C.J. Phillips, "Stuart's Cavalry: And How It Was 'Reviewed' by the Union Troopers at Brandy Station," *National Tribune*, March 10, 1887.

692. Wise, *The Long Arm of Lee*, 2:594.

693. Neese, *Three Years in the Confederate Horse Artillery*, 179.

694. O.R., vol. 27, part 2, 683–84.

695. Matthews, "The Great Cavalry Battles of the War."

696. Theophilus F. Rodenbough, "Cavalry War Lessons," *Journal of the United States Cavalry Association* 11, no. 5 (1889): 107.

697. *Richmond Sentinel*, June 12, 1863; and *Richmond Examiner*, June 12, 1863. Some historians have speculated that the harsh criticism of Stuart was an impetus to his absence from the Army of Northern Virginia during the first two days of the Battle of Gettysburg and that Stuart had gone on a joy ride around the Army of the Potomac in an effort to restore the luster to his tarnished reputation after the Battle of Brandy Station. For an interesting examination of this controversy, see Eric J. Wittenberg and

J. David Petruzzi, *Plenty of Blame to Go Around: Jeb Stuart's Controversial Ride to Gettysburg* (El Dorado Hills, CA: Savas-Beatie, 2006).

698. Mitchell, *The Letters of Major General James E.B. Stuart*, 323–24.

699. Borcke and Scheibert, *The Great Cavalry Battle at Brandy Station*, 102.

700. "The North Carolina Cavalry."

701. Quoted in Wert, *Cavalryman of the Lost Cause*, 247.

702. Rufus H. Peck, *Reminiscences of a Confederate Soldier of Co. C, 2ⁿᵈ Va. Cavalry* (Fincastle, VA: privately published, 1913), 31. ("We were near enough to hear the firing but not near enough to engage in it. [Pleasonton] did not attempt to cross where we were, so we just stood guard all day.")

703. Susan Leigh Blackford, comp., *Letters from Lee's Army: Memoirs of Life In and Out of the Army in Virginia During the War Between the States* (New York: Charles Scribner's Sons, 1947), 175.

704. Garnett, *Major-General J.E.B. Stuart*, 34–35.

705. Trout, *Memoirs of the Stuart Horse Artillery Battalion*, 50.

706. Sutherland, *Seasons of War*, 256–57.

707. John B. Jones, *A Rebel War Clerk's Diary at the Confederate States Capital*, 2 vols. (Philadelphia: J.B. Lippincott & Co., 1866).

708. O.R., vol. 27, part 2, 722.

709. Wade Hampton to Henry B. McClellan, January 14, 1878, H.B. McClellan Papers, Archives, Virginia Historical Society.

710. O.R., vol. 27, part 2, 750.

711. William G. Delony to Dear Rosa, June 12, 1863, Delony Papers.

712. Wade Hampton to Beverly H. Robertson, November 17, 1877. Published in the December 26, 1878 edition of the *Memphis Weekly Appeal*.

713. O.R., vol. 27, part 3, 881.

714. Hopkins, *From Bull Run to Appomattox*, 91.

715. Delony to Dear Rose, June 12, 1863.

Epilogue

716. Godfrey, *Sketch of Major Henry Washington Sawyer*, 4.

717. Ibid., 4–5.

718. O.R., series 2, vol. 5, 702.

719. Godfrey, *Sketch of Major Henry Washington Sawyer*, 5.

720. Ibid., 6.

721. *Richmond Whig*, July 7, 1863.

722. *Richmond Dispatch*, July 7, 1863.

723. Godfrey, *Sketch of Major Henry Washington Sawyer*, 8.

724. *Philadelphia Inquirer*, March 23, 1864.

725. Neal Dow, *The Reminiscences of Neal Dow: Recollections of Eighty Years* (Portland, ME: The Evening Express Publishing Co., 1898), 731.

726. O.R., series 2, vol. 6, 107.

727. Ibid., 109.

728. Ibid., 118.

729. Daughtry, *Gray Cavalier*, 141–45.

730. *Richmond Daily Dispatch*, June 27, 1863; and *New York Times*, June 29, 1863.

731. O.R., series 2, vol. 6, 1127.

732. Dow, *The Reminiscences of Neal Dow*, 730.

733. Godfrey, *Sketch of Major Henry Washington Sawyer*, 9.

734. *Philadelphia Inquirer*, March 23, 1864.

735. O.R., series 2, vol. 6, 707.

736. Ibid., 927. Major General Ethan A. Hitchcock, who replaced Ludlum, wrote on February 8, 1864, "It has been intimated from Richmond that if we will consent to exchange General Lee and two officers of the grade of captain the rebel authorities will give us General Dow and Captains Sawyer and Flinn. If you can obtain the assent of the rebel authorities to this exchange, making sure that we shall receive Captains Sawyer and Flinn, the exchange can be made, and General Lee will be sent to you for the purpose."

737. Godfrey, *Sketch of Major Henry Washington Sawyer*, 10; and O.R., series 2, vol. 6, 219. (Ludlum wrote on August 20, 1863, "I am satisfied, as I have been from the first, that Sawyer and Flinn will not be executed. This was settled by the prompt and significant selections of Lee and [Tyler].")

738. See, generally, Daughtry, *Gray Cavalier*, 277–303.

739. *Philadelphia Inquirer*, March 23, 1864.

740. John Y. Foster, *New Jersey and the Rebellion: A History of the Services of the Troops and People of New Jersey in Aid of the Union Cause* (Newark, NJ: Martin R. Dennis & Co., 1868), 871; and Godfrey, *Sketch of Major Henry Washington Sawyer*, 10–11.

BIBLIOGRAPHY

NEWSPAPERS

Aurora Beacon
Baltimore American
Boston Daily Globe
Charleston Mercury
Daily Morning News [Savannah, Georgia]
Memphis Commercial Appeal
Memphis Weekly Appeal
Morrison-Whiteside Journal
National Tribune
News & Observer [Raleigh, North Carolina]
New York Herald
New York Times
Philadelphia Inquirer
Philadelphia Press
Philadelphia Weekly Times
Pittsburgh Evening Chronicle
Richmond Daily Dispatch
Richmond Examiner

Richmond Sentinel
Rochester Daily Union and Advertiser
Savannah Republican
St. Mary's Beacon Sunny South
Vermont Chronicle
Washington Star
Weekly Raleigh Register
Western Reserve Chronicle

BIBLIOGRAPHY

MANUSCRIPT COLLECTIONS

Manuscripts Collection, Brandy Station Foundation, Brandy Station, Virginia:
  Thomas Hoskins letter of June 10, 1863
  Thomas Marshall letter of June 4, 1863
Special Collections, Brown University Library, Providence, Rhode Island:
  John B. McIntosh Letters
Archives, Charleston Library Society, Charleston, South Carolina:
  Edward Laight Wells Correspondence
Archives, College of Physicians, Philadelphia, Pennsylvania:
  Silas Weir Mitchell Papers
Special Collections, Spahr Library, Dickinson College, Carlisle, Pennsylvania:
  William Brooke-Rawle Papers
Special Collections, Perkins Library, Duke University, Durham, North Carolina:
  Munford-Ellis Family Papers
  John R. Porter diary
Archives, Fredericksburg Spotsylvania National Military Park, Fredericksburg, Virginia:
  Emmons Guild Letter of March 20, 1863
French Army Archives, Vincennes, France:
  Napoleon Alexandre Duffié Service Records
Special Collections, Hargrett Library, University of Georgia, Athens, Georgia:
  William G. Delony letters
Blair Graybill Collection, Charlottesville, Virginia:
  Virgil Brodrick Papers
Archives, Historical Society of Pennsylvania, Philadelphia, Pennsylvania:
  Cadwalader Family Collection
  Louis Henry Carpenter Letters from the Field, 1861–1865
  John Gibbon Papers:
    Henry Hazeltine notes
  Newhall Family Papers
  Tatnall Paulding Papers
Archives, Huntington Library, San Marino, California:
  Joseph Hooker Papers
Special Collections, Jefferson County Museum, Charles Town, West Virginia:
  Roger Preston Chew Papers
Manuscripts Division, Library of Congress, Washington, D.C.:
  Gilpin Family Papers
  Samuel J.B.V. Gilpin Diary
  David M. Gregg Papers
  Henry Jackson Hunt Papers
  Charles McVicar Memoirs

Alfred Pleasonton Papers

Louis T. Wigfall Papers

Monroe County Public Library System, Monroe, Michigan:

Lawrence A. Frost Collection of Custeriana

National Archives and Records Administration, Washington, D.C.:

RG 94, Letters Received, Telegrams, Reports, and Lists Received by Cavalry Corps, 1861–1865

RG 94, Letters Received by the Confederate Adjutant General and Inspector General, 1861–1865

Archives, Navarro College, Corsicana, Texas:

Pearce Civil War Collection

Tom K. Savage Collection, Atlanta, Georgia:

Alonzo West diary for 1863

Archives, Staten Island Historical Society, Staten Island, New York:

Pelton-Duffie Family Papers

Diaries and Letters, Friends Historical Library, Swarthmore College, Swarthmore, Pennsylvania:

Kimber L. John diary for 1863

Southern Historical Collections, Wilson Library, University of North Carolina, Chapel Hill, North Carolina:

William Penn Lloyd Papers

Peck Family Papers

Special Collections, United States Military Academy Library, West Point, New York:

George A. Custer Papers

James E. Harrison Papers

Henry McQuiston Papers

Archives, United States Army History and Education Center, Carlisle, Pennsylvania:

Civil War Miscellaneous Collection

Order Book for the Chief of Cavalry for the Year 1863

Jasper Cheney Diary

Civil War Times Illustrated Collection

James S. Brisbin Letters

Archives, Virginia Historical Society, Richmond, Virginia:

Hoskins Family Papers

Henry B. McClellan Papers

Francis Smith Robertson, "Reminiscences, 1861–1865"

James McClure Scott, "War Record"

Archives, Western Reserve Historical Society, Cleveland, Ohio:

Albinus Fell Papers

BIBLIOGRAPHY

PUBLISHED PRIMARY SOURCES

Articles

"The Beau Sabreur Of Georgia." *Southern Historical Society Papers* 25 (1897): 149.

Beck, Elias W., MD. "Letters of a Civil War Surgeon." *Indiana Magazine of History* (June 1931): 132–63.

Bliss, George N. "Duffié and the Monument to His Memory." *Personal Narratives of Events in the War of the Rebellion, Being Papers Read Before the Rhode Island Soldiers and Sailors Historical Society* VI. Providence, RI: Published by the Society, 1890.

Braskillien, Dr. T.M. "Chapters of Unwritten History: A Sharp Cavalry Clash: The Personal Recollections of a South Carolina Trooper at Brandy Station: Butler at Stevensburg." *Philadelphia Weekly Times*, March 24, 1883.

Bull, H.A. "Brandy Station: Where the 8th N.Y. Cav. Had Its Full Share of Fighting." *National Tribune*, January 20, 1887.

Chase, George H. "A Scrap of History." *National Tribune*, September 2, 1882.

Colley, Thomas E. "Brig. Gen. William E. Jones." *Confederate Veteran* 11 (1903): 266–67.

Cooke, Jacob B. "The Battle of Kelly's Ford, March 17, 1863." *Personal Narratives of Events in the War of the Rebellion, Being Papers Read Before the Rhode Island Soldiers and Sailors Historical Society* IV. Providence, RI: Published by the Society, 1887.

Cooke, John Esten. "General Stuart in Camp and Field." In *Annals of the War, Written by Leading Participants, North and South*. Philadelphia: Times Publishing Co., 1879.

Copeland, J.E. "The Fighting at Brandy Station." *Confederate Veteran* 30 (1922): 451.

Dabney, Chiswell. "The Battle of Brandy Station." *Writings of Maud Carter Clement*. Chatham, VA: Pittsylvania Historical Society, 1982.

Fitz Simmons, Charles. "Hunter's Raid." *Military Essays and Recollections, Papers Read Before the Commandery of the State of Illinois Military Order of the Loyal Legion of the United States* 4. Chicago, 1907.

Ford, Charles W. "Charge of the First Maine Cavalry at Brandy Station." *War Papers Read Before the Commandery of the State of Maine, Military Order of the Loyal Legion of the United States* 2. Portland, ME: LeFavor-Tower Co., 1902.

Graham, W.A. "From Brandy Station to the Heights of Gettysburg." *News & Observer*, February 7, 1904.

Gregg, David M. "The Union Cavalry at Gettysburg." In *The Annals of the War, Written by Leading Participants North and South*. Philadelphia: Times Publishing Co., 1879.

Holmes, James G. "The Fighting Qualities of Generals Hampton, Butler, and Others Related by Adjutant-General Holmes of Charleston." *Sunny South*, June 13, 1896.

Inram, Samuel G. "Beverly Ford: The Third Corps Helps the Cavalry Surprise Jeb Stuart and Give Him a Rough House." *National Tribune*, April 28, 1904.

Matthews, Henry H. "The Great Cavalry Fights of the War, Fleetwood Hill or Brandy Plains, June 9, 1863." *St. Mary's Beacon*, March 9, 1905.

McClellan, Henry B. "The Campaign of 1863—A Reply to Kilpatrick." *Philadelphia Weekly Times*, February 7, 1880.

Merritt, Wesley. "Personal Recollections—Beverly's Ford to Mitchell's Station, 1863." In *From Everglade to Canon with the Second Dragoons*, edited by Theophilus F. Rodenbough. New York: D. Van Nostrand, 1875.

Moffat, George H. "The Battle of Brandy Station." *Confederate Veteran* 14 (February 1906): 74.

Monie, J.M. "War Recollection: Cavalry Operations Relating to the Campaign of Gettysburg, Brandy Station or Fleetwood, and Stevensburg." *News and Observer*, August 29, 1894.

Moyer, William F. "Brandy Station: A Stirring Account of the Famous Cavalry Engagement." *National Tribune*, March 28, 1884.

Munford, Thomas T. "Reminiscences of Cavalry Operations." *Southern Historical Society Papers* 12 (1884): 32–350 and 13 (1885): 133–45.

Newhall, Frederic C. "The Battle of Beverly Ford." In *The Annals of the War as Told by the Leading Participants*. Philadelphia: Times Publishing Co., 1879.

News and Observer. "The North Carolina Cavalry: Its First Fight—War Records—Curious Reports—A Great Cavalry Battle—Virginia ad North Carolina Exultant." May 11, 1883.

Peake, John W. "Recollections of a Boy Cavalryman." *Confederate Veteran* 34 (1926): 260–62.

Phillips, C.J. "Stuart's Cavalry: And How It Was 'Reviewed' by the Union Troopers at Brandy Station." *National Tribune*, March 10, 1887.

Reno, Marcus A. "Boots and Saddles: The Cavalry of the Army of the Potomac." *National Tribune*, April 29, 1886.

Rodenbough, Theophilus F. "Cavalry War Lessons." *Journal of the United States Cavalry Association* 11, no. 5 (1889).

Saussy, G.N. "Anniversary of Brandy's Battle: Fought 46 Years Ago Today." *Memphis Commercial Appeal*, June 9, 1909.

Savannah Daily News. "A Savannah Boy in the Cavalry Fight at Brandy Station—A Perilous Scout." June 20, 1863.

Savannah Republican. "The Georgia Cavalry in the Brandy Station Fight." June 26, 1863.

Shaw, W.P. "Fifty-ninth Regiment (Fourth Cavalry)." In *Histories of the Several Regiments and Battalions from North Carolina in the Great War 1861–'65*, 5 vols., edited by Walter Clark. Goldsboro, NC: Nash Brothers, 1901.

Starnes, C.R. "A Few Incidents in My Life." *Recollections and Reminiscences 1861–1865 through World War I*. Columbia: South Carolina Division United Daughters of the Confederacy, 1990.

Waud, Alfred R. "The Cavalry Fight Near Culpeper." *Harper's Weekly*, July 10, 1863.

Wyndham, Percy. "The Wyndham Question Settled." *New York Herald*, September 16, 1863.

Young, T.J. "The Battle of Brandy Station." *Confederate Veteran* 23 (April, 1915): 171–72.

Books

Adams, M.K., ed. *Salt Horse and Sabers: Whitaker's War-Bull Run to Appomattox, 4 Years—82 Battles*. Privately published, 2003.

Alexander, Peter Wellington. *Writing & Fighting the Confederate War: The Letters of Peter Wellington Alexander, Confederate War Correspondent*. Edited by William B. Styple. Kearny, NJ: Belle Grove Publishing Co., 2002.

Avary, Myrta Lockett. *A Virginia Girl in the Civil War*. New York: D. Appleton & Co., 1903.

Baylor, George. *Bull Run to Bull Run; or, Four Years in the Army of Northern Virginia*. Richmond, VA: B.F. Johnson Publishing Company, 1900.

Beach, William H. *The First New York (Lincoln) Cavalry from April 19, 1861, to July 7, 1865*. New York: Lincoln Cavalry Association, 1902.

Beale, Richard L.T. *History of the Ninth Virginia Cavalry in the War Between the States*. Richmond, VA: B.F. Johnson Publishing Co., 1899.

Blackford, William W. *War Years With Jeb Stuart*. New York: Charles Scribner's Sons, 1945.

Bliss, George. *The First Rhode Island Cavalry at Middleburg*. Providence, RI: privately published, 1889.

Blue, John. *Hanging Rock Rebel: Lt. John Blue's War in West Virginia and the Shenandoah Valley*. Edited by Dan Oates. Shippensburg, PA: Burd Street Press, 1994.

Borcke, Heros von. *Memoirs of the Confederate War for Independence*. Philadelphia: J.B. Lippincott, 1867.

Borcke, Heros von, and Justus Scheibert. *The Great Cavalry Battle of Brandy Station*. Translated by Stuart T. Wright and F.D. Bridgewater. 1893. Reprint, Gaithersburg, MD: Olde Soldier Books, 1976.

Botts, John Minor. *The Great Rebellion: The Political Life of the Author Vindicated*. New York: Harper & Bros., 1866.

Bradshaw, Ada Bruce D., ed. *Civil War Diary of Charles William McVicar*. Washington, D.C.: privately published, 1977.

Brooke-Rawle, William. *History of the Third Pennsylvania Cavalry, Sixtieth Regiment Pennsylvania Volunteers, in the American Civil War 1861–1865*. Philadelphia: Franklin Printing Co., 1905.

Brooks, U.R., ed. *Butler and His Cavalry in the War of Secession, 1861–1865*. Columbia, SC: The State Co., 1909.

Bryant, Edwin E. *History of the Third Regiment of Wisconsin Veteran Volunteer Infantry 1861–1865*. Madison, WI: Published by the Veteran Assoc. of the Reg't., 1891.

Cheney, Newel. *History of the Ninth Regiment, New York Volunteer Cavalry. War of 1861 to 1865. Compiled from Letters, Diaries, Recollections and Official Records*. Poland Center, NY: Martin Merz & Sons, 1901.

Child, William. *A History of the Fifth Regiment New Hampshire Volunteers, in the American Civil War, 1861–1865*. Bristol, NH: R.W. Musgrove, 1893.

Cooke, John Esten. *Wearing of the Gray, Being Personal Portraits, Scenes & Adventures of the War*. New York: E.B. Treat & Co., 1867.

Crowninshield, Benjamin W. *A History of the First Regiment Massachusetts Cavalry Volunteers*. Boston: Houghton-Mifflin Co., 1891.

Dahlgren, John A. *Memoir of Ulric Dahlgren*. Philadelphia: J.B. Lippincott, 1872.

"David McMurtrie Gregg." Circular No. 6, Series of 1917, Military Order of the Loyal Legion of the United States, Commandery of Pennsylvania, May 3, 1917.

Davis, Sidney Morris. *Common Soldier, Uncommon War: Life as a Cavalryman in the Civil War*. Edited by Charles F. Cooney. Bethesda, MD: SMD Group, 1994.

Denison, Rev. Frederic. *Sabres and Spurs: The First Rhode Island Cavalry in the Civil War, 1861–1865*. Providence: The First Rhode Island Cavalry Veteran Assoc., 1876.

Doster, William E. *Lincoln and Episodes of the Civil War*. New York: G.P. Putnam's Sons, 1915.

Dow, Neal. *The Reminiscences of Neal Dow: Recollections of Eighty Years*. Portland, ME: The Evening Express Publishing Co., 1898.

Emerson, Edward W., ed. *Life and Letters of Charles Russell Lowell*. Port Washington, NY: Kennikat Press, 1971.

Ford, Worthington C., ed. *A Cycle of Adams Letters, 1861–1865*. 2 vols. Boston: Houghton-Mifflin, 1920.

Frost, Robert W., and Nancy D. Frost, eds. *Picket Pins and Sabers*. N.p.: privately published, 1971.

Gardner, Charles. *Three Years in the Cavalry: The Civil War Remembrances of Charles Gardner*. Tucson, AZ: A Plus Printing, 1998.

Garnett, Theodore S. *J.E.B. Stuart (Major General) Commander of the Cavalry Corps, Army of Northern Virginia, C.S.A.: An Address Delivered at the Unveiling of the Equestrian Statue of General Stuart, at Richmond, Virginia, May 30, 1907*. New York: The Neale Publishing Co., 1907.

Glazier, Willard. *Three Years in the Federal Cavalry*. New York: R.H. Ferguson & Co., 1873.

Godfrey, Dr. C.E. *Sketch of Major Henry Washington Sawyer, First Regiment, Cavalry, New Jersey Volunteers: A Union Soldier and Prisoner of War in Libby Prison Under Sentence of Death*. Trenton, NJ: MacCrellish & Quigley, 1907.

Gracey, Samuel L. *Annals of the Sixth Pennsylvania Cavalry*. Philadelphia: E.H. Butler & Co., 1868.

Grimsley, Daniel A. *Battles in Culpeper County, Virginia, 1861–1865*. Culpeper, VA: Raleigh Travers Green, 1900.

Hall, Hillman A., ed. *History of the Sixth New York Cavalry (Second Ira Harris Guards), Second Brigade-First Division-Cavalry Corps, Army of the Potomac 1861–1865*. Worcester, MA: Blanchard Press, 1908.

Hard, Abner N. *History of the Eighth Cavalry Regiment Illinois Volunteers*. Aurora, IL: privately published, 1868.

Hinkley, Julian Wisner. *A Narrative of Service with the Third Wisconsin Infantry*. Madison: Wisconsin History Commission, 1912.

Hopkins, Luther W. *From Bull Run to Appomattox: A Boy's View*. Baltimore, MD: Press of Fleet-McGinley Co., 1908.

Howard, Wiley C. *Sketch of Cobb Legion Cavalry and Some Scenes and Incidents Remembered.* Atlanta: Atlanta Camp 159, S.C.V., 1901.

Hubard, Robert T., Jr. *The Civil War Memoirs of a Virginia Cavalryman.* Edited by Thomas P. Nanzig. Tuscaloosa: University of Alabama Press, 2007.

Hunter, Alexander. *Johnny Reb and Billy Yank.* New York: Neale Publishing Co., 1905.

Hyndman, William. *History of a Cavalry Company: A Complete Record of Company "A," 4th Pennsylvania Cavalry.* Reprint, Hightstown, NJ: Longstreet House, 1997.

Jones, John B. *A Rebel War Clerk's Diary at the Confederate States Capital.* 2 vols. Philadelphia: J.B. Lippincott & Co., 1866.

Kidd, James H. *Personal Recollections of a Cavalryman in Custer's Michigan Brigade.* Ionia, MI: Sentinel Publishing Co., 1908.

Lee, Captain Robert E. *Recollections and Letters of Robert E. Lee.* Garden City, NY: Garden City, 1924.

Lee, Robert E. *The Wartime Papers of R.E. Lee.* 2 vols. Edited by Clifford Dowdey and Louis H. Manarin. Boston: Little, Brown, & Co., 1961.

Lee, Susan P. *Memoirs of William Nelson Pendleton, D.D.* Philadelphia: J.B. Lippincott, 1893.

Leon, Louis. *Diary of a Tar Heel Confederate Soldier.* Charlotte, NC: Stone Publishing Co., 1913.

Lloyd, William P. *History of the First Reg't Pennsylvania Reserve Cavalry, from Its Organization, August 1861, to September, 1864, with List of Names of All Officers and Enlisted Men.* Philadelphia: King & Baird, 1864.

Maury, Dabney Herndon. *Recollections of a Virginian in the Mexican, Indian, and Civil Wars.* New York: Charles Scribner's Sons, 1894.

McClellan, Henry B. *The Life and Campaigns of Major General J.E.B. Stuart.* Boston: Houghton-Mifflin, 1895.

McDonald, William N. *A History of the Laurel Brigade.* Baltimore, MD: Sun Job Printing Office, 1907.

McSwain, Eleanor D., ed. *Crumbling Defenses; Or Memoirs and Reminiscences of John Logan Black, C.S.A.* Macon, GA: privately published, 1960.

Merington, Margeurite, ed. *The Custer Story: The Life and Letters of General George A. Custer and His Wife Elizabeth.* New York: The Devin-Adair Co., 1950.

Merrill, Samuel H. *The Campaigns of the First Maine and First District of Columbia Cavalry.* Portland, ME: Bailey & Noyes, 1866.

Meyer, Henry C. *Civil War Experiences Under Bayard, Gregg, Kilpatrick, Custer, Raulston, and Newberry, 1862, 1863, 1864.* New York: Knickerbocker Press, 1911.

Mitchell, Adele H., ed. *The Letters of Major General James E.B. Stuart.* Richmond, VA: Stuart-Mosby Historical Society, 1990.

Mohr, James C., and Richard E. Winslow III, eds. *The Cormany Diaries: A Northern Family in the Civil War.* Pittsburgh: University of Pittsburgh Press, 1982.

Moore, Frank, ed. *The Rebellion Record: A Diary of American Events, With Documents, Narratives, Illustrative Incidents, Poetry, Etc.* 11 vols. New York: D. Van Nostrand, 1864–68.

Moore, James, MD. *Kilpatrick and Our Cavalry*. New York: W.J. Widdleton, 1865.

Mosby, John Singleton. *Stuart's Cavalry in the Gettysburg Campaign*. New York: Moffatt, Yard & Co., 1908.

Moyer, Henry P. *History of the Seventeenth Regiment, Pennsylvania Volunteer Cavalry*. Lebanon, PA: privately published, 1911.

Murray, R.L., ed. *Wayne County Troops in the Civil War*. Wolcott, NY: Benedum Books, 2003.

Myers, Frank M. *The Comanches: A History of White's Battalion, Virginia Cavalry*. Baltimore, MD: Kelly, Piet & Co., 1871.

Neese, George M. *Three Years in the Confederate Horse Artillery*. New York: Neale Publishing Co., 1911.

Ness, George T., Jr. *The Regular Army on the Eve of The Civil War*. Baltimore MD: Toomey Press, 1990.

Newhall, Frederic C. *With General Sheridan in Lee's Last Campaign*. Philadelphia: J.B. Lippincott, 1866.

Norton, Henry. *Deeds of Daring: or History of the Eighth New York Volunteer Cavalry*. Norwich, NY: Chenango Telegraph Printing House, 1889.

Oakey, Daniel. *History of the Second Massachusetts Regiment of Infantry: Beverly Ford. A Paper Read at the Officers' Reunion in Boston, May 12, 1884*. Boston: Geo. H. Ellis, 1884.

Oeffinger, John C., ed. *A Soldier's General: The Civil War Letters of Major General Lafayette McLaws*. Chapel Hill: University of North Carolina Press, 2002.

O'Ferrall, Charles T. *Forty Years of Active Service*. New York: The Neale Publishing Co., 1904.

Opie, John N. *A Rebel Cavalryman with Lee, Stuart, and Jackson*. Chicago: Charles B. Conkey, 1899.

Peck, Rufus H. *Reminiscences of a Confederate Soldier of Co. C, 2nd Va. Cavalry*. Fincastle, VA: privately published, 1913.

Perry, Bliss, ed. *Life and Letters of Henry Lee Higginson*. Boston: The Atlantic Monthly Press, 1921.

Poinsett, J.R. *Cavalry Tactics, Second Part, School of the Trooper, of the Platoon and of the Squadron Mounted*. Washington, D.C.: J. and G.S. Gideon Printers, 1841.

Porter, Burton B. *One of the People: His Own Story*. N.p.: privately published, 1907.

Preston, Noble D. *History of the Tenth Regiment of Cavalry, New York State Volunteers, August, 1861 to August, 1865*. New York: D. Appleton & Co., 1892.

Pyne, Henry R. *The History of First New Jersey Cavalry*. Trenton, NJ: J.A. Beecher, 1871.

Quint, Alonzo H. *The Potomac and the Rapidan: Army Notes, from the Failure at Winchester to the Reinforcement of Rosecrans, 1861–1863*. Boston: Crosby and Nichols, 1864.

———. *The Record of the Second Massachusetts Infantry, 1861–65*. Boston: James P. Walker, 1867.

Rodenbough, Theophilus F., ed. *From Everglade to Canon with the Second Dragoons*. New York: D. Van Nostrand, 1875.

Rosser, Thomas L. *Addresses of Gen'l T.L. Rosser at the Seventh Annual Reunion of the Association of the Maryland Line*. New York: L.A. Williams Printing Co., 1889.

Royall, William L. *Some Reminiscences*. New York: The Neale Publishing Company, 1909.

Schiebert, Justus. *Seven Months in Rebel States During the North American War, 1863*. Translated by Joseph C. Hayes. Tuscaloosa, AL: Confederate Publishing Co., 1958.

Shoemaker, John J. *Shoemaker's Battery, Stuart Horse Artillery, Pelham's Battalion, Army of Northern Virginia*. Memphis, TN: privately published, n.d.

Studenraus, P.J., ed. *Mr. Lincoln's Washington: Selections from the Writings of Noah Brooks, Civil War Correspondent*. South Brunswick, NJ: Thomas Yoseloff, 1976.

Summers, Festus P., ed. *A Borderland Confederate*. Pittsburgh: University of Pittsburgh Press, 1962.

Supplement to the Official Records of the Union and Confederate Armies. 100 vols. Wilmington, NC: Broadfoot, 1995.

Swank, Walbrook D., ed. *Sabres, Saddles, and Spurs*. Shippensburg, PA: Burd Street Press, 1998.

Taylor, Gray N., ed. *Saddle and Saber: The Letters of Civil War Cavalryman Corporal Nelson Taylor*. Bowie, MD: Heritage Books, 1993.

Taylor, James E. *The James E. Taylor Sketchbook*. Dayton, OH: Morningside, 1989.

Thomas, Hampton S. *Some Personal Reminiscences of Service in the Cavalry of the Army of the Potomac*. Philadelphia: L.R. Hamersly & Co., 1889.

Tobie, Edward P. *History of the First Maine Cavalry 1861–1865*. Boston: Press of Emory & Hughes, 1887.

———. *Service of the Cavalry in the Army of the Potomac*. Providence: N.B. Williams, 1882.

Tremain, Henry Edwin. *The Last Hours of Sheridan's Cavalry*. New York: Bonnell, Silver & Bowers, 1904.

Trout, Robert J., ed. *In the Saddle With Stuart: The Story of Frank Smith Robertson of Jeb Stuart's Staff*. Gettysburg, PA: Thomas Publications, 1998.

———. *Memoirs of the Stuart Horse Artillery Battalion: Moorman's and Hart's Batteries*. Knoxville: University of Tennessee Press, 2008.

———. *With Pen and Saber: The Letters and Diaries of J.E.B. Stuart's Staff Officers*. Mechanicsburg, PA: Stackpole Books, 1995.

Underwood, Adin B. *The Three Years Service of the Thirty-Third Mass. Infantry Regiment, 1862–1865*. Boston: A. Williams, 1881.

The War of the Rebellion: A Compilation of the Official Records of the Union and Confederate Armies. 128 vols., 3 series. Washington, D.C.: United States Government Printing Office, 1889.

Weygant, Charles H. *History of the One Hundred and Twenty-Fourth Regiment, N.Y.S.V.* Newburgh, NY: Journal Printing House, 1877.

Wister, Sarah Butler. *Walter S. Newhall: A Memoir*. Philadelphia: The Sanitary Commission, 1864.

Wright, Catherine M., ed. *Lee's Last Casualty: The Life and Letters of Sgt. Robert W. Parker, Second Virginia Cavalry*. Knoxville: University of Tennessee Press, 2008.

SECONDARY SOURCES

Articles

Bowmaster, Patrick A. "An Examination of Gen. Robertson in the Great Cavalry Battle." *Blue & Gray* 15 (Fall 1996): 22–33.

Brennan, Patrick. "Thunder on the Plains of Brandy." Part 1. *North & South* 5 (April 2002): 14–34.

———. "Thunder on the Plains of Brandy." Part 2, *North & South* 5 (June 2002): 32–51.

Gallagher, Gary W. "Brandy Station: The Civil War's Bloodiest Arena of Mounted Combat." *Blue & Gray* 9 (October 1990): 8–22, 44–53.

Hall, Clark B. "Auburn: Culpeper's Architectural and Historical Gem." *Culpeper Star Exponent*, May 1, 2008.

———. "The Battle of Brandy Station." *Civil War Times Illustrated* 29 (May/June 1990): 32–45.

———. "Long and Desperate Encounter: Buford at Brandy Station." *Civil War* (July/August, 1990): 12–17, 66–67.

———. "Robert F. Beckham: The Man Who Commanded Stuart's Horse Artillery After Pelham Fell." *Blue & Gray* 10 (December 1991): 34–37.

Longacre, Edward G. "Judson Kilpatrick." *Civil War Times Illustrated* 10 (April 1971): 25.

———. "Sir Percy Wyndham." *Civil War Times Illustrated* 8 (December 1968): 12, 14.

Wittenberg, Eric J. "'A Charge of Conspicuous Gallantry'": The 6th Pennsylvania Cavalry at Brandy Station, June 9, 1863." *Gettysburg Magazine: Historical Articles of Lasting Interest* 41 (July 2009): 7–32.

———. "John Buford and the Gettysburg Campaign." *Gettysburg Magazine: Historical Articles of Lasting Interest* 11 (July 1994).

———. "Ulric Dahlgren in the Gettysburg Campaign." *Gettysburg Magazine: Historical Articles of Lasting Interest* 22 (December 1999): 96–111.

Books

Alberts, Don E. *Brandy Station to Manila Bay: A Biography of General Wesley Merritt*. Austin, TX: Presidial Press, 1980.

Allardice, Bruce S. *Confederate Colonels: A Biographical Register*. Columbia: University of Missouri Press, 2008.

———. *More Generals in Gray*. Baton Rouge: Louisiana State University Press, 1995.

Andrew, Rod, Jr. *Wade Hampton: Confederate Warrior to Southern Redeemer*. Chapel Hill: University of North Carolina Press, 2008.

Arnold, James R. *Jeff Davis's Own: Cavalry, Comanches, and the Battle for the Texas Frontier*. New York: John Wiley & Sons, 2000.

BIBLIOGRAPHY

Balfour, Daniel T. *13th Virginia Cavalry*. Lynchburg, VA: H.E. Howard Co., 1986.

Bates, Samuel P. *Martial Deeds of Pennsylvania*. Philadelphia: T.H. Davis, 1876.

Beattie, Daniel. *Brandy Station 1963: First Step to Gettysburg*. London: Osprey, 2008.

Boatner, Mark M., III. *Civil War Dictionary*. New York: David McKay Co., 1959.

Burgess, Milton V. *David Gregg: Pennsylvania Cavalryman*. Privately published, 1984.

Busey, John W., and David G. Martin. *Regimental Strengths and Losses at Gettysburg*. Hightstown, NJ: Longstreet House, 1994.

Carter, William Harding. *From Yorktown to Santiago with the Sixth U.S. Cavalry*. 1900. Reprint, Austin, TX: State House Press, 1989.

———. *The Life of Lieutenant General Chaffee*. Chicago: University of Chicago Press, 1917.

Crouch, Richard E. *Brandy Station: A Battle Like None Other*. Westminster, MD: Willow Bend Books, 2002.

Daughtry, Mary Bandy. *Gray Cavalier: The Life and Wars of General W.H.F. "Rooney" Lee*. New York: DaCapo Press, 2002.

Davis, Burke. *Jeb Stuart: The Last Cavalier*. New York: Rinehart, 1957.

Devine, John E. *35th Battalion Virginia Cavalry*. Lynchburg, VA: H.E. Howard Co., 1985.

Downey, Fairfax. *Clash of Cavalry: The Battle of Brandy Station*. New York: David McKay Co., 1959.

Driver, Robert, Jr. *5th Virginia Cavalry*. Lynchburg, VA: H.E. Howard Co., 1997.

———. *1st Virginia Cavalry*. Lynchburg, VA: H.E. Howard Co., 1991.

———. *2nd Virginia Cavalry*. Lynchburg, VA: H.E. Howard Co., 1995.

———. *10th Virginia Cavalry*. Lynchburg, VA: HE. Howard Co., 1992.

Evans, Clement Anselm, ed. *Confederate Military History*. 13 vols. Atlanta: Confederate Pub. Co., 1899.

Fishel, Edwin C. *The Secret War for the Union: The Untold Story of Military Intelligence in the Civil War*. Boston: Houghton-Mifflin, 1996.

Fortier, John. *15th Virginia Cavalry*. Lynchburg, VA: H.E. Howard Co., 1993.

Foster, John Y. *New Jersey and the Rebellion: A History of the Services of the Troops and People of New Jersey in Aid of the Union Cause*. Newark, NJ: Martin R. Dennis & Co., 1868.

Freeman, Douglas Southall. *R.E. Lee: A Biography*. 4 vols. New York: Charles Scribner's Sons, 1951.

Frye, Dennis E. *12th Virginia Cavalry*. Lynchburg, VA: H.E. Howard Co., 1988.

Furgurson, Earnest B. *Chancellorsville 1863: The Souls of the Brave*. New York: Alfred A. Knopf, 1992.

Harrell, Roger H. *The 2nd North Carolina Cavalry*. Jefferson, NC: McFarland, 2004.

Hartley, Chris J. *Stuart's Tarheels: James B. Gordon and His North Carolina Cavalry*. Baltimore, MD: Butternut & Blue, 1996.

Heitman, Francis E. *Historical Register and Dictionary of the U.S. Army*. 2 vols. Washington, D.C.: U.S. Government Printing Office, 1903.

Helm, Lewis Marshall. *Black Horse Cavalry: Defend Our Beloved Country*. Falls Church, VA: Higher Education Publications, 2004.

Historic Culpeper. Culpeper, VA: Culpeper Historical Society, Inc., 1974.

Holland, Lynwood Mathis. *Pierce M.B. Young: The Warwick of the South.* Athens: University of Georgia Press, 1964.

Kester, Donald E. *Cavalryman in Blue: Colonel John Woods Kester of the 1ˢᵗ New Jersey Cavalry in the Civil War.* Highstown, NJ: Longstreet House, 1997.

Krick, Robert K. *Lee's Colonels.* 2ⁿᵈ ed. Dayton, OH: Morningside House, 1992.

———. *9ᵗʰ Virginia Cavalry.* Lynchburg, VA: H.E. Howard Co., 1982.

Lambert, Joseph I. *One Hundred Years with the Second Cavalry.* Topeka, KS: Press of the Caper Print Co., 1939.

Longacre, Edward G. *The Cavalry at Gettysburg: A Tactical Study of Mounted Operations During the Civil War's Pivotal Campaign, 9 June–14 July 1863.* Rutherford, NJ: Fairleigh-Dickinson University Press, 1986.

———. *Fitz Lee: A Military Biography of Major General Fitzhugh Lee.* New York: DaCapo, 2005.

———. *Gentleman and Solider: The Extraordinary Life of General Wade Hampton.* Nashville, TN: Rutledge Hill Press, 2003.

———. *Jersey Cavaliers: A History of the First New Jersey Volunteer Cavalry.* Hightstown, NJ: Longstreet House, 1992.

———. *Lee's Cavalrymen: A History of the Mounted Forces of the Army of Northern Virginia, 1861–1865.* Mechanicsburg, PA: Stackpole Books, 2002.

Martin, Samuel J. *"Kill-Cavalry": Sherman's Merchant of Terror—The Life of Union General Hugh Judson Kilpatrick.* Madison, NJ: Fairleigh-Dickinson University Press, 1996.

———. *Southern Hero: Matthew Calbraith Butler—Confederate General, Hampton Red Shirt, and U.S. Senator.* Mechanicsburg, PA: Stackpole Books, 2001.

Matteson, Ron. *Civil War Campaigns of the 10ᵗʰ New York Cavalry with One Soldier's Personal Correspondence.* Morrisville, NC: Lulu.com, 2007.

McFadden, Elizabeth. *The Glitter and the Gold: A Spirited Account of the Metropolitan Museum of Art's First Director, the Audacious and High-Handed Luigi Palma di Cesnola.* New York: Dial Press, 1971.

McKinney, Joseph W. *Brandy Station, Virginia, June 9, 1863: The Largest Cavalry Battle of the Civil War.* Jefferson, NC: McFarland, 2006.

Mesic, Harriett Bey. *Cobb's Legion Cavalry: A History and Roster of the Ninth Georgia Volunteers in the Civil War.* Jefferson, NC: McFarland, 2008.

Moore, Robert H. *The 1ˢᵗ and 2ⁿᵈ Stuart Horse Artillery.* Lynchburg, VA: H.E. Howard Co., 1985.

Musick, Michael P. *6ᵗʰ Virginia Cavalry.* Lynchburg, VA: H.E. Howard Co., 1990.

Nesbitt, Mark. *Saber and Scapegoat: J.E.B. Stuart and the Gettysburg Controversy.* Mechanicsburg, PA: Stackpole, 1994.

Nichols, James L. *Fitzhugh Lee: A Biography.* Lynchburg, VA: H.E. Howard Co., 1989.

Nye, Wilbur Sturtevant. *Here Come the Rebels!* Baton Rouge: Louisiana State University Press, 1965.

O'Neill, Robert F., Jr. *The Cavalry Battles of Aldie, Middleburg, and Upperville: Small But Important Riots, June 10–27, 1863.* Lynchburg, VA: H.E. Howard Co., 1993.

Pelton, Jeremiah M. *Genealogy of the Pelton Family in America.* Albany, NY: Joel Munsell's Sons, Publishers, 1892.

Phisterer, Frederick. *New York in the War of the Rebellion, 1861–1865.* 5 vols. Albany, NY: Weed and Parsons, 1890.

Price, George F. *Across the Continent with the Fifth Cavalry.* New York: Noble Offset Printers, 1883.

Raiford, Neil Hunter. *The 4th North Carolina Cavalry in the Civil War.* Jefferson, NC: McFarland, 2003.

Sears, Stephen W. *Chancellorsville.* Boston: Houghton-Mifflin, 1996.

———. *Gettysburg.* Boston: Houghton-Mifflin, 2003.

Staats, Richard J. *The History of the Sixth Ohio Volunteer Cavalry: A Journal of Patriotism, Duty and Bravery.* 2 vols. Westminster, MD: Heritage Books, 2006.

Stiles, Kenneth L. *4th Virginia Cavalry.* Lynchburg, VA: H.E. Howard Co., 1985.

Sutherland, Daniel E. *Seasons of War: The Ordeal of a Confederate Community, 1861–1865.* New York: Free Press, 1995.

Thomas, Emory N. *Bold Dragoon: The Life of J.E.B. Stuart.* New York: Harper & Row, 1986.

Thrapp, Dan L. *Encyclopedia of Frontier Biography.* 3 vols. Lincoln: University of Nebraska Press, 1991.

Tidball, Eugene C. *"No Disgrace to My Country": The Life of John C. Tidball.* Kent, OH: Kent State University Press, 2002.

Tischler, Allan L. *The History of the Harpers Ferry Cavalry Expedition, September 14 & 15, 1862.* Winchester, VA: Five Cedars Press, 1993.

Trout, Robert J. *Galloping Thunder: The Stuart Horse Artillery Battalion.* Mechanicsburg, PA: Stackpole Books, 2002.

———. *"The Hoss": Officer Biographies and Rosters of the Stuart Horse Artillery Battalion.* Myerstown, PA: JebFlo Press, 2003.

———. *They Followed the Plume: The Story of J.E.B. Stuart and His Staff.* Mechanicsburg, PA: Stackpole Books, 1993.

Urwin, Gregory J.W. *Custer Victorious: The Civil War Battles of General George Armstrong Custer.* East Rutherford, NJ: Combined University Presses, 1983.

———. *The United States Cavalry: An Illustrated History.* Poole, Dorset, England: Blandford Press, 1983.

Warner, Ezra J. *Generals in Blue: The Lives of the Union Commanders.* Baton Rouge: Louisiana State University Press, 1964.

———. *Generals in Gray: Lives of the Confederate Commanders.* Baton Rouge: Louisiana State University Press, 1949.

Wellman, Manly Wade. *Giant in Gray: A Biography of Wade Hampton of South Carolina.* New York: Charles Scribner's Sons, 1949.

Welsh, Jack D. *Medical Histories of the Confederate Generals*. Kent, OH: Kent State University Press, 1995.

Wert, Jeffry D. *Cavalryman of the Lost Cause: A Biography of J.E.B. Stuart*. New York: Simon & Schuster, 2008.

———. *Custer: The Controversial Life of George Armstrong Custer*. New York: Simon & Schuster, 1996.

Whittaker, Frederick. *A Complete Life of General George A. Custer*. New York: Sheldon, 1876.

Wilson, James H. *The Life and Services of Brevet Brigadier-General Andrew Jonathan Alexander, United States Army*. New York: privately published, 1887.

Wise, Jennings Cropper. *The Long Arm of Lee, or the History of the Artillery of the Army of Northern Virginia*. 2 vols. Lynchburg, VA: J.P. Bell Co., Inc., 1915.

Wittenberg, Eric J. *Gettysburg's Forgotten Cavalry Actions*. Gettysburg, PA: Thomas Publications, 1998.

———. *Like a Meteor Blazing Brightly: The Short but Controversial Life of Colonel Ulric Dahlgren*. Roseville, MN: Edinborough Publishing, 2009.

———. *Protecting the Flank: The Battles for Brinkerhoff's Ridge and East Cavalry Field, Battle of Gettysburg, July 2–3, 1863*. Celina, OH: Ironclad Publishing, 2002.

———. *Rush's Lancers: The Sixth Pennsylvania Cavalry in the Civil War*. Yardley, PA: Westholme, 2006.

———. *The Union Cavalry Comes of Age: Hartwood Church to Brandy Station, 1863*. Dulles, VA: Brassey's, 2002.

Wittenberg, Eric J., and J. David Petruzzi. *Plenty of Blame to Go Around: Jeb Stuart's Controversial Ride to Gettysburg*. El Dorado Hills, CA: Savas-Beatie, 2006.

Wittenberg, Eric J., J. David Petruzzi and Michael F. Nugent. *One Continuous Fight: The Retreat from Gettysburg and the Pursuit of Lee's Army of Northern Virginia, July 4–14, 1863*. El Dorado Hills, CA: Savas-Beatie, 2008.

ABOUT THE AUTHOR

An attorney in Columbus, Ohio, Eric J. Wittenberg has long been a student of Civil War cavalry operations. Wittenberg has published fourteen books on Civil War history, most of them centering on Virginia. Additionally, his articles have appeared in *Gettysburg Magazine, North & South, Blue & Gray, Hallowed Ground, America's Civil War* and *Civil War Times Illustrated.* He is very active in battlefield preservation and is affiliated with the Civil War Preservation Trust and the Brandy Station Foundation. He has worked extensively with the trust on the preservation of the Trevilian Station battlefield in Louisa County, Virginia, and is a member of the advisory board of the Trevilian Station Battlefield Foundation. He has also fought for the preservation of the Buffington Island battlefield in Meigs County, Ohio; Brandy Station in Culpeper, Virginia; and for various sites associated with the Battle of Gettysburg.